Scott Foresman
Advanced
Take-Home Readers

ISBN: 0-328-20018-2
Copyright © Pearson Education, Inc.
All Rights Reserved. Printed in the United States of America. This publication, or parts thereof, may be used with appropriate equipment to reproduce copies for classroom use only.
1 2 3 4 5 6 7 8 9 10 V084 14 13 12 11 10 09 08 07 06 05

Editorial Offices: Glenview, Illinois • Parsippany, New Jersey • New York, New York
Sales Offices: Needham, Massachusetts • Duluth, Georgia • Glenview, Illinois
Coppell, Texas • Sacramento, California • Mesa, Arizona

Contents

Unit 1 THIS LAND IS YOUR LAND

Week 1 The Story of Libraries

Week 2 Two Great Rivers

Week 3 Innocent Prisoners!

Week 4 The Diné

Week 5 John Muir: A Man of the Wilderness

Unit 2 WORK AND PLAY

Week 6 Equality in American Schools

Week 7 The Life of Cesar Chavez

Week 8 Geography Shapes Our World

Week 9 Danger! Children at Work

Week 10 The Power of Our People

Unit 3 PATTERNS IN NATURE

Week 11 Tracking Our Class Garden

Week 12 Birds of Flight

Week 13 Orbiting the Sun

Week 14 Wild Weather

Week 15 The Price of a Pipeline

Unit 4 PUZZLES AND MYSTERIES

Week 16 Tricking the Eye

Week 17 Echolocation: Animals Making Sound Waves

Week 18 Alexander Graham Bell, Teacher of the Deaf

Week 19 The Code Talkers

Week 20 Professor Science and the Salamander Stumper

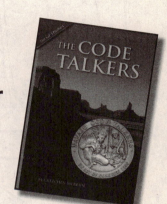

Unit 5 ADVENTURES BY LAND, AIR, AND WATER

Week 21 Thor Heyerdahl and the Kon-Tiki Raft

Week 22 Meet the Maya

Week 23 Two Women Astronauts

Week 24 Danger: The World Is Getting Hot!

Week 25 Life on Mars: The Real Story

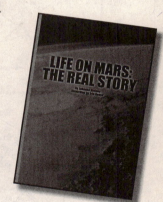

Unit 6 REACHING FOR GOALS

Week 26 The Women's Movement

Week 27 Jim Thorpe: The Greatest Athlete in the World

Week 28 Julia's New Home

Week 29 The Wheels on the Bike Go Round and Round

Week 30 Exploring the Mysteries of Space

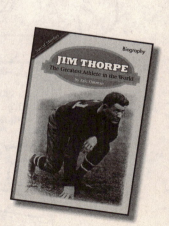

How to Use the Take-Home Leveled Readers

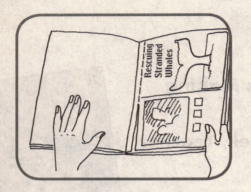

1. Tear out the pages for each Take-Home Leveled Reader. There are two pages back-to-back. Make a copy for each student.

2. Fold the pages in half to make a booklet.

3. Staple the pages on the left-hand side.

4. Have students read and discuss the Take-Home Leveled Readers with family members.

Suggested levels for Guided Reading, DRA,™ Lexile,® and Reading Recovery™ are provided in the Pearson Scott Foresman Leveling Guide.

Social Studies

The Story of Libraries

by Seth Williams

Genre	Comprehension Skill and Strategy	Text Features
Nonfiction	• Sequence • Summarize	• Captions • Heads • Labels • Glossary

Scott Foresman Reading Street 4.1.1

ISBN 0-328-13414-7

9 780328 134144

Reader Response

1. Using a chart similar to the one below, put the following events in the order in which they happened: Trajan's library founded; clay tablets found near Nippur; movable type invented by Gutenberg; Royal Library at Alexandria founded.

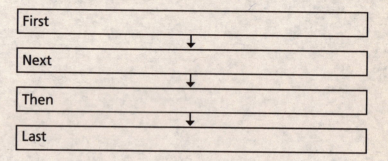

2. How would you summarize the major events in the life of Andrew Carnegie? Use pages 14-19.

3. Use a thesaurus. Make a ladder of synonyms for the word *peculiar*. Rank the synonyms from most peculiar (top) to least peculiar (bottom).

4. Look at the picture on page 6. How is the Royal Library different from the library at your school or in your town?

Glossary

codex *n.* an early book form with writing on both sides of the pages.

grand *adj.* excellent; very good.

memorial *adj.* helping people to remember some person, thing, or event.

peculiar *adj.* strange; odd; unusual.

positive *adj.* permitting no question; without doubt; sure.

prideful *adj.* haughty; having too high an opinion of oneself.

selecting *v.* picking out; choosing.

volume *n.* a book forming a part of a set or series.

The Story of Libraries

by Seth Williams

PEARSON
Scott Foresman

Editorial Offices: Glenview, Illinois • Parsippany, New Jersey • New York, New York
Sales Offices: Needham, Massachusetts • Duluth, Georgia • Glenview, Illinois
Coppell, Texas • Ontario, California • Mesa, Arizona

Here's How to Do It!

1. Think about how would you make the library useful for local residents. Where should it be located?

2. On a piece of paper sketch out a floor plan. Where will you put the children's section? Where will people go to find reference materials to do research? Will there be a quiet reading section? What kinds of furniture will be needed? Where will you put the audiovisual equipment?

3. After you plan your library, share it with the class and explain why you made the decisions that you did. Compare your floor plans with those of classmates.

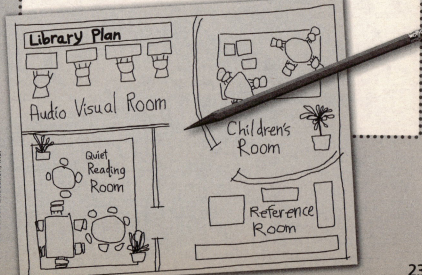

Now Try This

Libraries contain a lot of information for people to use. The resources found at libraries appeal to different age groups, reading abilities, and interests. Think about how your school library or a library in your community is organized, and then design your own library.

The Library of Congress in Washington, D.C.

Around 650 B.C. in ancient Assyria, King Ashurbanipal had just won a war against its neighbor Babylon. **Prideful** of his place in history, the king took valuable clay tablets from Babylon and added them to his library in Nineveh. The king left a message in one of the tablets, which said that anyone who broke, harmed, or removed the tablet and replaced it would be cursed by the gods.

There was nothing **peculiar** about the king's threat. Books in the ancient world were valuable because of the information they contained. Then, as it is now, knowledge was power. The information in a book could be as powerful as an army.

Early and modern forms of written communication

Early Libraries and the Written Word

The word *library* comes from *liber*, the Latin word for "book." The first books were written by hand on rolls of paper-like material, *papyrus*, around 3000 B.C. Other early books were handwritten on clay tablets from around the same time. Among the first libraries, or record rooms, was a group of tablets dating to around 2300 B.C. that was found near Nippur in Mesopotamia. The tablets listed geographical names, gods, names of professions, and a number of religious hymns.

Tablet writing from around 3000 B.C.

No doubt Carnegie would quickly see how far we have come from the days when he was allowed to borrow one book for a week from a rich man's private library. Even with his keen business sense, however, would he be able to predict what the library of our future might look like?

As exciting new technologies make it easier for people to find information, libraries will continue to help people sort through everything that is available. Libraries are more than just buildings that hold information. Libraries play important roles in our communities. They are places where people can educate and entertain themselves for free, just as Ben Franklin and Andrew Carnegie did. Libraries are places where people come together to learn, discuss, and share their knowledge. We are fortunate to have free access to these incredible places. Andrew Carnegie and Ben Franklin realized how valuable libraries were, and people today appreciate them just as much.

The Library Today and Tomorrow

Would Andrew Carnegie recognize what goes on in most libraries today? Certainly the activities of reading books, taking them out, discussing them, and returning them remain largely the same. But what would Carnegie think of using library catalogues online or reserving and renewing books by email? Could he have imagined downloading materials from the Internet, or sending them as email attachments? What about participating in online chats with authors or discussion groups with worldwide members of an email list?

These pictures show a modern library that opened in Alexandria, Egypt, in April 2002.

It was the Greeks who developed libraries with books on all subjects available to all readers. But it was not easy. The Dark Age of ancient Greece took place from 1200 B.C. to 900 B.C. During this time cities were destroyed and the knowledge of how to write was lost. Fortunately the Phoenicians, who lived in present-day Lebanon and Israel, had developed a form of writing that was fairly simple to learn. The Greeks adapted letters from this alphabet to make their own alphabet.

By the 400s B.C. the Greeks also had created a way to teach people about different subjects. Poetry and religious works were written down, as well as works in history, art, and even cooking.

Ancient Greek ruins

The Royal Library at Alexandria

The greatest center of ancient civilization in the Middle East was Egypt, home of the famous Royal Library at Alexandria. Founded around 300 B.C. by the Greek king Ptolemy I, it lasted for nearly six hundred years. It was the first library to offer a wide variety of books. It had about half a million handwritten rolls, or scrolls.

The Royal Library at Alexandria

Andrew remembered his promise to create free libraries. From 1886 to 1896, he contributed almost $2 million for urban community centers that included not only libraries but also places such as swimming pool areas. From 1896 to 1919, Carnegie's gifts of money, totaling over $39 million, went to small towns to construct buildings that would serve solely as libraries.

Carnegie did not give money to every town that wanted a library. Like any businessperson, he wanted his investment to succeed, so he set specific requirements for each applicant. The town had to own the land on which the library would be built. The land had to be large enough to allow for the library to grow if needed. Most important, Carnegie required that the town pay money each year to keep the building in good repair. More than fourteen hundred towns in forty-six different states benefited from these gifts.

In 1865, at the age of thirty, Andrew had become a private investor. **Selecting** carefully, he put money into industries, including oil, iron, and steel. Eventually he created the Carnegie Steel Company, which he sold in 1901 for $250 million. Carnegie spent the rest of his life giving away 90 percent of the money he had made.

One building that Andrew Carnegie funded is Carnegie Hall in New York City.

We know this because one man, Callimachus, put together an index of the entire library's Greek writings telling about each piece of work. His index filled 120 books! Sadly, any writer who hoped that the one copy of his book in the Royal Library at Alexandria would be a permanent **memorial** tribute to him would be disappointed. The library is thought to have been destroyed during a civil war in Alexandria around A.D. 270.

The Library at Alexandria was a great success in its time. The library and its contents were built from scratch. Books from other Greek cultures were brought to the library. The kings would bring great thinkers of the day to the library to meet, study, and give speeches. These people were housed, fed, and paid to live there.

A scroll

More Libraries and Learning

Other libraries were built during the Roman Empire, a time when Rome was trying to take over other lands. Julius Caesar planned a **grand** library that would have both Greek and Latin sections, but he did not live to see it through. The emperor Trajan's library was established in A.D. 114. It was one of the most famous Roman libraries. It held about twenty thousand scrolls.

The fall of the Roman Empire in A.D. 476 also marked the end of its libraries. Yet libraries continued to flourish in the East, especially in Syria and Persia. The followers of the prophet Muhammad, the founder of the Islamic religion, preserved the libraries of those they conquered. Starting in the 600s, they translated the books they found into Arabic.

By the end of the 700s, Baghdad was a world center of learning. From the Chinese, Arabs learned the art of making paper from linen or cotton rags. They adopted the form of the **codex** to replace the scroll. This changed the book into the basic shape we know today. Copying and translating books preserved many that might have been lost forever during the Dark Ages of Europe.

The library's rules allowed only apprentices, or people learning a trade, to borrow books for free. Messengers, like Andrew was at the time, had to pay. Andrew wrote a protest letter for the newspaper. He wanted to borrow books too. His complaints were heard. As a result, any young worker, apprentice or not, could borrow books without charge. Andrew decided that if he ever became rich, he would use some money to build free libraries.

Andrew Carnegie

A Working Boy

Andrew worked in cotton mills, and he was able to work his way up to billing clerk and messenger. After a while he got a job in a telegraph office as a messenger. Soon he was supervising the other messengers, which gave him a little extra time to learn how to operate the telegraph machine. Using the telegraph, one could send messages over telegraph wires. The messages were sent in an instant through a system of dots and dashes called Morse code, named after its inventor, Samuel F. B. Morse. Once Andrew learned to translate Morse code he became a telegraph operator.

Andrew also enjoyed skating on the river and discussing current events with his young friends. He, too, formed a debate club. Despite the efforts of Ben Franklin and others, there were still very few books available for borrowing in the Pittsburgh area. There was no public library either.

One day Andrew was reading the newspaper. Colonel James Anderson, a wealthy local resident, was opening his four hundred **volume** personal library on Saturday afternoons to young workers. Andrew leaped at the chance to become a regular borrower.

The printing press was invented by a German printer named Johannes Gutenberg in the mid-1400s. Books were then printed rather than written by hand. As public libraries started to be built, wealthy nobles usually provided books and money. By the end of the 1500s there were libraries in almost every major European city, and many were open to the public. Valuable books were sometimes fastened to bookshelves with long chains to keep them from being stolen.

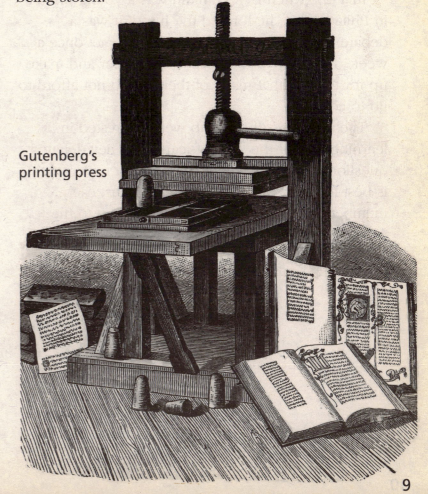

Gutenberg's printing press

Libraries in Early America

The earliest settlers of the American colonies brought some books with them, mainly for religious reasons. The wealthiest merchants and planters may have had their own libraries, but most people who could read probably only read the Bible. During the 1700s, as ways to print books improved, more people could afford to buy them, but books were still too expensive for most people.

In 1727, when Ben Franklin was a young printer in Philadelphia, he formed the Junto. It was a debate, or discussion, club. The group met once a week. They hoped to educate each other and make up for the fact that many of them could not afford to go to college.

The members of the club were interested in learning just for the sake of learning. They debated questions such as whether one form of government is best for everyone. Every three months, each member had to write an essay and read it to the whole group.

When children began school at the age of five, Andrew refused to go. His parents allowed him to wait until he was ready, but after three years they were concerned. They asked their local schoolmaster to convince Andrew that school was exciting.

Finally when he was eight years old, Andrew started attending school. There were 150 children of all ages in one big classroom. Though he attended school for only five years, young Andrew was an ambitious and bright student. He especially loved to memorize poetry.

As Andrew grew up, his father could not continue to support his family by weaving. Steam-powered machinery was beginning to replace hand looms. Soon work became harder and harder for Will Carnegie to find. Machine-woven textiles were here to stay. Will was very discouraged, but Margaret had an idea. Two of her sisters had already moved to America to seek a better life. So in 1848, the Carnegie family did the same. They left Scotland for the United States and settled in what is now Pittsburgh, Pennsylvania.

Carnegie the Great

In 1835, forty-five years after Ben Franklin's death, Andrew Carnegie was born to a poor family of weavers in Scotland. Andrew grew up in a small stone house with a younger brother, Tom. His father, Will, weaved at his hand loom on the ground floor. Andrew's mother, Margaret, became a skilled shoemaker. Andrew enjoyed being at home with his parents so much that he was not **positive** he wanted to go to school. He found life in his small town interesting. Andrew enjoyed hearing stories of Scottish history from his uncle, George Lauder, who ran a local grocery store.

Andrew Carnegie as a young man

Benjamin Franklin sits at a desk during a meeting.

A statue of Benjamin Franklin stands above the front door of a reconstruction of the Library Company in Philadelphia.

Not everyone in the group could afford to have his own personal library of books to read to prepare these essays. So Ben Franklin suggested that the group put their earnings together and buy books that the members could borrow. In 1731 the Library Company became the first lending library in America.

Fifty people gave money to the Library Company to keep it running. By 1741 the library listed 375 titles in its catalogue. Members could borrow books without charge. Non-members had to leave a security deposit equal to the value of the book borrowed.

A few years later, the Second Continental Congress met in Philadelphia to write the Declaration of Independence. Nine signers of the Declaration were also members of the Library Company. In fewer than fifty years, with over two thousand books and hundreds of subscribers, the Library Company had come a long way from Ben Franklin's small debate club. In fact, the Library Company still exists today.

The idea of independent libraries eventually spread throughout the colonies and, later, the young United States. The Providence Athenaeum, in Rhode Island, was founded in 1753, and the New York Society Library was founded in 1754. In Philadelphia, the Union Library, which itself had been formed from two smaller libraries in 1746, merged with the Library Company in 1769.

The Boston Athenaeum, founded in 1807

Suggested levels for Guided Reading, DRA,™ Lexile,® and Reading Recovery™ are provided in the Pearson Scott Foresman Leveling Guide.

Social Studies

Two Great Rivers

by Stephanie Sigue

Genre	Comprehension Skill and Strategy	Text Features
Nonfiction	• Author's Purpose • Answer Questions	• Heads • Map • Captions • Glossary

Scott Foresman Reading Street 4.1.2

scottforesman.com

ISBN 0-328-13417-1

Reader Response

1. The author probably had two purposes for writing this book: to inform and to persuade. Make a chart like the one below. Find two facts to support each of the author's purposes for writing this selection.

Author's Purpose	Facts

2. What questions do you have about floods and flooding? What strategy can you use to answer your questions? Where can you find more information about these two great rivers?

3. The Mississippi Delta is home to many types of birds. Many of these birds migrate there. Use the words *migrating* and *migratory* in a sentence.

4. Suppose you want to compare the Missouri River to the Mississippi River. What four headings from the selection would you use in your comparison?

Glossary

barges *n.* large, strongly built, flat-bottomed boats for carrying freight on rivers, canals, etc.

conservationists *n.* people who want to preserve and protect the forests, rivers, and other natural resources of a country.

diminishing *v.* making or becoming smaller.

expedition *n.* a journey for some special purpose, such as exploration, scientific study, or for military purposes.

reservoirs *n.* places where water is collected and stored for use.

route *n.* way to go; road.

silt *n.* very fine particles of dirt carried by moving water and deposited as sediment.

tributaries *n.* streams or rivers that flow into a larger one.

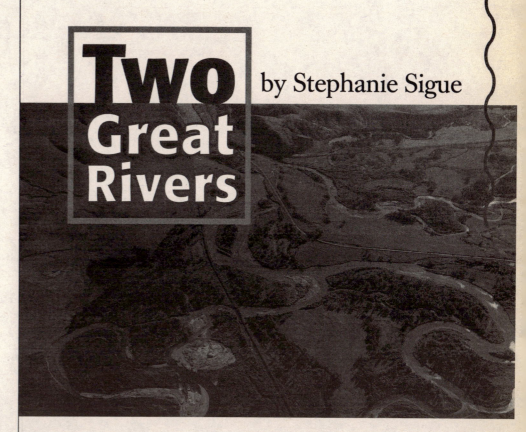

Two Great Rivers

by Stephanie Sigue

PEARSON
Scott Foresman

Editorial Offices: Glenview, Illinois • Parsippany, New Jersey • New York, New York
Sales Offices: Needham, Massachusetts • Duluth, Georgia • Glenview, Illinois
Coppell, Texas • Ontario, California • Mesa, Arizona

Here's How to Do It!

1. Find a partner. Look at a map of the world. Pick out another major river in the United States or in another country in the world.

2. Next decide what you would like to learn about the river. Make a list of questions you have and choose questions to answer.

3. Now it is time to do research. Look at encyclopedias and other reference books for more information about the river you selected.

4. Assemble your findings in a format that you can present to the class. Include a map. Share your findings with the group and answer questions regarding your river.

Now Try This

Study a River

In this book you read about two of the great rivers in the United States. Now it is time to find out about other great rivers.

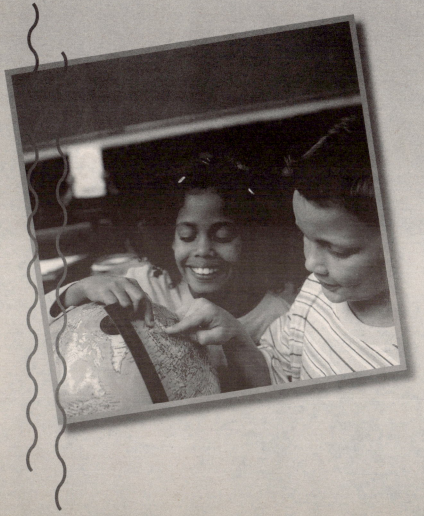

The Mighty Mississippi

The Mississippi River is one of the most famous rivers in the world. It is the widest river in the United States, and the second longest. Mark Twain gave a vivid description of the river in his book *Life on the Mississippi*. Many other writers, poets, and songwriters have been inspired to write about it.

The Mississippi River is divided into three parts: the Headwaters, which is where the river begins, the Upper Mississippi River, and the Lower Mississippi River. This river begins as a small stream from Lake Itasca in northern Minnesota. It flows from north to south for over two thousand miles and passes through many states before emptying into of the Gulf of Mexico.

Two great United States rivers

As the Mississippi meanders along, it is joined by the waters of several other rivers. The Platte, Yellowstone, Minnesota, St. Croix, Illinois, Missouri, Ohio, Wabash, Tennessee, Arkansas, Red, and Atchafalaya rivers all meet the Mississippi somewhere along the way. More than 250 **tributaries** from the east and west flow into the Mississippi. It is no wonder that so many Native American tribes–the Illinois, the Kickapoo, and the Ojibway–that lived in the upper Mississippi Valley called it "Big River" and the "Father of Waters."

History of the River

The Mississippi was formed about 100,000 years ago. At that time glaciers covered the Northern Hemisphere. As the glaciers began to melt, they carved out channels. Meltwater filled the channels to form the Mississippi River.

The beautiful city of St. Louis would not be the same without the two great rivers.

The Two Rivers

The Mississippi and the Missouri are important waterways. What would the United States be like without these two powerful rivers? How big an impact would it have on the lives of people? How big an impact would it have on the wildlife? Industry and commerce would suffer. Wildlife and ecosystems would disappear. Plants, animals, and fish that we think of as common might not exist.

Besides their scenic beauty, the rivers sustain a way of life for millions of people. From north to south, east to west, these two rivers are a part of American history and culture that has existed since before the days of the pioneers. They are both mighty rivers, although one may be a little muddy.

Life along the Mississippi River near Fountain City, Wisconsin

Hernando de Soto, a European explorer, crossed the river in 1541 near what is now Memphis, Tennessee. Later, French explorers traveled the river and claimed the Mississippi Valley for France. Finally, the United States bought this land from France in the Louisiana Purchase of 1803.

Hernando de Soto

The river became an important transportation and trade **route.** After the development of steamboats in the early 1800s, the river became even more important. Cities along the river—St. Louis, Memphis, and New Orleans—became the best places to buy supplies before heading west.

The Louisiana Purchase

After the Civil War, railroads and bridges were built to make it easier to cross the river. However, the river continued to be a major trade route. River transportation increased in the early twentieth century. Using tugboats and **barges**, large quantities of cargo and freight began to be transported along the great river.

The locks, or gates, in this section of the Mississippi River raise and lower the water level so that ships can pass through.

Missouri River Wildlife

Since part of the Missouri runs through the mountains, bear, elk, deer, moose, and other large animals are plentiful. In the middle and lower parts of the river valley, smaller animals are more visible. These include beavers, foxes, muskrats, and weasels.

Rainbow trout and mountain whitefish live in the parts of the river that are clear. Bass, catfish, carp, and perch live in the muddier waters.

Environmental Dangers

Today **conservationists** and the federal government disagree about how much water should flow into the river. Conservationists think that some fish and wildlife are in danger if the water flow is controlled by the dams. They want the natural flow of the river restored.

Conservationists say that the high level of water necessary to support barge traffic is harmful to animals. It floods the nesting habitats of two species of endangered river birds and reduces the survival rate of an endangered fish. A court will have to decide the outcome. For now the dam system continues to be used.

A white-tailed deer fawn in a Missouri tall grass prairie (top) and a mink by the water in Montana (bottom) are samples of wildlife found along the Missouri River.

More than 60 percent of the United States' grain exports are carried down the Mississippi River each year. Aluminum, petroleum, coal, and steel products are transported on the river. Even food, such as corn, soybeans, and wheat, moves along the Mississippi.

The port of New Orleans is the busiest port in the United States. You can sit on the wharf and scan the city's docks as ships from all over the world are loaded and unloaded. The Mississippi is also popular with tourists. Steamboat and riverboat cruises provide wonderful views of the river and its surrounding beauty.

Tourists ride a riverboat along the scenic Mississippi River.

Floods and Flood Control

Flooding along the Mississippi can be a problem. When melting snow or heavy rains add lots of water to the river, it overflows its banks. If the surrounding land is unable to absorb the water, flooding occurs. Since many acres of wetlands along the river have been drained and turned into farmland, more water has been forced into the river. Paved roads, parking lots, and even the roofs on buildings prevent rainwater from soaking into the ground. This increases run-off into the river and the chance of flooding. Severe flooding often results in damage to nearby homes and communities.

Several methods are used to control floods. One way is to plant trees, grass, and other plants to absorb the water. Another way to protect the land from flooding is to build levees. Levees raise the banks of the river so that it can hold more water. Floodways are areas of land that provide outlets for draining water when the river reaches flood level. They help to decrease flooding.

Levees help flooding control along the Mississippi.

No More Floods

Wherever there is a large amount of free-flowing water, there is a danger of flooding. However, this danger has been eliminated along the Missouri River. Six huge dams were built on the river to form a chain of **reservoirs.** These reservoirs run from north to south along the river. They are Fort Peck, Garrison, Oahe, Big Bend, Fort Randall, and Gavins Point. There are also sixty smaller dams and reservoirs along the Missouri's tributaries that keep the Missouri from overflowing.

Besides **diminishing** the chances of flooding, the dams provide electrical power to the farms, homes, and industries along the river's banks. The reservoirs provide recreation spots too. Boating, fishing, waterskiing, swimming, and other water sports are all popular.

The River and Its Uses

The Missouri River has an upper, middle, and lower part. The upper Missouri, near Montana, is a clear mountain stream. The middle part of the river begins when the river leaves the mountains and crosses the Great Plains. This part of the river is slower and muddier. The lower part of the river is the slowest and muddiest of all. It begins in South Dakota and flows until the Missouri and Mississippi meet in St. Louis.

The river is muddy because it picks up sand as it moves through the mountains. The river runs over a thick bed of **silt** and carries it to the Mississippi. Much of the mud and silt is trapped by reservoirs on the Missouri River, but some of it empties into the Mississippi. Before meeting the Missouri in St. Louis, the Mississippi is actually clear.

The Missouri River has always been a trading route. In earlier times fur traders moved furs from the West to the East on the river. Today most of the river traffic above Sioux City, Iowa, is recreational. The activity on the lower part of the river is commercial. Between Sioux City and St. Louis, tugboats push barges along the Missouri loaded with farm and industrial products.

Big Bend Dam at Fort Thompson, South Dakota

Flood water from the Mississippi River engulfs the city of Keithsburgh, Illinois.

Plant and Animal Life

Forests and wetlands border much of the Mississippi River. These natural areas provide important habitats for plants, fish, and wildlife.

The clear waters of the upper Mississippi are home to freshwater fish such as bass, sunfish, and trout. In the muddy waters of the lower Mississippi, carp, catfish, and buffalo fish make their home. The coastal wetlands of Louisiana provide areas where oysters, crabs, and shrimp are raised.

Wildlife is found along most of the Mississippi. More than four hundred species of animals live along this stretch of water. Mink, muskrats, opossums, otters, skunks, and rodents called nutrias live in the swamps and marshlands along the Mississippi Delta. Forty percent of the nation's migrating birds flock to the area during the winter. These include ducks, geese, and other migratory birds. Pelicans, herons, and egrets live in the area year-round.

A nutria in the wild

Lewis and Clark's expedition began in May of 1804 and ended in September of 1806. During that time they met Sacagawea, the Shoshone wife of a Canadian fur trapper. She helped guide them up the Missouri River and across the Rocky Mountains.

Lewis and Clark exploring in the Bitterroot Mountains in Montana (top)

An antique wooden compass with leather pouch used on the expedition (right)

Missouri River History

The Wind River Shoshone and Atsina Native American nations lived near the headwaters of the Missouri in western Montana. The river was a hunting ground, a canoe route, and a source of water.

French explorers Louis Joliet and Father Jacques Marquette were most likely the first to explore the eastern Missouri in 1673. Later, in 1738, another group of French explorers traveled the upper parts of the river. They reported seeing herds of buffalo and Native American villages in the area that would later become North Dakota.

Lewis and Clark

In 1803 President Thomas Jefferson chose Meriwether Lewis and William Clark to lead an **expedition** that would take them from Missouri to the Pacific Ocean. Jefferson wanted them to form peaceful relations with the Native American tribes along the way and to establish trade with them. The expedition also was to gather and record information. Jefferson wanted to know about the geography of the terrain, the types of plants and animals they found, and the mineral resources.

Dangers to the River

The Mississippi River has faced two problems in recent years. One is the amount of sediment that flows into the Mississippi from the Missouri River. The construction of a series of reservoirs along the Missouri, however, now traps sediment and stops it from flowing into the river.

Pollution is another problem. Poor water quality threatens the habitats of many plant and animal species. Wildlife was threatened when fertilizers and chemicals were washed into the river by farms and industries. Now the government has made severe regulations that forbid the use of harmful chemicals that damage the environment.

Great blue heron (left); Mississippi alligator hiding among the lily pads (below)

The Muddy Missouri

The Missouri River is not as famous as the Mississippi River, but it's longer. It flows 2,315 miles through seven states, starting from the Jefferson River at Red Rock Creek in southwestern Montana.

The Platte River in Nebraska is the largest of the Missouri River's tributaries. Other major rivers that flow into the Missouri are the Big Sioux, Cheyenne, James, Kansas, Milk, Osage, and Yellowstone.

Native Americans and early explorers called the river "Big Muddy" because of the amount of mud in the water. The name, Missouri, probably comes from the name of the Indian village *Ou-Missouri* or *Oue Messourit* that was located near the mouth of the river.

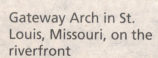

Gateway Arch in St. Louis, Missouri, on the riverfront

Aerial view of the headwaters of the Missouri River

Suggested levels for Guided Reading, DRA,™ Lexile,® and Reading Recovery™ are provided in the Pearson Scott Foresman Leveling Guide.

Social Studies

INNOCENT PRISONERS!
Life in a Japanese American Internment Camp

by Gretchen McBride
illustrated by Tom McNeely

Genre	Comprehension Skill and Strategy
Fiction	• Sequence • Graphic Organizers

Scott Foresman Reading 4.1.3

PEARSON
Scott Foresman

ISBN 0-328-13420-1

9 780328 134205

90000

Reader Response

1. Make a list of the events in the story. Then review the story and put the events on your list in order from the first event that happened to the last.

2. Contrast the life of Japanese Americans before Pearl Harbor and after. Use a chart like the one below.

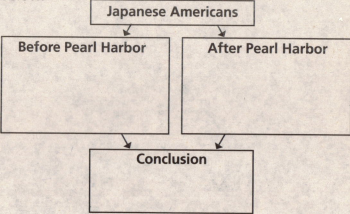

3. Make a glossary of the words in the story that relate to the internment camp setting. You might begin with the word *barracks*. Write a definition and then check your definition against a dictionary definition.

4. Do you think it was wrong for the United States government to intern the Japanese Americans? Explain your answer. What do you think would happen in a similar situation today?

America Makes Amends

When the Japanese launched a surprise attack on the ships in Pearl Harbor, the United States was horrified. Japanese Americans were horrified, too. But what horrified them more was how they were treated by some of their neighbors and by their own government. They acted as if the Japanese were no longer Americans. They treated them as if they were to blame for the attack on Pearl Harbor.

The U.S. government, worried that they might be spies, and put Japanese Americans into special camps called "relocation centers." After the war ended, the camps were closed. The last camp was closed in 1945.

Since that terrible time, America has realized that Japanese Americans were treated unjustly. In 1988, Congress gave money to every Japanese person who had been in a camp. In 1990, President Bush sent letters of apology to them.

INNOCENT PRISONERS!
Life in a Japanese American Internment Camp

by Gretchen McBride
illustrated by Tom McNeely

PEARSON
Scott Foresman

Editorial Offices: Glenview, Illinois • Parsippany, New Jersey • New York, New York
Sales Offices: Needham, Massachusetts • Duluth, Georgia • Glenview, Illinois
Coppell, Texas • Ontario, California • Mesa, Arizona

"What do you want to do?" Father asked Yukiko. She thought long and hard. "I want to stay in America," she said. "This camp was a terrible thing. But this is still our country, isn't it?"

"I want to stay, too," said Mama. "It will be hard, but how else can I practice my English? I do not want to give up either language, or either country. Someday, we will all visit Japan."

"I would like to see Mount Fuji," Yukiko said. She suddenly knew the first thing she would do when they got out of the camp and into a new home. She would hang the old man's drawing of Mount Fuji next to a drawing of Mount Whitney. Both mountains and both countries were important to her.

Three long years passed. Every year was harder than the one before. Yukiko thought they would never get out of the camps. And then, one morning, Yukiko heard great excitement outside. "The war is over! We're going home!" someone cried. Everyone was laughing and cheering.

Everyone gathered in the mess hall. Some people said they were going back to Japan. Other people wanted to go back to their American homes. They were worried. Would their homes still be there?

"What will we do?" Yukiko asked her parents.

"When will we be able to go back to our farm, in the San Fernando Valley, big brother?" Yukiko asked. She was Japanese. So were all the families in the camp.

"I don't know," said Aki. He spoke in Japanese. That was the language of their parents. "Mama and Papa don't know."

Yukiko knew there was a war going on. She knew Japan had attacked Pearl Harbor, a naval base in Hawaii, on December 7, 1941. Since then, people in the United States treated their Japanese neighbors differently. People who used to smile at Yukiko now frowned and looked away.

The government moved all Japanese and Japanese Americans to internment camps or relocation centers in early 1942 because of fears that they might become a threat to national security. The small rooms in the camps were called barracks. Every house was covered in tar paper. There was no kitchen or shower.

Yukiko went to find her father. He was sitting on a chair he had made from scraps of woods. There wasn't enough furniture here. Everyone made their own.

How is it possible the family had been living here for six whole months? "Come," said Papa to Yukiko, "let's go get breakfast at the mess hall. We'll join the whole family there."

Everyone ate in the mess hall. Some families ate together. But many people now ate with the friends they had made at the camp. Yukiko liked sitting with her friends. But she missed the way her family used to eat in their own farmhouse. She even missed helping out on the farm.

The wind began to blow the dust. "Another dust storm!" cried Aki. Talking was now impossible. Aki drew his jacket up to cover his nose and mouth with one hand. He put his other arm around Yukiko's shoulder.

Once inside the house, Father passed out rags. They pressed the rags into the cracks in the walls and the floor so the dust couldn't get in.

After dinner, the family walked back to their home. "Mother," Yukiko asked suddenly, "What is your secret?"

This brought a smile to her mother's face. "Yukiko," she said, "What did you do in school today?"

The family was still. They were stunned. Finally, Aki spoke. "English! Mother, you spoke in English!"

"This is my secret," she said proudly. "I have no cooking to do, so I take class. I study English every morning."

Yukiko knew Papa was not an American citizen. Neither was Mama. But she and Aki were born in the United States. "Someday you will vote in elections!" Papa told them.

The whole family sat at a big table together. Aki began telling a noisy story.

"Speak softly," Mama said. She was proud of her children's independent American ways, but she could not get used to the loud voices Americans used. She could not understand their American speech.

That evening at dinner, Aki sat with the older boys. This evening there were many complaints about the hot dogs and beans.

Suddenly a man stood up. "When this is over, we need to turn our backs on the United States and go back to Japan!" he shouted.

"You are wrong! We are not Japanese. We are Japanese Americans! America is our home, too," cried another man.

A shadow of a small woman fell across their table. It was Mama! "We must not disturb the peace of the other diners," she said in Japanese. "Let us all think hard about what is the right thing to do."

Mama got up. "Aki, make sure your sister gets to school on time," she said.

"Where are you going, Mama?" Yukiko asked in Japanese, taking her mother's hand.

"Ah," Mama said with a slight smile. "That is a secret I am keeping. Now do not be late for school."

After breakfast, Aki walked his sister to school. School was a small building across the dusty yard of the camp.

"Do you know what kind of secret Mama is keeping?" Yukiko asked. Aki shook his head.

"Are you going to be an American soldier after you graduate?" Yukiko asked Aki. Some of Aki's friends were in the war. Yukiko felt proud of them, but scared, too. She loved America but she didn't want Aki fighting any Japanese in the war.

"Here you go. Study hard," Aki said. This school was covered in dull black tar paper to keep out the dust. Yukiko thought of her brick school building at home. She missed her classmates.

The old man smiled once more and handed Yukiko the drawing of Mount Fuji. Then he picked up his walking stick and slowly made his way along the dusty path.

Aki and Yukiko walked a little ways and then stopped and gazed at the snow-covered peak.

"Imagine," Aki said, "how clean the snow must be so far above the dust."

"Maybe after the war, you'll return to Japan," said Aki. "You can see Mount Fuji again."

"I will never return to Japan," said the old man. "I loved my homeland, but my life there was a hard one because we were poor. I urged my children to move to America for a better life, and they did. Soon, they sent for me."

He smiled sadly. "It is a mystery how we could all end up here behind these wires. I come here to think about this in the shadow of this great American mountain. It is now my Mount Fuji."

"Have you solved the mystery?" Aki asked. "Do you understand why we are here?"

"Ah," the old man said," I see that even you—so young—struggle with the mystery."

"Well, students, I have an exciting announcement to make!" the teacher said. "Some wonderful people have given our school another blackboard! It will be mounted on our classroom wall very soon."

Yukiko was quiet. Her teacher wrote math problems on a piece of paper tacked to the wall. She thought how nice it would be to have a blackboard.

Yukiko wondered how people could be so nice sometimes, and other times be so mean. She had asked her father about this. He shook his head. "It's wrong and unfair, but that is the way it is, and we cannot change it," he said. Yukiko wanted a better answer.

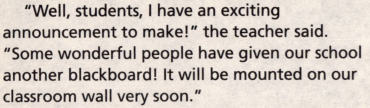

"I know the very best place to see the peak," Aki said. "Follow me!" They rounded a growth of sage brush. Then they stopped, amazed and bewildered. There, seated on a rock, was the oldest man Yukiko had ever seen.

The old man was drawing something on a large pad of paper. He looked up and saw them and gave them a big smile.

"Young ones," the old man said. "Before us is a great mountain! Mount Whitney. I come here often to admire it and to remember."

"Remember what?" asked Yukiko.

"This," the old man said. He showed them his drawing, but it was not Mount Whitney. "This is Mount Fuji," the old man said. "It is in Japan, and it is sacred."

After school, Yukiko met Aki in the yard. At this time of day, they always loved to look at Mount Whitney in the distance. Today they would walk to the edge of the camp where they could get the best view of the mountain.

Although it felt good to walk after sitting at her school desk, Yukiko did not like the route they took. She hated seeing the barbed wire, the guard towers, and American soldiers holding real guns. Most of the time, she could pretend these things were not there. Sometimes she could pretend that she and her family were living in a strange new town, but not now.

The wire and the guards made Yukiko feel as if she had done something wrong. They made her feel like a prisoner. But she and her family had done nothing wrong! They made her angry. How could her own government treat her and her family this way?

"Look at the beautiful mountain peaks!" said Aki.

Yukiko lifted her eyes to the horizon. There was snow-capped Mount Whitney towering above the desert.

Suggested levels for Guided Reading, DRA,™ Lexile,® and Reading Recovery™ are provided in the Pearson Scott Foresman Leveling Guide.

Social Studies

THE DINÉ

by Kathleen Cox

Genre	Comprehension Skill and Strategy	Text Features
Nonfiction	• Author's Purpose • Text Structure	• Map • Captions • Labels • Glossary

Scott Foresman Reading Street 4.1.4

PEARSON

Scott Foresman

scottforesman.com

ISBN 0-328-13423-6

9 780328 134236

90000

Reader Response

1. Why do you think the author wrote this book? Use a chart like the one below to help organize your ideas.

Question the Author	
1. What does the author tell you?	
2. Why do you think the author tells you that?	
3. Does the author say it clearly?	
4. What would make it clearer?	
5. How would you say it instead?	

2. The author organizes this book into four parts: Before Columbus; the Diné and the Spanish; the Diné and the U.S. Army; the Diné today. Write a sentence to tell about each part.

3. List two words from the Glossary and write synonyms for them.

4. Look at the map on page 3. What is the northern body of water? What is the southwestern body of water?

Glossary

ancestors *n.* people from whom you are descended, such as your great-grandparents.

cardinal points *n.* the Diné expression for the four principal directions on the compass: north, south, east, and west.

edible *adj.* something that is safe to eat.

environmentalists *n.* people who want to protect the land.

hogans *n.* circular buildings, made from logs and earth, used by the Diné.

inhabited *v.* lived in a place.

nomads *n.* people who move from place to place.

The Diné

by Kathleen Cox

Editorial Offices: Glenview, Illinois • Parsippany, New Jersey • New York, New York
Sales Offices: Needham, Massachusetts • Duluth, Georgia • Glenview, Illinois
Coppell, Texas • Ontario, California • Mesa, Arizona

Here's How to Do It!

1. Find two same-sized pieces of construction paper in two of your favorite colors.
2. Cut one piece of paper into one-inch-wide strips going the long way, shown in example A. Cut the other piece of paper into one-inch-wide strips going the short way, shown in example B, leaving the last inch of the strip connected to the paper. This will be your base to start weaving.
3. Weave the strips of the first piece of paper over and under the strips of the second piece of paper. If one row begins by going "over," then the next row should begin by going "under." This will create your pattern. You may want to use small pieces of tape on the last strip to keep it in place.
4. Try experimenting with thinner or wider strips. Try different colors to make unique designs. Decorate your woven art with symbols that represent who you are as a person.

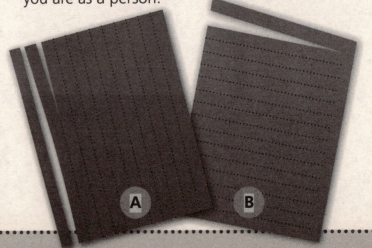

Now Try This

Be a First-Class Weaver

The Diné are known for their beautiful weaving work. As you know, they wove cotton into cool clothing and wool into warm blankets and rugs. The skilled art of weaving is an important part of the Diné culture. Their artistry represents who they are as a people. You can be a first-class weaver too!

Diné woven blanket

Long before Christopher Columbus, there were many groups of Native American people in North America. Thousands of years ago, their **ancestors** probably crossed from what is now Russia into what we now call Alaska. At that time a narrow strip of land connected the two continents where the Bering Strait is today. The Diné, who are also known as the Navajo, were one of these groups of Native Americans.

For a long time the Diné **inhabited** the land that is now western Canada. They were hunters and gatherers. Diné ancestors did not have horses. They hunted on foot with spears and clubs. They also collected **edible** flowers, leaves, and roots of wild plants for food.

Native American ancestors probably crossed from Russia to Alaska where the Bering Strait is today.

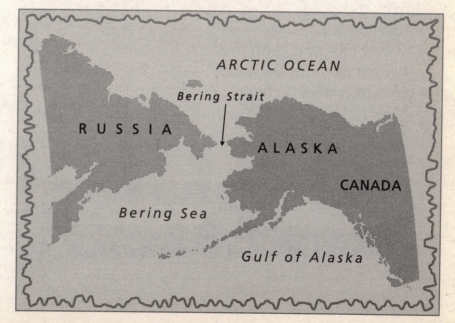

The ancestors of the Diné were **nomads.** They never stayed in one area for very long. Since the Diné moved around, they had few possessions. They carried little more than their weapons and the simple tools they used for cooking. Too many possessions would slow them down.

Because they understood that their survival depended on the gifts of nature, the Diné might be called early **environmentalists**. They protected and respected the land. Never killing for sport, the Diné hunted only to get food for themselves. Very little of an animal was left behind. The Diné used animal skins for clothing, animal bones to create jewelry and weapons, and bird feathers for headgear.

The Diné's religion and folklore celebrated nature. They worshipped Father Sky and Mother Earth. They revered the mountains, the rainbow, the Sun, the rivers, and all animal species. Even plants were sacred to the Diné.

Over time the Diné drifted south through the Western plains. By the 1400s the Diné had migrated to southwestern North America.

The Code Talkers did not fight with guns. They fought with their language. The Diné sent important secret messages to other Marines so that they could defeat the Japanese. The Japanese, who had skilled code-breakers, could not understand the secret Diné code.

Since World War II, the Diné nation has worked to create new opportunities for its people and the country. The Diné are allowing oil wells on their land, and already companies are searching for valuable minerals.

The Diné teach their children to respect their culture, and they want them to know the Diné nation's history. They want them to learn their language and to revere their land and traditions—to have a respect for the old teachings. People across America also have learned to respect and understand the Diné culture, as it is a special part of our diverse country.

In the 1940s the Diné joined forces with the people who once captured them. More than three thousand Diné became members of the U.S. military during World War II. Many of them trained to become Code Talkers. The Code Talkers were Marines stationed in the Pacific.

World War II Code Talkers

These carvings were found at the Canyon de Chelly in Arizona, where the Diné lived.

Part of the Southwest was a desert grassland. Though the area was very dry, part was covered with evergreen forests. Another part was thick with berry trees and nut trees. The Diné used the fibers of the beautiful yucca plant to weave sandals and baskets. Juniper and oak trees offered shade from the sun. The nuts from the pinion tree were good food.

Rock formations, Monument Valley, Arizona

Beans

The U.S. government finally let the Diné sign a second peace treaty in 1868. In return the Diné were given land in the Southwest. Their new reservation included their sacred Dinétah. The Diné were also given some livestock to replace what had been taken. They were given the right to make their own laws on this new reservation. Their days of raiding were over. The Diné had to promise to keep the peace, and they could no longer fight against the U.S. government.

The cavalry had destroyed Dinétah. Weeds grew throughout the once-plowed fields, dirt filled the ditches where water once flowed, and the lovely peach trees were reduced to tree stumps. But the Diné still had their four sacred mountains.

The Diné wanted to repair the damage. They performed ceremonies in honor of their Mother Earth. They prayed that Mother Earth would bless them again. Over time the Diné made a comeback. By 1890 their population had doubled to eighteen thousand people. The Diné also increased the size of their reservation until they owned more than fifteen million acres of land. Most of their land is in New Mexico and Arizona. The Diné also built up their livestock.

Diné women weaving on their reservation

The Diné appreciated Mother Earth for all the wild animals—the many bears, mountain lions, mountain goats, elk, deer, rabbits, and raccoons. There were lots of birds, including eagles and wild turkeys, and plenty of fish in rivers.

In the Southwest the Diné discovered rivers and streams and the beauty of the land. Majestic rock formations stood like monuments inside huge canyons. Towering cliffs rose up on either side of narrow ones. The beautiful land made the nature-loving nomads want to stay in one place.

The Southwest was also home to other Native Americans, including the Pueblo, who were farmers and lived in villages. When the Diné met the Pueblo, the Diné saw how these people benefited from planting corn, squash, and beans in nearby fields. These crops provided a steady source of food. The Pueblo taught the Diné how to make pottery. They showed them how to mix water into the clay dirt, mold the mixture, and fire it to make useful pots, containers, and tools.

The Diné learned the art of weaving from the Pueblo, who wove cloth from the cotton that they grew. The Diné used this cotton cloth to make more comfortable clothing for the hot summers. During the cold, snowy winters, the Diné continued to wear their warm animal skins.

In the 1600s Spanish explorers came to the Southwest. They traveled on powerful horses they had brought from Spain.

The Diné saw the strength and speed of these animals. They realized that it would be much easier to hunt on horses. They could travel much faster. Horses could also carry and pull heavy loads.

The Diné also admired the flocks of sheep that the Spanish had brought from Spain. The Diné realized that if they owned sheep, they would have a good supply of food. They would not have to hunt every day. The Diné decided they needed to get as many horses and sheep from the Spanish as they could.

Many Diné died from starvation, illness, and exhaustion during the march, called the Long Walk. It took at least forty days for the Diné to get to Fort Sumner.

Once the Diné reached their new reservation, they continued to suffer. They tried to farm the new land, but the soil was poor. The weather was not much better. Part of the year brought no rain and too much sun, which dried out the land. The other part of the year brought floods from too much rain.

In four years, 25 percent of the Diné died from hunger and disease. The Diné who managed to survive those difficult years at Fort Sumner longed to return to their sacred homeland.

U.S. soldiers stand watch over the captured Diné at Fort Sumner.

The Diné threw stones and spears at the invaders, but the cavalry had powerful rifles. The Diné could not stop their rivals from destroying the last of their peach trees and fields of corn, squash, and beans. They could not stop the destruction of their herds.

The Diné were overwhelmed and weak from many days with little food. They were exhausted from so many battles with the American soldiers. They were freezing from the harsh winter cold.

By the end of 1864, thousands of Diné had surrendered to the U.S. Army. Long lines of Diné men, women, and children walked about three hundred miles to Fort Sumner in New Mexico. The cavalry watched every step.

The Diné raided the Spanish settlements. In time they became skilled raiders. They stole thousands of animals for their herds. The Diné liked how much these animals helped them in their everyday lives.

Raising livestock became important to the Diné.

The horse became the Diné's preferred way to travel, and sheep supplied much of their food. The Diné wove the wool from the sheep into warm blankets and rugs. In time the Diné became known as first-class weavers. They also were first-class raiders who raided other Native American settlements. Soon, many people feared the Diné.

A Diné woman weaves a rug.

Portrait of Diné men

The general ordered Kit Carson, a famous trapper, hunter, and frontier scout, to defeat the Diné. The general told Carson that when the Diné surrendered to him, they would be taken from their homeland. Any Diné who didn't agree to surrender would be shot. The Diné soon discovered that they were fighting for their survival.

Carson rode his troops into Canyon de Chelly in Dinétah. Many Diné, who were starving, hid from them behind the rocks.

In the 1800s the population of the United States was expanding rapidly. People began settling in the Southwest. Soon, the Diné discovered they had a new rival: the U.S. cavalry and the American settlers.

The two groups battled each other off and on. Then, in 1846, the Diné signed a peace treaty with the U.S. government. Disagreements ended the peace by 1849.

A new general, James Henry Carleton, took control of the U.S. territory of New Mexico in 1862. The general decided he disliked Native Americans.

U.S. cavalry chasing Native Americans

The Spanish stirred up their own trouble with the Diné. The Spanish were devout Catholics. They wanted to turn the Diné into Catholics, but the Diné would not give up their sacred beliefs.

Fighting continued between the Diné and the Spanish. So, in time, the Diné moved to a remote part of the Southwest. They chose an area bordered by four mountains that cut into the sky from each of the four **cardinal points.** There was a towering peak in the north, in the east, in the south, and in the west. The Diné considered these four mountains sacred, along with the land within their boundaries.

This area was also a good hiding place for the Diné. Their scouts could conceal themselves behind rocks jutting up from the canyons, or they could hide out behind the rocky ledges on the top. When a warrior spotted trouble, there was be plenty of time to signal other Diné to warn of danger.

Peaks of La Plata Mountain (Dibé Nitsaa) in Colorado, one of the four sacred mountains of Dinétah

The Diné called this rugged land Dinétah, or homeland. For thousands of years small groups of Diné had roamed North America. Usually, everyone in each group was related. Once these small groups moved to Dinétah, the Diné began to think of themselves as a nation of people who shared a common land.

Once the Diné got horses and sheep, their lifestyle changed. They continued to hunt, but now they hunted on horseback. They needed a constant source of food and water for the people and their herds.

The Diné farmed the surrounding land and grew crops of corn, squash, and beans. The Diné also grew splendid orchards of peach trees.

The Diné built **hogans.** Hogans were circular structures supported by logs or poles that were normally covered with earth and bark. A fire was built inside for both heat and cooking. A smoke hole in the top of the hogan let smoke escape. The entrance to the hogan always faced east so the Diné could honor and greet the rising sun each morning. They lived in some of the hogans, but other hogans were used only for sacred ceremonies.

A Diné hogan

Suggested levels for Guided Reading, DRA,™ Lexile,® and Reading Recovery™ are provided in the Pearson Scott Foresman Leveling Guide.

Science
Science

Biography

John Muir: A Man of The Wilderness

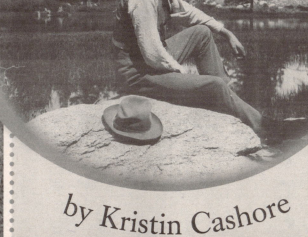

by Kristin Cashore

Genre	Comprehension Skill and Strategy	Text Features
Nonfiction	• Main Idea and Details • Graphic Organizers	• Heads • Captions • Time Line • Glossary

Scott Foresman Reading Street 4.1.5

ISBN 0-328-13426-0

scottforesman.com

Reader Response

1. Think about the book you have just read. Use a chart similar to the one below to tell a main idea in this book. Then tell three supporting details.

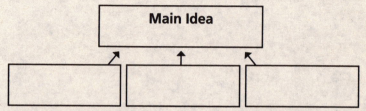

2. Use a map of the world. Trace the travels Muir made that you read about on page 8. What continents did he cover?

3. Work with a group to make a list of "nature words" from Muir's biography. Write each word on two cards. Turn the cards face down and mix them up. Turn over two cards at a time looking for a match. Use the word in a sentence when you make a match. See who has the most matches at the end of the game.

4. How did the time line on pages 14 and 15 help you understand what happened in Muir's life?

Glossary

botany *n.* the science of plants; study of plants and plant life.

conservation *n.* preservation from harm or decay; protection from loss or from being used up.

glaciers *n.* great masses of ice moving very slowly down a mountain, along a valley, or over a land area.

naturalist *n.* a person who makes a study of living things.

preserve *v.* to keep from harm or change; keep safe; protect.

species *n.* a set of related living things that all have certain characteristics.

John Muir: A Man of The Wilderness

by Kristin Cashore

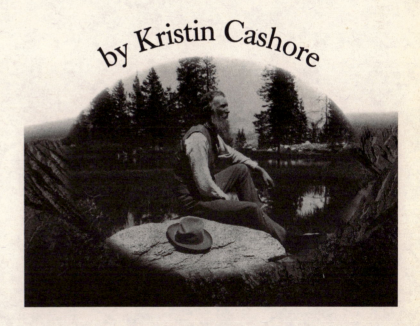

Editorial Offices: Glenview, Illinois • Parsippany, New Jersey • New York, New York
Sales Offices: Needham, Massachusetts • Duluth, Georgia • Glenview, Illinois
Coppell, Texas • Ontario, California • Mesa, Arizona

Here's How to Do It!

1. First, you need to decide what changes you will make. What things lived and grew here before your home was built? What kinds of trees, shrubs, and flowers would you like to plant? Do you want to include any bird feeders? A fountain or pond? A bee hive? Make a list!

2. Next, make a plan. Where will you get the materials you need? How will you learn the steps involved in planting a tree or caring for a garden? How will you learn to garden in ways that are good for the environment? Make a list of the questions you will need to ask in order to complete your plan.

3. Draw a rough diagram of how your yard will look when you have planted your trees and plants. Where will each tree go? Which flowers will go in which garden? Where will you hang the bird feeders?

4. Plan for the future. Will you plant more trees later on? Will you plant the same flowers every year? How can you continue to encourage birds, squirrels, spiders, and other creatures to use your yard as their home?

Now Try This

Be a Settler and a Conserver

It is your turn to conserve nature! Often when a house is built, the land around the house is cleared. Trees are chopped down, shrubs are uprooted, and weeds and other plants are removed. After the house is built, the owners may plant grass, but the wild growth from before is lost. Insects and animals are pushed away. But there are ways to bring the wildness back. Take charge of this conservation effort and see what you can do to restore what has been lost!

Planting and taking care of the plants and flowers in your home and garden is one way to conserve nature.

A Preserver Among the Settlers

Imagine a beautiful land with forests and hills, lakes and rivers, and lots of wildlife. The land has plenty of wood to build houses, plenty of land to farm, plenty of animals for food, and plenty of water. But what happens if we start to cut down the trees for houses? What happens when our cows begin to eat all of the grass on the hills? What if we need to dam the river to gather water and make electricity? What if we drive the animals away?

When people settle a new place, the landscape must change. In the nineteenth century, the American West was a wilderness, and people moved in to "tame" it. As a result, our country prospered and grew. At the same time, the environment changed.

Many people were full of ideas about how they could use the American West. Only a few people realized what Americans were doing to the American West. Only a few were thinking about the land, the plants, the animals, and the trees. One of those people was John Muir.

John Muir

An American Hero from Scotland

John Muir may have spent his life fighting to **preserve** America's natural wonders, but he was not an American. Muir was born in Dunbar, Scotland, on April 21, 1838. Even as a young boy, he loved the outdoors. Whenever Muir could sneak away from his schoolwork, he walked along the Scottish coast and wandered through the countryside. When he was eleven years old, his life changed. His family moved to the United States.

A street banner that honors John Muir in the town of Dunbar

The Scottish coast near Muir's childhood home in Dunbar, Scotland

Muir Opens America's Eyes

In the nineteenth century, America was full of settlers. Many of these settlers saw mountains, trees, and valleys as an opportunity to build homes, farms, and towns. These settlers weren't worried about the trees they cut down or the animals they drove away. They didn't realize how much America had to lose. It took a young man from Scotland to see these same mountains, trees, and valleys as national treasures.

Nature was John Muir's escape from a hard day's work on the farm, and it was his comfort after a scary eye injury. Nature taught him at the University of the Wilderness. Nature showed him one of life's truths: All living things, no matter how big or small, are important. Muir knew the value of nature, and he made nature the work of his lifetime. It took him a lifetime of work to open America's eyes to its own beauty.

If you ever have a chance to visit a national park, remember John Muir. Our country's natural wonders might not be here today if Muir had not seen them and loved them. Our wilderness might have disappeared long ago if Muir had not defended it.

In 1849 the Muir family settled in Wisconsin and started a farm. Until he was twenty-one, Muir spent almost all of his time working on this farm. He did not go to school, but he found time to teach himself math, literature, and other subjects that interested him. Muir developed a skill for building and inventing things. He made working clocks from scratch and even invented a machine that tipped him out of bed in the morning!

Life in Wisconsin was very hard work, and Muir did not have a lot of free time. Whenever he could, though, Muir roamed through the fields and the forests. He loved the outdoors, and even farmwork led him to become an amateur **naturalist,** or person who studies living things.

Yosemite National Park

Muir's home in Wisconsin

The Wanderer Leaves Home

In 1860 Muir left the farm and went to the Wisconsin State Fair in Madison. He took clocks that he had built to the fair, and he won prizes for them!

The next year, Muir studied at the University of Wisconsin. Because he had learned so much on his own, Muir passed a high school program and got right into college. He did very well in his classes and became fascinated with **botany,** the study of plants.

In 1863 Muir left Wisconsin and entered what he called "The University of the Wilderness." He walked all the way from Wisconsin to Mississippi, studying the trees and plants along his path.

John Muir invented and built clocks that kept good time.

Even Muir's Hetch-Hetchy Valley is still an open question. Today the Sierra Club is working to reverse the Hetch-Hetchy Valley decision. It wants to empty the dam and return the river and the valley to their original state. In the meantime, the Sierra Club works to prevent other destructive dams from being built.

The Muir Woods National Monument in California is named after John Muir.

Muir's Legacy

John Muir was one of our country's most important naturalists. Millions of people have read his books. His writing has changed people's attitudes. It is thanks to John Muir and others like him that many Americans today care about nature and the environment. People who work toward conservation today are acting in the spirit of John Muir.

John Muir is so admired that many parks, trails, and organizations are named after him. The John Muir Trust is a Scottish organization that works to protect the environment. The Muir Woods National Monument is a forest of protected redwood trees in California. The John Muir Trail runs for 211 miles through some of the most beautiful mountains in California. The John Muir Wilderness is a large area in California full of mountains, lakes, and streams. The Sierra Club has also grown over the years, and today it does important conservation work all over the world.

The California quarter and some stamps have John Muir's image on them.

For the next few years, Muir explored the northern United States and Canada. While he wandered, he worked odd jobs. In Canada, he worked at a sawmill and a broom and rake factory. In Indiana, he worked at a carriage factory.

In 1867 when Muir was almost thirty years old, there was a terrible accident in the carriage factory. Muir, who had always found the natural world so beautiful, became blind. After a few difficult weeks, his eyesight began to return. It took months for him to recover completely and regain his sight. When he did, he chose to leave his work in the factory.

Muir's accident made him realize that he wanted to spend his life in forests and on mountains, not in factories. He set out on a long walk to Florida. This was the beginning of a lifetime of wandering and study. For the rest of his days, Muir traveled, studied, and learned from the University of the Wilderness.

The University of Wisconsin

California and the World

Where did Muir go? So many places! From Florida, he sailed to New York, Cuba, Panama, and California. He explored California's mountains, valleys, and rivers. He traveled through the American West and made his way to the mountains and **glaciers** of Alaska. He visited the Appalachian Mountains and explored the eastern states. He returned to Alaska many times.

In later years, Muir's wanderings took him to parts of Europe as well as Russia, Korea, Japan, China, India, Egypt, Australia, New Zealand, Indonesia, the Philippines, Hong Kong, and Hawaii. He visited Brazil and Chile, South Africa, and parts of eastern Africa. He went to museums, and he visited the great bridges and buildings that people had built. But it was the natural world that thrilled him; it was the rivers and the forests that he traveled to see.

This is California's Yosemite National Park.

In 1906 there was an earthquake in San Francisco and a fire destroyed most of the city. After the earthquake, city officials decided that they wanted to dam the Tuolumne River and flood the Hetch-Hetchy Valley. This would create a reservoir of water to supply San Francisco. It would also make it easier to put fires out the next time there was an earthquake.

John Muir and the Sierra Club battled to protect the Hetch-Hetchy Valley from the city's decision. The fierce fight lasted seven years. In 1913 President Woodrow Wilson signed a bill that gave the city of San Francisco the right to dam the Tuolumne River and flood the Hetch-Hetchy Valley. Muir and the Sierra Club had lost the fight, and the world had lost the valley.

The fight against damming of the Tuolumne River and flooding of the Hetch-Hetchy Valley was Muir's last battle. One year later, while visiting one of his daughters in Los Angeles, he caught pneumonia. At the age of seventy-six, John Muir died, but this lover and protector of our country's wilderness has not been forgotten.

The Tuolumne River

One Last Fight

In the later years of Muir's life, he spent time with his wife and two daughters and wrote even more than he had earlier. During his life he published more than three hundred articles and ten books. He never stopped traveling the world, and he never stopped fighting for the cause of conservation.

Unfortunately, Muir did not always win his fights. One of his greatest disappointments involved the Hetch-Hetchy Valley in Yosemite. The Hetch-Hetchy Valley was a gorgeous part of Yosemite through which the Tuolumne River flowed.

The Tuolumne River dam

Yosemite's Hetch-Hetchy Valley

Muir visited many places, but California became his home, and he loved his surroundings. The Sierra Nevada were the most beautiful mountains he had ever seen. Muir did not think anything compared to the valleys, waterfalls, and cliffs of Yosemite.

California is also the home of the giant redwood trees. These trees can grow to be more than three hundred feet tall, with trunks twenty feet wide. Some of the giant redwoods are more than three thousand years old. John Muir loved these trees and always returned to them after his wanderings.

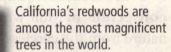

California's redwoods are among the most magnificent trees in the world.

The background shows the Sierra Nevada.

Words Can Save Mountains

But there was no denying it: The acts of humans were harming the Sierra Nevada, Yosemite, and other parts of California. As people settled in California, they chopped down the magnificent redwoods. Muir could not bear to see people destroying nature. So what did he do? He began to write.

Muir wrote articles about animals and plants. He wrote about bees, salmon, sheep, birds, and trees. He wrote about glaciers and earthquakes. Everything in nature interested Muir, and he shared his knowledge by writing it down.

Some of his most important writing was about **conservation.** Muir wrote passionately about saving nature from the carelessness of humans. He fought for the preservation of the redwoods. He wrote about sheep and cows whose grazing was ruining the environments of California. In his writing, Muir begged people to be more careful and to preserve the natural world.

Muir loved writing as much as he loved nature.

Muir's hard work led to the creation of Yosemite National Park and Sequoia National Park in California, and Mount Rainier National Park in Washington. It also led to the protection of the Petrified Forest and the Grand Canyon in Arizona. Muir's writing was so important and influential that today he is often called the father of our national park system.

In 1892 Muir and some of his followers decided to start an organization to preserve the Sierra Nevada. They called this organization the Sierra Club, and Muir served as its president from 1892 to 1914. Muir wrote that the Sierra Club would "do something for wilderness and make the mountains glad." Today the Sierra Club continues working to preserve nature and educate people all over the world.

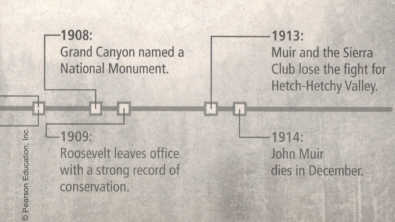

1908: Grand Canyon named a National Monument.

1909: Roosevelt leaves office with a strong record of conservation.

1913: Muir and the Sierra Club lose the fight for Hetch-Hetchy Valley.

1914: John Muir dies in December.

Muir Creates the National Park System

President Roosevelt left the mountains of California and returned to the White House, but he did not forget the beauty of California. He did not forget what Muir had said about conserving nature.

While Roosevelt was president he started the U.S. Forest Service, which works to protect our forests. He created 150 national forests, five national parks, eighteen national monuments, and fifty-one new wildlife refuges. Today President Theodore Roosevelt is famous for conservation. Without his actions, many of our most beautiful lands might not exist.

Muir did not stop after encouraging the President. He continued to write long articles explaining that lands should be protected, and he worked hard to educate people about conservation. He fought for the creation of national parks.

Conservation in the Time of John Muir

- **1890:** Yosemite and Sequoia National Parks formed.
- **1892:** Muir and friends found Sierra Club.
- **1899:** Mount Rainier National Park formed.
- **1903:** Roosevelt visits Muir in California.
- **1906:** The fight for Hetch-Hetchy Valley begins.
- **1906:** Petrified Forest named a National Monument.

Muir also wrote down his own philosophy, or beliefs, about the way the world worked. Muir believed that all living things were connected and that no living thing was more important than any other. A worm was just as important as a human, and all living things worked together to keep Earth healthy. Muir wanted humans to stop acting as if they were more important than other living things. He wanted humans to respect Earth and every **species** on it.

Important magazines started publishing Muir's writings, and people all over the country began to read what Muir had to say. Many people agreed with his ideas and opinions. Because of Muir, people joined the fight to protect nature. Muir began to gain some very powerful friends.

Muir at work in his den

Famous Friends and Allies

Muir's writings caught the attention of many famous people of his time. Asa Gray was a famous professor who studied botany. Gray visited Muir in California, and they traveled and studied together. Gray even named a few plants that he discovered for Muir!

The great philosopher and writer Ralph Waldo Emerson also visited Muir. This was exciting for Muir, who was a fan of Emerson's works. Emerson respected Muir's ideas, and the two men became good friends.

Ralph Waldo Emerson

Asa Gray

Muir's most powerful friend and visitor was the President of the United States, Theodore Roosevelt. President Roosevelt had read Muir's writings and liked what he had to say. Roosevelt wrote a letter to Muir asking Muir to show him the mountains of California.

Muir agreed, and for three days in 1903, John Muir went camping with the President of the United States! They sat under the trees in Yosemite and talked about conservation. Muir explained to President Roosevelt that the wilderness was in danger of being destroyed. He asked the President to help preserve America's natural beauty. He stressed that the mountains and forests were important to all people.

President Roosevelt and many others took Muir's message seriously, and because of Muir, the country began to change.

In 1903 John Muir showed President Roosevelt the natural beauty of California.

Suggested levels for Guided Reading, DRA,™ Lexile,® and Reading Recovery™ are provided in the Pearson Scott Foresman Leveling Guide.

Social Studies

EQUALITY IN AMERICAN SCHOOLS

by Lillian Forman

segregation vs. integration

Genre	Comprehension Skill and Strategy	Text Features
Nonfiction	• Cause and Effect • Prior Knowledge	• Captions • Labels • Heads • Glossary

Scott Foresman Reading Street 4.2.1

PEARSON
Scott Foresman

scottforesman.com

ISBN 0-328-13429-5

9 780328 134298

Reader Response

1. Use a chart similar to the one below to tell some causes of the fight for equality for African Americans. What are some of the effects?

Cause	Effect

2. What did you know about segregation before reading this book? How did that help you while you were reading?

3. Define the word *legal*. Then add a prefix to make it mean its opposite. Add a suffix to make it a verb. Use the dictionary to help you.

4. Using the section headings, find out how many years passed between the time the Fourteenth Amendment was passed and the end of Reconstruction?

Glossary

aspiring *adj.* having an ambition for something; desiring earnestly; seeking.

discrimination *n.* the act of showing an unfair difference in treatment.

diversity *n.* variety.

doctrine *n.* what is taught as true by a church, nation, or group of persons; belief.

integration *n.* inclusion of people of all ethnic backgrounds on an equal basis in schools, parks, neighborhoods, and so on.

jeering *v.* laughing at rudely or unkindly; mocking; scoffing.

tactics *n.* ways to gain advantage or success; methods.

EQUALITY IN AMERICAN SCHOOLS

by Lillian Forman

Editorial Offices: Glenview, Illinois • Parsippany, New Jersey • New York, New York
Sales Offices: Needham, Massachusetts • Duluth, Georgia • Glenview, Illinois
Coppell, Texas • Ontario, California • Mesa, Arizona

Here's How to Do It!

1. First, set a goal. You will need to focus on a problem that seems possible to solve. For example, you might decide to help students with language differences.
2. Next, make a plan. List the steps needed to solve the problem. Enlist the help of your classmates. Ask your teachers for suggestions. What else might help you make a plan?
3. Form a group and assign a task to each member of the group. If you want to deal with a language difference, the group might help a student learn English by holding practice conversations with him or her. One member of the group might pick a topic and another might make a list of English words that suit the topic. All members of the group should take part in the conversations.
4. You might want to turn the group into a club. Think of a name for the club. How will the name reflect the club's goal?

Thurgood Marshall on the cover of *Time* magazine

Now Try This

Make a Difference at Your School

When asking for integration of the schools, Thurgood Marshall reminded the Supreme Court justices that African American and white children played together on the way to and from school. He asked what harm it would cause if they also went to school together. In making this point, Marshall suggested that if young people went to school together, they would remain friendly and helpful to each other.

What can you do to help people of different ethnicities and cultures in your school? Are some students being left out of social groups? Is anyone having difficulty with language? List the problems that you have observed. Interview students of other cultures to find out what they need in order to be happy at your school.

1868 The Fourteenth Amendment

Before the 1950s the laws of some states forced African Americans to use different facilities from those that white Americans used. They had to drink from separate water fountains, eat in separate restaurants, go to separate hospitals, and learn in separate schools.

In 1868 the Fourteenth Amendment to the Constitution of the United States officially recognized that African Americans, recently freed from slavery, were citizens. It gave them all the rights of citizens, including "equal protection under the law." The Fifteenth Amendment, passed in 1870, made it illegal for anyone to prevent a citizen from voting because of the color of his or her skin.

Segregated movie theater

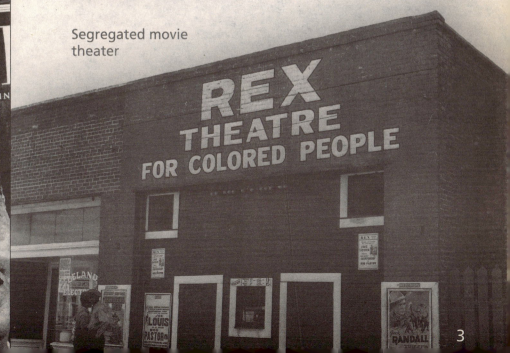

1865-1877 Reconstruction

There were many acts of **discrimination** against African Americans. After the Civil War ended on April 26, 1865, the U.S. government sent soldiers to the South. They were there to protect African Americans and to make sure that no one prevented them from voting. During this period, called Reconstruction, many African Americans became leaders in their state governments and representatives in the U.S. Congress.

Children of different ethnic backgrounds share the same classroom as a result of desegregation.

Today: The Fight Continues

The people who were against integration became more active. Newspapers showed photographs of mobs **jeering** at African American students, who only wanted an equal education.

Instead of being discouraged, African Americans continued to fight. New laws were made ending segregation in all public facilities. In 1967 Thurgood Marshall became the first African American U.S. Supreme Court justice.

Integration did not progress quickly, though. In 2004, on the fiftieth anniversary of the *Brown v. Board of Education* decision, educators met at Central Missouri State University. They found that schools were becoming segregated again, partly because our nation had not been paying attention to desegregation. The educators restated the importance of **diversity** in U.S. schools and vowed to renew the fight to make it happen.

Reconstruction ended in 1877, and the federal troops withdrew. This left African Americans unprotected. Many white Southerners wanted African Americans to live in separate communities. They kept African Americans from voting. As a result, after Reconstruction, people who had supported the Confederacy still governed the South. These legislators wanted to keep African American and white people separate. They turned such practices into laws.

Soldiers of different ethnic backgrounds at a camp in Pennsylvania.

1896 Separate But Equal

In the late 1800s the Supreme Court said that segregation of African Americans and white people was in agreement with the Constitution, as long as they were separate but equal. The places for African Americans had to be equal to those for white people.

Did this really mean that African Americans had the same rights as white people? Suppose you find out that a group of students has taken over a table in the cafeteria. When you try to sit there, the group tells you to go somewhere else even if there is room. They point out that the other tables are the same. As a result you feel that the members of the group think that they are better than you and do not want you around.

Shortly after the Supreme Court had declared school segregation unconstitutional, a group of people in Mississippi formed the White Citizens Council to fight integration. The members of the White Citizens Council and similar groups took legal and illegal measures to prevent African American children from entering white schools. Besides handing out leaflets to advertise their own point of view, they hurt those who did not agree with them. The members boycotted, or refused to buy from, businesses whose owners did not support segregation. They fired African American employees who tried to insist on the rights of their children.

Separate But Equal?

Do you think the students in these pictures have equal opportunities?

Southern politicians found three ways to fight the *Brown* v. *Board of Education* decision. One of these **tactics** was to do nothing about helping integration along. Another was to refuse to obey the laws against segregation. The third involved violence. Mobs of people threatened and insulted African American students who tried to attend white schools.

Brown v. *Board of Education* National Historic Site in Topeka, Kansas

The **doctrine** of "separate but equal" does not make segregation right. Political leaders of the late 1800s failed to provide equal facilities for African Americans. Little money was spent on African American facilities. African American schools, for example, were not as good as those used by white people.

Perhaps the most important public facility is school. It is in school that people learn about citizenship and prepare themselves for the future. It is in school that people learn about their own culture as well as other people's cultures. A poor school leaves its students at a disadvantage.

James Weldon Johnson

Supreme Court justices, 1953 (left) and a newspaper announcing the Court's decision (below)

This landmark decision was a great victory for African Americans, but it was just the beginning of a long and difficult struggle. The Supreme Court justices knew that many white people would fight against allowing African American children into their schools. They decided that integration should take place in a slow but steady manner.

In 1952 Thurgood Marshall brought Brown's case before the Supreme Court. The Court did not make a decision at that time. The case was opened again in 1953 and was argued using the Fourteenth Amendment, which gives all citizens, of any ethnic background, equal rights and equal protection under the law. In 1954 Chief Justice Earl Warren read the Court's unanimous, or fully agreed upon, decision in favor of Linda Brown. The Court concluded that separate schools are unequal. It also stated that anyone forced to go to a segregated school is "deprived of the equal protection of the laws guaranteed by the Fourteenth Amendment."

1909-Present NAACP

In the mid-1920s African Americans in a group called the National Association for the Advancement of Colored People (NAACP) decided to do something about this inequality. James Weldon Johnson, a poet, led the group in a series of lawsuits to force school boards to spend as much money on African American schools as they did on white schools.

These lawsuits were also meant to start **integration,** or the inclusion of people of all racial backgrounds in public places. The NAACP planned to do this in three ways:

- by advertising to the American public how African Americans were discriminated against
- by showing African Americans that they could fight against inequality
- by making it so expensive to provide "separate but equal" facilities that white Southern taxpayers would accept the idea of integration

The NAACP was not able to carry out this plan at the time. They needed more money and more African American lawyers to do so. Fortunately, in the 1930s, a group of African American leaders took up the challenge.

One of these leaders was a lawyer named Thurgood Marshall. He worked with another African American lawyer, Charles Hamilton Houston, to fight segregation in public schools. At first Marshall and Houston tried to win equal conditions for African American graduate students, or people continuing their studies after college. They felt that white judges would respect the achievements of these young people.

Marshall and Houston went on to win many cases. Two of the most important victories were in the late 1940s. They both involved aspiring lawyers—Herman Sweatt and George McLaurin.

Herman Sweatt applied to the University of Texas School of Law and was rejected. True to the doctrine of separate but equal, the state of Texas gave the university money to build a law school for African Americans. Until the new school was built, however, Sweatt had to attend a makeshift school in the basement of a building. When the new school was built, it was not as good as the University of Texas School of Law.

1951-1954 *Brown v. Board of Education*

Many parents asked their local NAACP to help them get better school conditions for their children. Some parents just wanted their segregated schools to be as good as the white schools. Marshall and other NAACP leaders persuaded these people to demand that their children be admitted to white schools.

Oliver Brown of Topeka, Kansas, did not want his nine-year-old daughter, Linda, to have to cross train tracks and a busy street to get to her bus stop. At first he wanted safer transportation for her, but then he realized that the white school was only a few blocks away. It made more sense to ask that Linda be allowed to attend that school.

Linda Brown's case was first tried in the U.S. District Court for the district of Kansas in 1951. This court agreed that segregation made African American children feel less valued. However, Linda Brown still was not allowed to go to school with the white students.

Linda Brown, as a child (above)

Cheryl Brown Henderson, Linda's sister, speaking at a celebration fifty years after the *Brown* v. *Board of Education* decision, along with President George W. Bush (left)

© Pearson Education, Inc.

Thurgood Marshall

George McLaurin is forced to sit alone in a classroom of white students.

George McLaurin applied to the University of Oklahoma. Since Oklahoma had no law school for African Americans, the university had to accept McLaurin as a student. He sat in the same classroom as white students, but he sat alone.

In 1950 Marshall brought these cases to the Supreme Court and won. In Sweatt's case, the Supreme Court justices agreed that the facility for African American students was not equal to the one for white students. In McLaurin's case, they recognized that sitting alone prevented him from participating in class.

The Supreme Court ruled that Sweatt and McLaurin should be treated the same as other students. However, separate but equal facilities were still allowed in other places.

These Supreme Court rulings gave Marshall a way to fight segregation in elementary and high schools. The rulings proved that McLaurin's isolation within the classroom had made his education inferior. Marshall hoped that this would make it easier for the NAACP to show that all forms of segregation were harmful.

Suggested levels for Guided Reading, DRA,™ Lexile,® and Reading Recovery™ are provided in the Pearson Scott Foresman Leveling Guide.

Social Studies

Biography

The Life of César Chávez

Genre	Comprehension Skill and Strategy	Text Features
Nonfiction	• Draw Conclusions • Prior Knowledge	• Captions • Heads • Map • Glossary

Scott Foresman Reading Street 4.2.2

PEARSON
Scott Foresman

scottforesman.com

ISBN 0-328-13432-5

9 780328 134328

by Gretchen McBride

Reader Response

1. Why do you think César Chávez was so successful in his effort to better the farm workers' lives?

2. What did you already know about nonviolent protests before reading this book? How did it help you when you were reading?

3. Using a chart similar to the one below, make a list of the words in the book that are Spanish. Write the English translation for each word and tell how you know that's what it means.

Spanish Word	Definition

4. How do the headings help you when you are reading? Under which heading can you find information about *La Causa*?

Glossary

boycotts *v.* refusals to buy or use a product or service.

discrimination *n.* act of showing an unfair difference in treatment.

fast *v.* to go without food; eat little or nothing.

grueling *adj.* very tiring; exhausting.

predetermined *v.* determined or decided beforehand.

strikes *n.* acts of stopping work.

The Life of César Chávez

by Gretchen McBride

Editorial Offices: Glenview, Illinois • Parsippany, New Jersey • New York, New York
Sales Offices: Needham, Massachusetts • Duluth, Georgia • Glenview, Illinois
Coppell, Texas • Ontario, California • Mesa, Arizona

Here's How to Do It!

1. Think about images to represent the different backgrounds of people in your class and the different hobbies or special interests they might have.
2. Draw some pictures for your banner, or gather photographs or pictures from magazines.
3. What do you all have in common? Consider how you might represent this with a drawing or other image.
4. Choose two or three colors that have a special meaning to the group. What do your colors represent to you?
5. Decide what your group is called. You might also decide to use a slogan.
6. Create your banner!

Now Try This

A Banner for Identity

What might a banner that represented your school or your class look like? César Chávez and his farm workers' union followed a banner to declare their group identity when they demonstrated and marched. That banner was designed by César's brother, Richard, with the help of a graphic designer. They decided to show an eagle on the banner because an eagle appears on the Mexican flag. Some say that the eagle they designed has the look of an ancient Aztec temple, bringing to mind the ancient culture of Mexico. César chose the colors for the banner: Black stood for the struggles of the farm workers, red for the sacrifices that they would make, and white for hope.

The workers carried their banner proudly, telling everyone who they were and what they stood for.

César Estrada Chávez (1927–1993)

César Chávez

After a life filled with struggle and triumph, misery and happiness, César Chávez died unexpectedly at age sixty-six. César was in San Luis, Arizona, on union business, when he passed away due to natural causes.

Although there had been many long journeys in his life, César died not far from the farm his family had lost in the Great Depression of the 1930s. The family farm was a place that held happy memories of hard work rewarded, independence, and self-respect.

César met many hardworking people living under difficult circumstances during his lifetime. César wanted these people to experience some of the good things in life that he saw as possible.

César's grandfather, Cesario Chávez, was born in Chihuahua, Mexico. His life was one of servitude, or forced labor, on a hacienda, or ranch. He worked as a ranch hand to pay the owner of the hacienda so that his days of servitude would be over. But the owner took so much from the wages of his *peones,* or farm workers, for room and board that Cesario could never save any money.

Deep Roots

Finally, in the late 1880s, Cesario ran away. Crossing the Rio Grande into Texas, he made his way to Arizona. Cesario worked hard and saved money for a small ranch. The land he bought was near Yuma, Arizona. It was desert land, but the new dam that was being built in the Gila River valley would provide irrigation for the crops. Cesario would finally be his own master.

Saying Farewell to a Hero

Richard Chávez had run and swum and played with his brother César when they were young, before their family lost their small businesses and precious land. He worked beside him in the fields and on the picket lines. In the end, Richard built his brother's casket. It was a simple pine box that was carried during César's funeral, along with the union's banner bearing its proud black eagle, and the flags of Mexico and the United States.

Approximately forty thousand people would pay their last respects to this man on the day of his funeral. His mourners followed the banners and the handmade casket for more than three miles. They walked along part of the route that César had traveled for *La Causa*, a route that had led many to self-respect and better lives for themselves and their families.

Statue of César Chávez at California State University

The Legacy of César Chávez

César Chávez would continue his work for more than twenty years after the triumph of July 1970. In fact, before a month had passed, he was organizing the lettuce workers. Once again, a boycott was called. When a judge ordered César to call off the boycott, he refused, was fined, and spent twenty days in jail.

César was now a public figure of great importance, but many people did not agree with what he was doing for the workers. He received death threats and was convinced by others that he should have guard dogs to protect him. But no matter what the challenge—or even the threat—César Chávez never wavered from his belief in nonviolence. There would be more demonstrations, strikes, and fasts for what he believed in, but never would he raise his hand against another. He never forgot the advice of his mother, to use his mind instead of his fists.

Cesario met his wife in the United States. Her family was also from Mexico. Dorotea—or "Mama Tella" as her grandchildren would call her—was literate. She had learned to read and write both Spanish and Latin in a Catholic orphanage in Mexico. Eventually, she would pass on her education to her children and then her grandchildren. Cesario and Dorotea would have fifteen children, including César's father, Librado.

Cesario and Dorotea built a large adobe farmhouse with thick walls to keep out the heat of the Arizona desert's summer days and the cold of winter nights. All of the children worked on the farm as they grew up.

When Librado was thirty-eight years old, he married Juana Estrada. Her family had come to the United States from the same area of Mexico as Librado's father. The couple owned and ran a small grocery store, a garage, and a pool hall. They also raised a family. Their second child, César Estrada Chávez, was born on March 31, 1927.

César's grandfather moved from Chihuahua, Mexico (pictured), to land near Yuma, Arizona.

Growing Strong

There would be difficult—even terrible—times ahead for the Chávez family, but César's early years gave him many pleasures, and the memory of those years would later help to keep him strong.

His father taught César about farming. His mother, like his grandmother, was a religious person, and she passed on her values to her children. From her, César learned that instead of fighting, it was best to "turn the other cheek." She taught him that he did not need to resort to violence; instead, he should use his mind to find a solution to a problem. This lesson would be one of the most important of César's life.

He and his brothers helped with the farming and all three of the family businesses. César liked the freedom he had to roam the family farm. He and his brother Richard swam, hiked, and explored at will. They loved to build forts for fun out on the open land.

In October 1929, on Wall Street in New York City—very far from the Chávez's home—the stock market "crashed." Many people lost all of their money. Businesses failed and even banks closed all over the United States.

César's brother Richard holds the first crate of Coachella Valley grapes to display the union logo.

Thanks to César, his union, and its supporters, the workers in the grape vineyards got a hiring hall, which meant the end of discrimination by labor contractors. Higher wages, protection against pesticides, and other benefits were negotiated too. With great ceremony, the agreements were signed.

César and his followers had completed an important mission, but there were other struggles ahead. *La Causa* had never been just about the workers in the grape vineyards—it was about the plight of all poor people.

Following the example of Gandhi, César Chávez stopped eating. He called a meeting to explain that he would fast until union members recommitted themselves to nonviolence. The **fast** also showed he would not be promoting the grape industry, or consuming grapes, from which supermarkets profited. Once again, César had the attention of the country. Martin Luther King Jr. and Robert Kennedy both expressed their support. On the **predetermined** date of March 10, 1968, César stopped fasting.

A Reason to Celebrate

It was clear that the strikes and the boycotts of nonunion growers were paying off. After Schenley signed the union contract, pressure on other growers continued. Finally, in July 1970, César could make an exciting announcement: Twenty-three companies were ready to negotiate with the union. By the mid-1970s, two-thirds of grape growers in California were under contract with César's union.

This economic disaster also reached the Chávez family. By 1932, they could no longer pay their bills. They lost their businesses. Then a great draught came. With no rain, the states of the Great Plains turned into a "dust bowl." Farms failed. The Chávez family could not pay the taxes on their land, and they lost their beloved farm. It was 1937. César Chávez was ten years old.

The soil that had produced good crops in the past turned into useless dust during the long drought of the 1930s.

The Migrant Life

The Chávez family packed up their belongings and headed to California to find work. César's father hoped they could earn enough money to recover their farm.

Migrant workers, such as the Chávez family, moved from place to place, following the seasonal crops. They lived in rented houses that were often shacks. Usually, their basic living expenses ate up the low wages they earned picking grapes, lettuce, peas, or beans. The labor was **grueling,** workers often spent the entire day crouched, or bent low, to the ground.

Even the children worked in the fields, attending school only once in a while. César was fifteen years old when, after attending more than thirty different schools, he completed the eighth grade. He decided then that he must concentrate on earning money for the family and did not go back to school.

Like these workers, César and his family worked long hours in fields that were not their own.

By 1968 some strikers were turning to violence. César found guns on one picket line, and someone burned a number of packing sheds belonging to a grape grower. The people were forgetting César's lessons about the importance of nonviolence. Something, he decided, must be done to remind the members of the NFWA and their supporters that only peaceful acts would bring them nearer to a better life for everyone.

On March 17, 1966, César and seventy other members of the NFWA began a march of over three hundred miles from Delano to Sacramento, the state capital of California. They marched for *La Causa*.

As the marchers followed the NFWA banner, with its proud eagle, from town to town, more supporters joined the march. People all over the country watched the marchers on television. Americans were impressed with the dedication of the marchers, and they listened to what the NFWA had to say about the working conditions in the grape vineyards. The marchers asked that people not buy grapes from companies that treated their employees unfairly. They urged buyers to look for the NFWA eagle on the grapes they bought.

Finally, there was a breakthrough. Schenley Industries, one of the country's largest grape growers, agreed to sign a contract, or agreement, with the farm workers' union. This was the first contract for farm workers ever signed in the United States.

The Schenley contract did not bring an end to the struggle. Strikes, demonstrations, and **boycotts** against nonunion grape growers continued so that more farm workers could enjoy the protection of a contract.

César marched in 1966, and met with strikers in 1968, to encourage nonviolence.

César and his family often had to live in shacks such as these.

In addition to the hardships of the road and field, the Chávez family also suffered from **discrimination** because of their Mexican heritage. In some small towns in California, businesses hung out signs saying "Whites Only." Once, César watched as his father was cursed at and thrown out of a café where he had gone for a cup of coffee. César would never forget the pain he saw in his father's eyes.

Along with discrimination, the Chávez family and other workers faced very poor working conditions. Sometimes there were **strikes** in the fields. The workers would stop working to protest their terrible working conditions, low wages, and other unfair treatment. César and his family often participated. *"Huelga!"* the people would shout. Strike!

Changing Times

In 1944 the United States was in the middle of World War II. César Chávez was seventeen. He and his family were still living the life of migrant workers, and their dream of buying back the family farm had long ago faded away. César decided that he had to make a change in his life. There were few opportunities for a young Mexican American man with little education, so César decided to join the U.S. Navy.

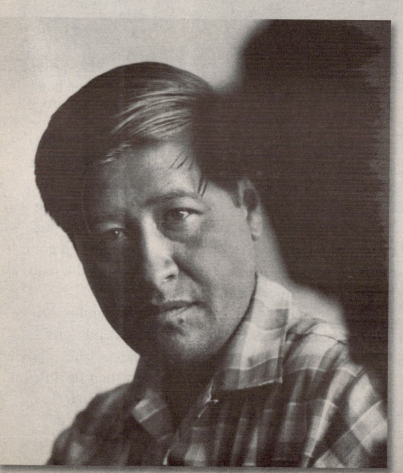

The arguments of the NFWA in support of better working conditions for farm laborers, and their belief in nonviolent protest gained the attention of Senator Robert F. Kennedy, a Democrat from New York. Senator Kennedy supported the NFWA. He criticized the local sheriff for his treatment of the strikers, and he remained an important ally, or partner, of the NFWA.

Senator Robert F. Kennedy and César Chávez (both seated), in early 1968. Kennedy would be assassinated later that year. César was deeply hurt by his death.

Viva La Causa!
"Long live the cause!"

In 1962 César left his job at the CSO to pursue an even bigger dream. He had never forgotten the hard life that he lived as a migrant farm worker. He knew that the people who worked in the fields, gathering the harvests to feed the nation, had a right to be paid fairly for their hard labor and to be treated with dignity and respect. This would be his life's cause: to ensure a better life for the farm workers of America.

The Chávez family moved to Delano, California, where Helen had family, and where César's brother Richard lived. Here he formed the National Farm Workers Association (NFWA). To support the family while the union was being set up, César and his wife returned to work in the fields, harvesting grapes.

In 1965 the NFWA took a stand in support of striking grape harvesters. César made sure the union members understood that all demonstrations were to be nonviolent. They would raise their voices and speak their minds, to convince people of their cause.

The voices of the NFWA were heard loud and clear. Many people supported the cause by agreeing not to buy the grapes sold by companies that did not treat their workers fairly.

If, in joining the navy, César expected to escape the discrimination he suffered in California, he was disappointed. But César was learning from all his experiences—bad and good—and he would use what he learned to better the lives of many people.

When César returned to California after the end of World War II, he did not want to go back to work in the fields. The Great Depression was over, but no one wanted to give a good job to a young Mexican American man with only an eighth-grade education. César had to return to harvesting grapes.

But returning to California did bring César back to Helen Fabela. She was a young woman who he had met a few years earlier when he was a teenager. In 1948 Helen and César married. The couple lived in a one-room shack with no electricity or running water.

But change was on the horizon. At first, the whole Chávez family tried renting a farm in San Jose to grow strawberries. This did not prove profitable, but it was better than life on the road. Finally, after César and Richard had worked at a rainy northern California lumber mill for a while, the Chávez family returned to sunny San Jose where César got work at another lumber mill.

César Chávez discovered that Mexican Americans also suffered from discrimination in the navy.

Sal Si Puedes
"Get out if you can"

Within San Jose there was a barrio, or community of Spanish-speaking people, called *Sal Si Puedes*. This means, loosely translated, "Get out if you can." Most residents of the barrio hoped that one day they would escape from the crowded narrow strip of land. César, Helen, and their three children moved to *Sal Si Puedes* in 1952. In this unlikely place, César would meet two men who would influence his life greatly.

Father Donald McDonnell, the Catholic priest in the barrio, sympathized with the troubles of the Mexican Americans he served. César grew to trust Father McDonnell, and the priest had great respect for César. Father McDonnell introduced him to Mahatma Gandhi's ideas about nonviolent protest. César recognized how much in common those ideas had with the advice he had gotten from his mother so long ago, to use his mind instead of his fists.

The other important man César met in *Sal Si Puedes* was Fred Ross. Ross worked with the Community Service Organization (CSO). The CSO knew that there was power in the vote. The first important job Chávez had with the CSO was helping to register four thousand new voters.

These voters helped to elect a Mexican American representative to the city council so that the voice of their community might be heard. César realized what gaining a voice in the government could accomplish, and so he volunteered to work with the CSO. After working all day, César knocked on doors all night, encouraging his fellow Mexican American citizens to vote. In 1958 César became director of the CSO.

The people of *Sal Si Puedes* often lacked basic services, such as indoor plumbing.

Suggested levels for Guided Reading, DRA,™ Lexile,® and Reading Recovery™ are provided in the Pearson Scott Foresman Leveling Guide.

Social Studies

Geography Shapes Our World

by Stephanie Sigue

Genre	Comprehension Skill and Strategy	Text Features
Nonfiction	• Drawing Conclusions • Answer Questions	• Captions • Glossary • Heads • Maps

Scott Foresman Reading Street 4.2.3

ISBN 0-328-13435-9

Reader Response

1. Give two examples of how geography affects culture.

2. Choose three captions and tell what questions they answer.

3. Look at the word *miscommunication*. Name the prefix and the suffix. Then tell what the word means.

4. What do you think the author's purpose was in writing about a day in the life of these different children?

Glossary

climate *n.* the usual weather in a place

continents *n.* seven large land masses of the earth (Asia, Africa, Europe, North America, South America, Australia, and Antarctica)

geography *n.* the study of the earth, including its people, resources, climate, and physical features

industry *n.* manufacturing companies and other businesses

irrigate *v.* to supply water to crops by artificial means, such as channels and pipes

native *n.* a person, an animal, or a plant that originally lived or grew in a certain place

plantation *n.* a large farm found in warm climates where crops such as coffee, tea, rubber, and cotton are grown

product *n.* something that is manufactured or made by a natural process

typhoon *n.* a violent tropical storm

Geography Shapes Our World

by Stephanie Sigue

Editorial Offices: Glenview, Illinois • Parsippany, New Jersey • New York, New York
Sales Offices: Needham, Massachusetts • Duluth, Georgia • Glenview, Illinois
Coppell, Texas • Ontario, California • Mesa, Arizona

Here's How To Do It!

1. Use an atlas. Turn to the maps of Africa, Europe, South America, Asia, or the Caribbean, and decide where you might like to live.

2. After you have chosen a country, use at least two resources, such as the Internet and books from the library, to find out more about it.

3. Think about living in one of those countries. Write a diary page about your day. What is the geography of your country like? What happens when you wake up? What happens in school? Is the weather hot or cold? What do you eat for breakfast? What sights do you see during your busy day?

4. Be sure to include some interesting facts in your report. Don't forget to tell what people do for fun. Make your report thorough and lively.

5. Add visuals to help describe the country.

6. Present your report to the group.

Now Try This

You've read about a few of the countries of West Africa, Western Europe, South America, Asia, and the Caribbean and about some children who live in them. What do you think your life might be like if you lived in one of those countries? You can write a diary page to tell what your life is like in one of those countries.

Geography Shapes Culture

Imagine living by the ocean in Portugal. The ocean supplies your family with lots of fish to sell and to eat. But if you live in the grassy plains of Uruguay in South America, your family may raise cattle. And if you live in the city of Paris, you don't have to depend on what grows in the area. Food is shipped in from all over the world. Where you live has a lot to do with *how* you live.

The Earth is made up of seven different **continents**, connected by the Pacific, the Atlantic, the Indian and the Arctic Oceans. The continents are Asia, Africa, North America, South America, Antarctica, Europe, and Australia. Each continent has a different **climate** and **geography** and **industry**. Let's take a look at a few!

You can find maps like this in an atlas. An atlas provides information about the world.

Waking Up in Mali

"Wake up, Aminata!" calls her mother. Aminata wakes to another warm, **humid** day in Mali. She squats on the floor with her family and has a delicious breakfast of maize porridge. The maize is a kind of corn, which her family grows in a small plot of land just behind their house.

After eating, Aminata helps her mother sweep and wash dishes. By eight, her parents leave to work in the nearby cotton fields. Part of the money they make pays for Aminata's schooling.

Today at school, they are studying the Dogon people. The Dogon used to live high in the cliffs, in protective dwellings made of pink sandstone. They now live in the villages because life is easier, and they are closer to the Niger River.

Mali is the largest country in West Africa.

In school, Gina is learning about the dance *Tarantella*, which means spider. The dance began long ago as a cure for the spider bite. Dancers spun around wildly and danced away the poison!

At dinner that night, Gina's mother makes homemade pasta and sauce, which she calls gravy. They dip bread in olive oil that is made locally.

After dinner, Gina's father gives Gina a music lesson. She is learning to play the *organetti*, which is Italy's accordion. "Did you know the Italians invented the way we set down musical notes?" he asks. "That was the beginning of 'do re mi'."

Gina is so excited by her grandfather's stories she can hardly go to sleep. Her mind is as busy as Rome, the city she calls home.

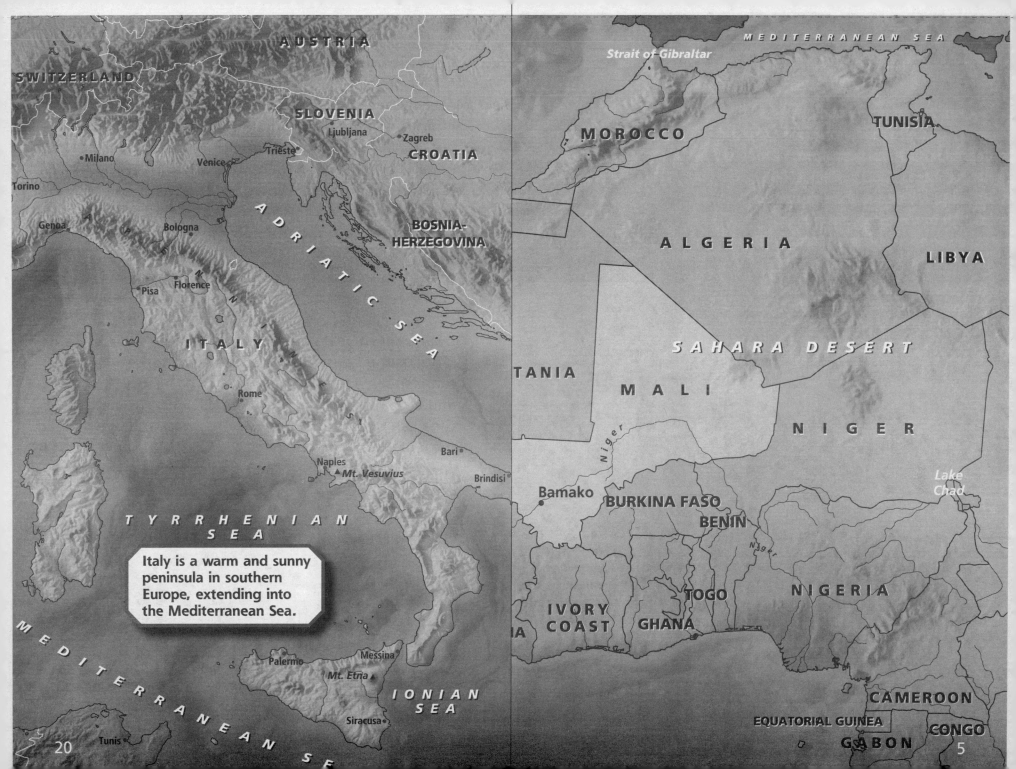

The 21-string Kora

Gina Introduces Us to Rome

"Honk! Honk!" A car horn blasts and Gina's eyes fly open. She wakes up in one of the most famous cities in the world, Rome, Italy.

Gina lives in a modern apartment with her parents and her grandparents. Everyone has breakfast together, eating eggs and toast and cereal. On her way to school Gina dodges the honk of scooters and the rush of people coming and going.

Gina loves the city. You can walk just about anywhere, from the Forum to the Spanish Steps. Her favorite place is by the Coliseum, which is thousands of years old. And right on the same block as the Coliseum is a brand new store selling fancy shoes. There is a great sense of history here and also a sense of modern life. Living in Rome, Gina can't help but appreciate her past and her present.

These are the ancient ruins of the Temple of Saturn and the Arch of Severus in Rome.

At night, Miko practices the *sanshin*, a kind of banjo. Her grandfather helps her because he wants to pass down the music traditions. He tells her that in Okinawa, where he once lived, the workers used to take their instruments right into the rice fields. "After work was done, we would play," he said. "It made working so much easier!"

Miko has seen a picture of her grandfather's house in Okinawa, where he lived before coming to live with them. It is surrounded by heavy stone walls. These protected his house from Japan's frequent typhoons.

Finally, Miko lays down on her mat to sleep. The scent of the cherry blossoms comes in through the window and lulls her to sleep.

The sanshin is a traditional three string banjo.

Aminata knows how important the Niger river is. Without it, how would her family irrigate crops? How would they travel to visit relatives?

When Aminata gets home, she helps her mother prepare the *poulet yassa,* which is the grilled perch that her father caught in the Niger.

After dinner, Aminata's father plays the *kora*, a instrument of 21 strings. It's made of rosewood which is found in Mali. The government prizes this music because it is native. Her uncle plays the drums. "Drums used to be played by people to send messages across the land," her uncle tells her.

That night, in her bed, Aminata listens to the crickets outside. Everything here seems to have a beat, and like the drums, she wonders what messages the crickets are repeating to one another.

This sandstone mosque, a place where muslims worship, is in Timbuktu in Mali. Timbuktu was once a great center of trade and learning in the Muslim world.

Maria in Brazil

Maria wakes to beeping cars and loud conversations. Two out of three Brazilians live in a city, including Maria and her family, who live in São Paulo. Maria gets ready for school. She's luckier than Aminata because her schooling is free.

Brazil is close to the equator. From December to February it's summer, which is just one month away, and Maria can't wait! It's so hot that most people take vacation and school is then closed. Maria and her family will go to the beach and to the five-day Carnival, which is celebrated all over Brazil.

Today at school, Maria learns about the Amazon, the largest river in the world. Many people fish here and hunt along its banks.

São Paulo, the biggest city in South America.

South America is the 4th largest continent in the world.

At school, they are learning about Japan's geography. Miko knows that there are many volcanoes and earthquakes which cause damage, but the country has learned to track them. Miko's school was even built to be quake resistant.

When Miko comes home for dinner, she takes off her shoes and puts on soft slippers. For dinner they are having sushi, which is raw fish and rice wrapped in seaweed. They will also have tempura, which is fish and vegetables fried in batter.

The family talks about what they will do in the fall. "We'll go see *Kagura*," Miko's father says. The dancers in this ceremony wear fancy costumes and masks. Kagura was originally a way to ask for good harvest.

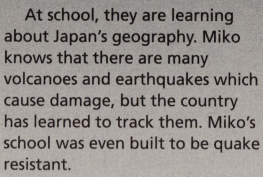

Japan has several thousand islands. Most of Japan is mountains and hills, so people tend to live in crowded cities along the coastlines.

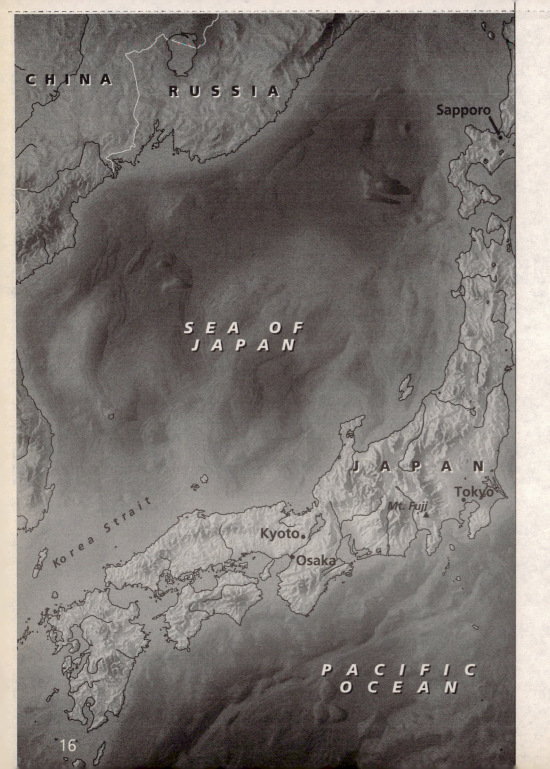

In the evening, Maria and her family eat rice, beans and fish that her father caught. Brazil is famous for coffee and all the adults drink it throughout the meal.

After dinner, Maria practices a little *repitismo* with her mother. It is a kind of call and response singing. "It's like a conversation," Maria's mother tells her. "In Brazil, music is the way to have a social gathering of family and friends. This is very important, especially in the rocky, arid areas where there aren't a lot of people."

By the time Maria goes to sleep, she is very tired. She thinks of what her mother told her about how important family and music are. She's glad she has her music and her family around her.

Brazilians eat the foods they grow locally. A typical Brazilian meal is arroz, or white rice, and black beans and fish.

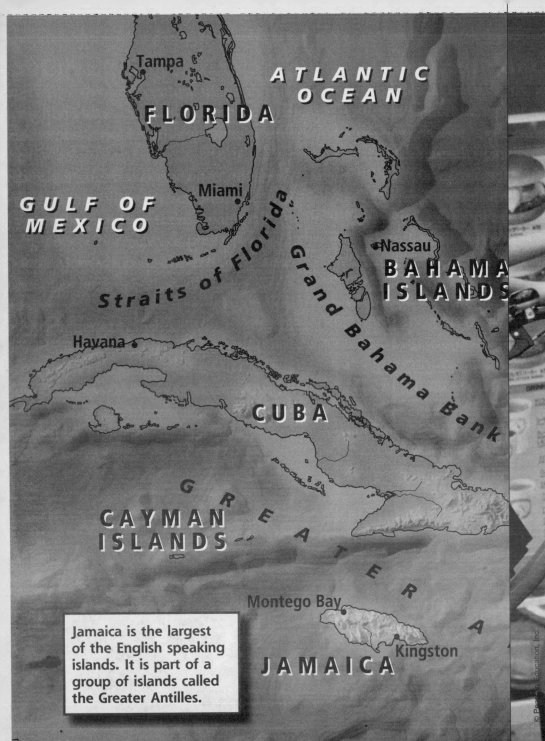

Jamaica is the largest of the English speaking islands. It is part of a group of islands called the Greater Antilles.

Miko in Japan

The delicious smell of miso soup wakes Miko. Miso is made of fermented soybeans, which are one of Japan's natural products. Miko gets up from the straw mat where she sleeps. Japan is very humid, but these mats keep the floor cool now, and they will keep the floor warm in winter.

After Miko eats, she heads outside to school. The cherry blossoms are in bloom! Japan has more kinds of cherry trees than any other place on Earth, and when they bloom in April, everyone celebrates. The blossoms mean new beginnings. That's why the school and business years begin at this time. Later that evening, Miko and her family will go to the park to see the blossoms. Lots of other families will also be there. Miko's mother pickles the blossoms and makes a delicious hot drink from them.

In Japan, the roads are so crowded that many people find it easier to bicycle to work or to do the daily shopping.

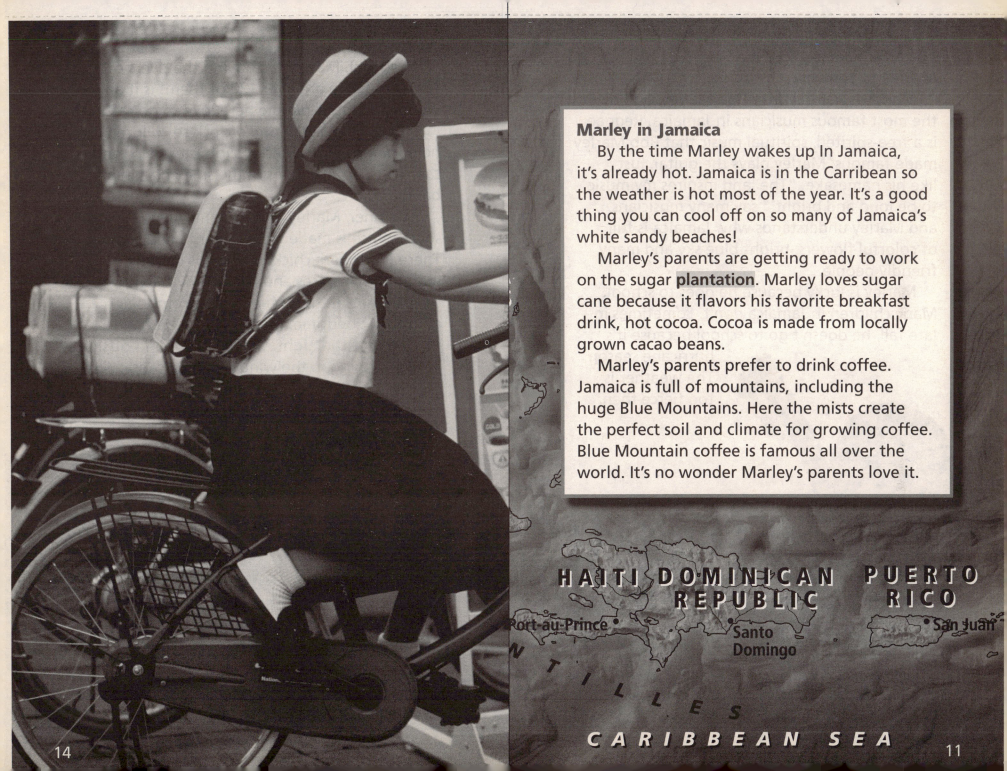

Marley in Jamaica

By the time Marley wakes up In Jamaica, it's already hot. Jamaica is in the Carribean so the weather is hot most of the year. It's a good thing you can cool off on so many of Jamaica's white sandy beaches!

Marley's parents are getting ready to work on the sugar plantation. Marley loves sugar cane because it flavors his favorite breakfast drink, hot cocoa. Cocoa is made from locally grown cacao beans.

Marley's parents prefer to drink coffee. Jamaica is full of mountains, including the huge Blue Mountains. Here the mists create the perfect soil and climate for growing coffee. Blue Mountain coffee is famous all over the world. It's no wonder Marley's parents love it.

Marley in Jamaica

Marley is named after Bob Marley, one of the most famous musicians in Jamaica. Reggae is a free-spirited, spiritual music that Bob Marley made famous. Marley plays the guitar, just like his namesake. "The land inspires my music to be loud and bright," say many musicians, and Marley understands why. Jamaica is full of colorful flowers, bright blue sky and many friendly people.

Marley is lucky because he goes to school. Many children in Jamaica don't. Sometimes in late fall, he doesn't go to school because it's hurricane season. The weather is too fierce then.

Bob Marley and his band The Wailers popularized Reggae music.

At school, Marley is studying the rivers of Jamaica. There are over 120 of them! Is it any wonder so many people here love to go rafting?

School gets out at one o'clock so children can help their parents. Marley's job is to help tend the sweet potato crops in the small plot in his backyard.

At dinner, Marley and his family eat cowcod soup, which is made from bananas and yams. There is also jerk chicken which is chicken marinated in spices and fried. They also have sweet potatoes that Marley dug from their garden. At bedtime, Marley lays in bed and looks out at the night. There is a cooling offshore breeze coming in the window. Jamaicans call it "the doctor breeze" because it makes you feel better. Even the breeze, Marley thinks, has music in it.

Jamaican children love to play soccer.

Suggested levels for Guided Reading, DRA,™
Lexile,® and Reading Recovery™ are provided
in the Pearson Scott Foresman Leveling Guide.

Social Studies *Social Studies*

Danger!
Children at Work

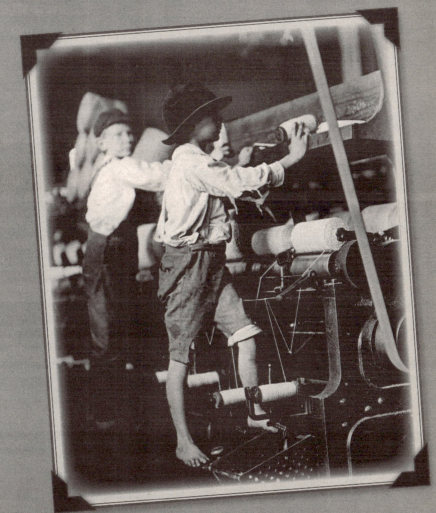

Genre	Comprehension Skill and Strategy	Text Features
Nonfiction	• Fact and Opinion • Monitor and Fix Up	• Heads • Captions • Time Line • Glossary

Scott Foresman Reading Street 4.2.4

PEARSON
Scott Foresman

scottforesman.com

ISBN 0-328-13438-4

9 780328 134380

90000

by Sharon Franklin

Reader Response

1. Reread pages 6-8. Make a chart stating of facts and opinions about child labor from these pages.

Fact	Opinion

2. In the beginning, if you did not understand the difference between child labor and the work you do in your family, what would be one good way to answer your question?

3. If you wanted to find out more about child labor in the library or on the Internet, list three Glossary terms you could use in a search to get more information.

4. Look carefully at the photographs in this book. What do you notice from seeing these photographs of children working that you might miss if you only read an encyclopedia article about child labor?

Glossary

bobbins *n.* reels or spools for holding thread, yarn, etc.

breaker boys *n.* workers who pull slate out of the coal cars in coal mines.

child labor *n.* the abuse and misuse of children at work in ways that profit only employers.

dismay *n.* sudden, helpless fear of what is about to happen or what has happened.

doffers *n.* workers who remove full bobbins and replace them with empty bobbins.

payroll *n.* list of persons to be paid and the amount that each one is to receive.

spinners *n.* workers who brush lint off the machines and watch for breaks in the thread in textile factories.

sweatshops *n.* places where workers are employed at low pay for long hours under bad conditions.

tenement houses *n.* buildings, especially in poor sections of the city, divided into sets of rooms occupied by separate families.

textile mills *n.* factories that make fabric.

Danger!
Children at Work

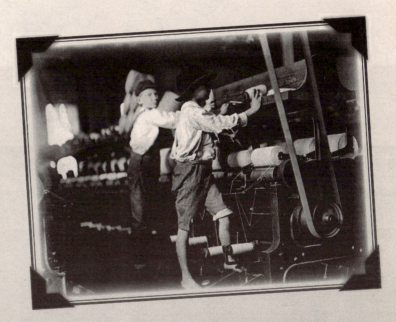

by Sharon Franklin

Editorial Offices: Glenview, Illinois • Parsippany, New Jersey • New York, New York
Sales Offices: Needham, Massachusetts • Duluth, Georgia • Glenview, Illinois
Coppell, Texas • Ontario, California • Mesa, Arizona

Here's How to Do It!

1. ***Child's point of view.*** Think about working at one of the jobs mentioned in this book. Write a journal entry that describes one day in your life. What do you do and see? How do you feel? What do you think about while you work?

2. ***Employer's point of view.*** As the owner of a cotton mill, you depend on child labor. You believe strongly that children love to work and benefit from working. Write a paragraph questioning those who wish to reform child labor laws. Make your case in favor of it.

3. ***Parent's point of view.*** It is 1915. Even with everyone working, there is barely enough money to buy food. You want your children to have a happy life like the children you see playing in the park. Still, you desperately need the money your children can make, even though it is dangerous work that threatens their health and well-being. Make a chart that presents the pros and cons of sending your children off to work.

4. ***Your point of view.*** Lewis Hine's photographs capture the terrible truth about child labor in a way that words alone cannot do. Create a poster or drawings that express your ideas about children's rights as expressed in the Declaration of Dependence.

Now Try This

Point of View

All people in history have a point of view. When studying any event in history, past or present, it is important to identify whose voices are heard and whose voices are silent. In this activity you will create the voice of one person's view about child labor. Share with partners who chose different points of view.

Who has a point of view about child labor?

What responsibilities do you have at home? Maybe you have to feed the dog and clean your room. Perhaps you have to do the dishes or take out the trash. Do you think it is unfair, having to do so much work?

Believe it or not, the chores you and other young people do today are nothing compared to the hard, dangerous work many children did less than one hundred years ago! Picture this.

What kinds of chores do you do?

It is dark outside, as you would expect it to be at 3 A.M., when most people are sleeping. But Nellie, a thin, scraggly-haired seven-year-old with sad green eyes, is waiting at the dock, as she has done nightly for nearly a year. She is waiting for the oyster boats to unload their cargo. Near the dock in the dim light you can see a huge pile of oyster shells. Soon she hurries off to take her place shucking oysters. Later in the day, she will start peeling shrimp.

Nellie uses her small hands and a sharp knife to pry open the oyster shells and drop the meat into a pail. When Nellie's pail is full, she carries it off to be weighed. Nellie usually fills one or two pails each day.

The oyster shells are sharp on little fingers, but the shrimp are even worse. When peeled, they ooze acid that eats holes in shoes and even in Nellie's tin pail. Many children, including Nellie, have swollen, bleeding fingers. Nellie, and many other children like her, stand up to do this job for ten to twelve hours, sometimes working until midnight. They do not get a short break until late afternoon. They earn less than fifty cents a day.

Shucking oysters is tough work on little fingers.

Child Labor Today

All fifty U.S. states now have child labor laws to protect children in the workplace. Most states set a minimum wage, safety standards that include a required minimum age, and limits on the number of hours children under eighteen may work per week. However, labor laws have had little effect on the children of migrant farm workers who may number in the hundreds of thousands.

Tonight as you wash the dishes or feed your cat, think about your life and how different it might have been if you had lived one hundred years ago. Also, think about the people whose hard work to change child labor practices and laws made a difference for so many children. What could you do to make a difference in the world in your lifetime?

This worker meets her state's minimum age requirement to work.

Declaration of Dependence
By the Children of America in Mines and Factories and Workshops Assembled

Whereas, We, Children of America, are declared to have been born free and equal, and

WHEREAS, We are yet in bondage in this land of the free; are forced to toil the long day or the long night, with no control over the conditions of labor, as to health or safety or hours or wages, and with no right to the rewards of our service, therefore be it

RESOLVED, I — That childhood is endowed with certain inherent and inalienable rights, among which are freedom from toil for daily bread; the right to play and to dream; the right to the normal sleep of the night season; the right to an education, that we may have equality of opportunity for developing all that there is in us of mind and heart.

RESOLVED, II — That we declare ourselves to be helpless and dependent that we are and of right ought to be dependent, and that we hereby present the appeal of our helplessness that we may be protected in the enjoyment of the rights of childhood.

RESOLVED, III — That we demand the restoration of our rights by the abolition of child labor in America.

National Child Labor Committee, 1913

The Start of Child Labor

Since ancient times, many children have worked with their families to do their part as a family member. The practice of **child labor,** however, is different. Child labor misuses and abuses children in a workplace that benefits only employers. It started in Europe in the 1700s with the production of iron and the use of coal to power machines. The new industrial societies used child labor.

Society was changing in the United States as well. Many factories were being built there in the 1800s. Children were often forced to work alongside their parents in the factories or mines to make ends meet.

Factories filled with big machines churned out products that were once made by hand by skilled workers in small workshops. To the workers' **dismay,** the factories did not need their skills anymore. Unskilled workers could tend the machines and perform the repetitive, boring work for much less money.

Children were highly desirable as a source of unskilled labor. They kept production costs down because they worked for lower pay than adults. They did not question authority, and employers thought were not likely to cause problems.

1912
Florence Kelley fights to establish the United States Children's Bureau, a government group whose purpose is to improve the lives of children in society.

1913
The National Child Labor Committee writes the Declaration of Dependence.

1924
Congress passes an amendment to the Constitution to protect children under the age of eighteen in the workplace. But it fails to win approval of three-quarters of the states, and so does not become law.

1929
The stock market crashes, marking the beginning of the Great Depression.

1938
The Fair Labor Standards Act of 1938 helps promote child labor reform and prevents children from doing dangerous work.

Time Line of Child Labor Reforms

1903
Labor organizer Mother Jones organizes a march of child textile workers and adult reformers from Philadelphia, Pennsylvania, to Long Island, New York.

1904
The National Child Labor Committee forms to publicize the truth about child labor. Photographer Lewis Hine is hired to take pictures in 1908. His powerful photos shock citizens and help change public opinion.

1906
John Spargo writes a book telling how child textile workers breathe in dust from animal fur and skin as they make felt hats.

1908
Elizabeth Beardsley Butler reports on factory working conditions for girls, who work for even less pay than boys.

1909
Clara Lemlich, a twenty-three-year-old garment worker, organizes a strike of more than twenty thousand garment workers.

Children and their mothers work cutting string beans.

Children and their mothers work shucking oysters.

Large numbers of poor people immigrated to the United States during the time when factories needed unskilled labor. Immigrants came from Germany, Italy, Ireland, and other countries. Between 1901 and 1910 more than eight million people came to live in the United States. Many of these new immigrants had little education and desperately needed money.

Many immigrant children were sent off to work at a young age. They were willing to work hard for money just to survive. In some places, for adults to get jobs, they had to have children who could work. Others lied about their children's ages in order to get them on the factory **payroll.**

These people are Italian immigrants at Ellis Island.

A family eats lunch by the side of a road during the Great Depression.

During the Great Depression, about one fourth of the labor force was out of work. People began to rely on the government to help end the suffering. In 1938 the government decided that children under the age of sixteen could not work during school hours. It also decided that businesses could not give jobs to children instead of adults. These decisions were called the Fair Labor Standards Act.

Technology was changing too. Factories needed skilled workers to run and maintain the machines. Many jobs required more education, and states responded by increasing the number of years children were required to be in school.

In order to protect children, concerned citizens took responsibility to change child labor. The actions of these people, along with the effects of the Great Depression, brought positive reforms.

Winds of Change

At the turn of the twentieth century, more than two million children in the United States worked. They could not attend school, and few of them knew how to read or write.

Things were changing though. At one time child labor was seen as a fact of life, but reformers began to call attention to the problem. Lewis Hine gave a human face to child labor with his photos of working children. Mother Jones, Clara Lemlich, and other reformers organized marches and strikes to protest child labor.

In 1929 the stock market crashed. As a result many people lost their jobs, their savings, and their businesses. This was the beginning of the Great Depression, a worldwide drop in business that lasted from 1929 to the end of the 1930s. Slowly people began to change their minds about child labor being good for children, for industry, or for the family.

Lewis Hine

Mother Jones

Clara Lemlich

Wanted: Child Workers

In the early 1900s not all children went to work. Children from wealthy families did not need to earn money. They played outside, went swimming, ate healthy meals, enjoyed ice cream during the summer, and snuggled next to warm coal fires in the winter.

Their lives were very different from the lives of the poor children working on the street. These young laborers sold newspapers to the fortunate children's parents. They dug the coal that warmed their houses or made the fabric for their clothes. Poor children often worked ten to twelve hours a day, six days a week. They worked in cramped, dimly lit factories, in the darkness of the mines, or in the freezing cold or blistering hot sun outside. Children often worked in dangerous, unhealthy environments to earn a week's wages that might only buy their family a loaf of bread. They could not attend school because they were always working.

These boys, called newsies, are ready to sell newspapers.

Many children worked for businesses called **sweatshops.** In sweatshops boys and girls worked long hours under dangerous and dirty conditions for low wages. Children working in fabric-making **textile mills** often experienced the worst sweatshop conditions.

The textile process begins with the making of cotton, wool, or silk thread. It ends with fabric that is made from the thread. In cotton mills many girls as young as five years old were hired as **spinners.** Boys younger than seven were hired as **doffers.**

The spinners brushed lint off of the machines. They watched the **bobbins,** as they filled with thread, for any breaks in the thread. When they spotted a break, they had to fix it quickly by tying the ends of the thread together. Spinners usually worked eleven or twelve hours a day, six days a week, and were on their feet nearly all that time.

Doffers removed the full bobbins and replaced them with empty bobbins. Most doffers worked barefoot so they could climb onto the machines. Some slipped, losing fingers and toes in the process. Others fell to their deaths if they slipped into the moving machines.

One of the most dangerous places to work for children was in and around the dark, damp, and dusty coal mines. In mining a breaker is a machine used to break rocks and coal. The youngest boys, often nine or ten years old, worked outside the mines as **breaker boys.** They sat on boards that hung over the coal chutes to work. They bent over and pulled out any slate or rock mixed in with the coal in the coal cars that sped by. It was dangerous work. These boys could reach down too far, fall, and be killed. The boys grew sick from bending over and breathing in coal dust all day long. Many developed chronic, or constant, coughs.

Breaker boys did back-breaking work, but they also had some power. Sometimes boys threw wood into the mining machinery, causing it to shut down for repairs so they could have a little rest.

Life was just as hard for older boys who worked down in the mines. There was always the danger of explosions and cave-ins. These boys worked nine or ten hours, sometimes twelve hundred feet or more below the surface, in absolute darkness except for their small oil lamps. They were paid as little as eight cents an hour.

Young miners pose for a picture.

Spinners (above) and doffers (below) tend their machines.

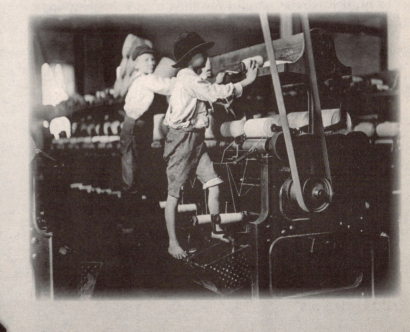

Children help make artificial flowers.

Other businesses paid families to do finish work from their homes in **tenement houses.** These buildings were small, overcrowded, dirty apartments where poor immigrant families lived. Some families worked ten to twelve hours a day in miserable conditions doing piecework such as sewing buttons on coats. This was a good system for employers because they could pay these workers very little for valuable work.

Some families worked making artificial flowers. A family who made 2,000 roses in one day might earn $1.20. Even three-year-old children were put to work making forget-me-not flowers. The small children could make 540 flowers a day. They were paid five cents.

No matter how bad the weather, newsies, or young newspaper sellers—some as young as five years old—got up at five in the morning and worked until after midnight. Many of these children died. Some delivery boys froze to death in their wagons. Many children grew sick from being outside in the cold weather or from the long hours of standing.

Other children and families worked out in the fields when the weather was warmer. These people traveled from farm to farm, trying to survive. Children as young as three worked in any kind of weather doing hard physical labor. They picked cranberries, cotton, and sugar beets. Many worked fourteen hours a day until the picking was done.

Young laborers carry heavy loads of berries out of the fields.

The Power of Our People

by Ellen Sutherland

Genre	Comprehension Skill and Strategy	Text Features
Nonfiction	• Main Idea and Details • Summarize	• Captions • Charts • Glossary • Photographs

Scott Foresman Reading Street 4.2.5

ISBN 0-328-13441-4

9 780328 134410

Reader Response

1. You have read about some of the differences between the Declaration of Independence and the Constitution. Use a chart, like the one below, to help you describe the main idea of each document. Then list three details that support each main idea. This will help you understand how the documents are alike and different.

	Declaration of Independence	Constitution
Main Idea		
1.		
2.		
3.		

2. Summarize the events that led to the creation of the Declaration of Independence.

3. *Confederation* is a word that may be new to you. Look up its root word, *confederate*, in a dictionary to see if it can be used as a noun, a verb, or even an adjective. Give examples of how it can be used, even in your school setting, and how it has been used in history.

4. Use some or all of the glossary words to write a paragraph of fiction about how a group might come together to form a nation and write its own constitution.

Glossary

amendments *n.* formal revisions to a document.

bicameral *adj.* composed of two legislative branches.

compromised *v.* settled by concessions.

confederation *n.* a political union of persons, parties, or states.

politics *n.* the art or science of government or governing.

ratified *adj.* approved and given formal sanction to.

representatives *n.* delegates or agents acting on behalf of others.

responsibilities *n.* things for which one must be accountable.

sovereignty *n.* supremacy of authority or rule.

unanimously *adv.* in a manner reflecting complete agreement.

THE POWER OF OUR PEOPLE

THE DECLARATION OF INDEPENDENCE, THE CONSTITUTION, AND THE BILL OF RIGHTS

by Ellen Sutherland

Editorial Offices: Glenview, Illinois • Parsippany, New Jersey • New York, New York
Sales Offices: Needham, Massachusetts • Duluth, Georgia • Glenview, Illinois
Coppell, Texas • Ontario, California • Mesa, Arizona

Here's How To Do It!

1. After you are all in agreement about what you want, write a constitution for your new government. This will not be easy. Use reference materials and primary source documents as a model. Give the leaders responsibilities and the citizens rights. You will probably have to debate and compromise quite a bit.

2. Now for ratification. Who has to ratify the document, and how many votes will be needed? Will you vote or do a canvass (survey) of citizens? Remember, many documents or amendments have gotten to the point of ratification only to stop there. The process can be very challenging. You may have to go back and revise the document before you can get it ratified.

3. Once the document is ratified as a constitution, use your art skills to draw a map of your new nation. Give your new nation a name and a capital—the names can reflect important people or shared beliefs.

© Pearson Education, Inc.

Now Try This

Establishing a New Nation

Have you ever wondered what it would be like to start your own country—or just a place to call your own? What rules and ideas might you use to run it? Brainstorm some ideas with a group, write those ideas down, debate their various merits, and then agree on a set of rules, or a constitution.

But wait a minute. You can have a constitution, but what are the principles behind it? What caused your nation to come into being? You probably need to write something like a Declaration of Independence!

Decide what you need independence from. What kind of place do you want to claim as your own? Brainstorm with a group and then work together to describe it.

Working to build a new nation is hard work.

What does the United States stand for? What do we value and what do we want for our people? How do we know what our laws are? Two important and honored documents can tell us: the Declaration of Independence and the Constitution with its Bill of Rights. These documents were written a long time ago. But they have lasted to this day. Let's take a look at how and why they were written. That will help us understand why they are still so important to us today.

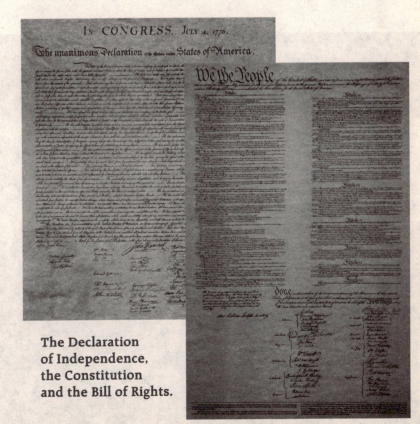

The Declaration of Independence, the Constitution and the Bill of Rights.

Think of July 4, and you probably think of fireworks. July 4 is called Independence Day, and it dates back to 1776. That's the day the Declaration of Independence was signed in Philadelphia, Pennsylvania. But did you know that signing the Declaration of Independence was a dangerous and revolutionary act?

Let's go back in time to colonial America. At that time, Americans had been fighting their British rulers for more rights. They didn't like the high taxes they had to pay Britain.

Delegates at the Continental Congress

As our country grew and changed, far-reaching amendments were added. One of them was the 19th Amendment. This gave women the right to vote.

Our Constitution really is a living document. It was designed to meet the needs of a new and growing country. It continues to meet the needs of our country today.

Women fought hard for the right to vote.

These amendments guarantee American citizens certain rights and freedoms. We have freedom of religion and speech. We can hold meetings, and we have freedom of the press.

The rights guaranteed by the Bill of Rights, however, are not necessarily absolute or without limits or restrictions. The wording of the original amendments has led to lots of political debate. For example, many people are not happy with the Second Amendment's "right to bear arms." This gives people the right to keep firearms. Those against this amendment feel it leads to more violence in today's society.

Our right to free speech is one of the amendments in the Bill of Rights.

They also didn't like being told what to do by a country far away from them. Even so, most colonists didn't think the colonies would ever break from British rule.

But as British rule dragged on, the colonists began to think that the best thing to do was to form their own nation. A Continental Congress, comprised of **representatives** from each of the colonies, began to meet to discuss the problems with British rule. Each colony (except for Georgia, which joined later) appointed a delegation to the Congress.

This action made England angry. In late 1775, it granted Parliament sovereignty over the colonies. This meant the colonists could not govern themselves. This made the colonists furious.

So, the colonists formed an army. In May of 1776, the Continental Congress advised each of the colonies to adopt a government of its own choosing. On June 7, 1776, Virginia made a motion to Congress that all states be declared independent from England.

People were shocked! Should they really do this? What would England do?

Quickly, colonial leaders Thomas Jefferson, John Adams, Benjamin Franklin, Roger Sherman, and Robert R. Livingston began to prepare a special document. It would outline reasons the colonies should separate from England and declare independence. The men worked on the document for the month of June.

Benjamin Franklin and Thomas Jefferson

It took a long time to get all the states to ratify the Constitution. One reason was that it didn't contain a Bill of Rights—a description of all the rights that belong to the people. Many of the writers of the Constitution had worried that if they listed citizens' rights, they might actually be limiting them. But because everyone was so concerned, the writers promised to add a Bill of Rights once the new government was in place.

On September 25, 1789, the First Congress of the United States proposed to the state legislatures an amendment, or change, to the Constitution. There were twelve Articles. The first two would be ratified later. But Articles 3 through 12 were ratified on December 15, 1791. These ten amendments became known as the Bill of Rights.

The Bill of Rights

The nine states that ratified the Constitution were Delaware, Pennsylvania, New Jersey, Georgia, Connecticut, Massachusetts, Maryland, South Carolina, and then, later, New Hampshire. But the writers of the Constitution wanted every state to agree to it.

So they decided to advertise! Alexander Hamilton, John Jay, and James Madison published essays about the Constitution in New York newspapers. A collection of these essays was later published and became known as *The Federalist Papers*.

The signing of the Constitution

Thomas Jefferson, John Adams, Benjamin Franklin, Roger Sherman, and Robert R. Livingston worked on the Declaration of Independence.

Thomas Jefferson wrote much of the Declaration of Independence. His fellow committee members asked him to write the first draft. When Jefferson was finished, they made minor changes. The Declaration was written on parchment, and it had two parts. First was a preamble, or introduction. This listed the rights of every man. Second was a list of the wrongs they felt the King of England had committed against them.

By July 1, the men were ready to present the document to the Second Continental Congress.

The Congress **unanimously** adopted the Declaration on July 4, 1776—the day we now celebrate as Independence Day.

The signing of the Declaration of Independence, as shown in a painting by John Trumbull

After much arguing, Connecticut suggested "The Great Compromise." This created a legislature that was **bicameral**, or made up of two rooms, or chambers. This government had a Senate and a House of Representatives. Each state had two senators, but the number of representatives each state sent to the House would be based on population.

The Constitution had to be approved, or **ratified**, by the people. Nine of the thirteen states had to approve it. And they did!

Delegates argued over the writing of the Constitution, but in the end, they compromised.

The Constitutional Convention was attended by representatives from each of the thirteen states (except Rhode Island). They met in secret during the hot summer in the Pennsylvania State House.

To create the document, they discussed, argued, and compromised for six months. James Madison's "Virginia Plan" called for a state and national government. The more people a state had, the more representatives it sent to the national government. If Madison's plan passed, the small states would have almost no say! The small states drew up their own plan, "The New Jersey Plan." This plan gave each state the same number of representatives.

John Adams would later say that he did not think the Declaration of Independence was really unique in its politics. He said that it borrowed heavily from the works of the philosopher John Locke. The Declaration also had a lot in common with Thomas Paine's pamphlet *Common Sense*. Paine, a political thinker and writer, had also argued passionately for independence from England.

Still, this was the first time that a whole people had asserted their right to choose a government for themselves.

John Locke and Thomas Paine

People come from all over the world to view the Declaration of Independence at the National Archives

It quickly became clear that it would be too difficult to change this document. Instead, a new one would have to be written. George Washington, Benjamin Franklin, and James Madison worked to decide what this new document should cover.

Gouveneur Morris is probably responsible for how the Constitution sounds. But Jacob Shallus, a Pennsylvania General Assembly clerk, is credited with actually writing down the words. He did it for just $30, which today would be about $260!

James Madison, the "father of the Constitution"

The U.S. Constitution was written in 1787, more than 200 years ago. If some of its ideas sound familiar, that's because many of its authors were the same people who wrote the Declaration of Independence.

Between May and September of 1787, a Federal Constitutional Convention met in Philadelphia to change the Articles of **Confederation**, a document that outlined our government. Some didn't really like this document because it gave most of the power to the states and little to the central government. Congress had to depend on the states for its funding.

The Assembly Room in Independence Hall

Some historians refer to the signing of the Declaration of Independence as the "Miracle of Philadelphia." Think about it: thirteen separate and very different colonies had sent representatives to the Second Continental Congress in Philadelphia. There, they had managed to agree on a vision for our new nation.

Today, you can visit the site of the signing—the former Pennsylvania State House, now known as Independence Hall. You can also see the original Declaration at the National Archives in Washington, D.C.

In many ways, the Declaration of Independence set the stage for our Constitution. The Constitution is the highest law in the United States. All other laws come from it. The Constitution describes how our government works. It also explains the rights and **responsibilities** enjoyed by each citizen. If it weren't for our Constitution, we wouldn't have the President, or Congress, or the Supreme Court.

The U.S. Constitution uses simple language to describe our government. It is the oldest written set of principles in use today. It is also the shortest, at about 4,500 words! The Constitution is called a "living document." That means that it was designed to work in 1776 as well as right now!

It's not easy to make changes to the Constitution. The Constitution can only be changed by **amendments** that have been approved by a majority of the states. Think about this: eleven thousand amendments have been proposed, but just twenty-seven amendments have been approved!

The first ten of these amendments are considered special, and are known as the Bill of Rights.

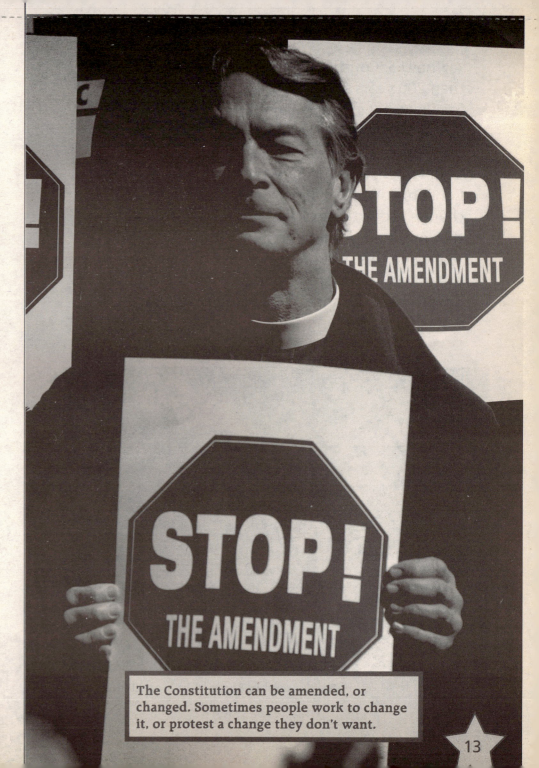

The Constitution can be amended, or changed. Sometimes people work to change it, or protest a change they don't want.

Suggested levels for Guided Reading, DRA,™ Lexile,® and Reading Recovery™ are provided in the Pearson Scott Foresman Leveling Guide.

Genre	Comprehension Skill and Strategy
Fiction	• Cause and Effect • Ask Questions

Scott Foresman Reading Street 4.3.1

PEARSON

Scott Foresman

scottforesman.com

ISBN 0-328-13444-9

9 780328 134441

Tracking Our Class Garden

by Rena Korb

illustrated by Ginna Magee

Reader Response

1. Why did the students do research? What happened as a result of their research? Write your answers in a chart similar to the one below.

Why did it happen?	What happened?

2. What questions did you have about gardening as you read this book? How did this book help you answer your questions? Where could you go to find more information on gardening?

3. Reread page 17 and think about what the borers did to the zucchini plants. What do you think the word *borer* means?

4. How did Sandra change from the beginning of the story to the end?

Indoor Gardening

An egg carton filled with potting soil makes a nice place to plant seeds and grow them indoors. A variety of seeds can be planted. The different seeds can be identified by sticking a flat wooden stick with the plant's name on it at the edge of each egg cup.

The seeds need to be planted just underneath the surface of the soil in each egg cup so that they can sprout. As you know, plants need water to grow. An old, clean spray bottle filled with water is great for watering plants. The fine mist of the spray will keep the soil moist, and the plants will grow best in a warm spot.

Eventually, tiny green shoots will pop out of the soil, and the plants will need water and sunlight. Soon the tiny green shoots will grow into stalks with two leaves. At this point, the plants will need more room to grow. A larger pot, careful handling, and soil around the roots will help the plants stay healthy.

Tracking Our Class Garden

by Rena Korb

illustrated by Ginna Magee

PEARSON
Scott Foresman

Editorial Offices: Glenview, Illinois • Parsippany, New Jersey • New York, New York
Sales Offices: Needham, Massachusetts • Duluth, Georgia • Glenview, Illinois
Coppell, Texas • Ontario, California • Mesa, Arizona

That fall the fourth graders returned as fifth graders. They knew another class would take over their garden, but Ms. Stinson had one more surprise for them. She asked them to join her new fourth-grade class to harvest the final crop of the year: the acorn and butternut squash.

As they worked, the older students gave the younger students helpful tips. The fifth graders remembered when Ms. Stinson first introduced them to the garden—a big patch of messy dirt. Now it was a rich garden that had produced good food, hard work, and new friends, and it had been an amazing year of gardening fun.

On the last day of school, the class carried out its final task. The children planted a new crop of vegetables. Most of the crop would ripen over the summer.

"But who's going to take care of our garden?" Melinda asked.

"I'll be here all summer long," Ms. Stinson told the class. "And you are welcome to help out whenever you can."

It turned out to be one of the hottest summers on record! Still, the students, often with their families, came out to work in the garden. They didn't care that the Sun was blazing hot or that sweat ran down their faces. They wanted to take care of their prized plants.

In July the ground started to dry out, and it seemed that no amount of water was enough for the plants. Sandra, Darrell, Cal, and Melinda got together and came up with an idea. They covered the plant beds with dry grass clippings to help keep in moisture.

As the summer went on, the plants grew larger and stronger, and brightly colored vegetables covered green stalks. In August Ms. Stinson invited the children and their families to a party. After they all helped gather the fresh vegetables, everyone sat down to a garden picnic.

Chapter 1 The New Garden

One warm afternoon in September, Ms. Stinson surprised her fourth-grade class by saying, "We're going to hold class outside. Follow me."

All the students jumped out of their chairs and formed a line. With the Sun shining brightly, any chance to go outside was a real treat.

As always, Cal rushed to be first in line. Sandra, the new girl, stood by herself at the end. Everyone else joined the line in groups of friends. As they made their way from the classroom, they talked quietly about what might be in store for them outside.

Ms. Stinson led the class outside. Melinda looked concerned as she walked through the grass because, after all, she was wearing her new shoes. Darrell cracked jokes to anyone who would listen. "Shh!" ordered Cal, frowning. Sandra simply walked slowly at the back of the line, keeping her eyes down.

Ms. Stinson brought the line to a halt. "Here we are," she said. She gestured to the ground with her hands, and the students looked around curiously. All they saw was a patch of dirt. "Meet your future garden!" exclaimed Ms. Stinson.

The students murmured in confusion. There were no vegetables, no flowers, not even any plants. All they saw was dry pale dirt with some weeds and a bit of grass.

Melinda raised her hand and asked the question on all their minds. "But where is the garden?"

"We have to grow it," said Ms. Stinson with a broad smile.

The garden was going to be a special class project. After they returned to the classroom, Ms. Stinson divided the class into four groups to research what to plant and how to care for the garden.

Melinda's group led the search for the cherry tomatoes. They picked only the tomatoes that looked red all over, leaving the green ones on the stems. To see if the carrots were ready, Cal grabbed a carrot top sticking out of the ground. When he pulled out a long orange carrot, the class knew it would be a good harvest. Darrell's group had decided against growing one big zucchini. "Smaller ones taste better," he explained.

Everyone did some snacking before they piled up the crisp crop in a wheelbarrow and pushed it to Ms. Stinson's car. The vegetables would go to a nearby food bank for people in need of food.

Chapter 5 The Harvest

The class spent the rest of the spring taking care of the garden. The week before school let out for the summer, they had their first harvest. All the students worked together to gather the ripened crop.

Under the bright Sun, the class picked the long stalks of the chives. To find the garlic and onions, they looked for green stems sticking straight up in the air. Then they wrapped their hands around the stalks and pulled the bulbs gently from the ground.

Cal instantly took charge by telling about books and Web sites he knew of that they could study. "Great, we've got another teacher," grumbled his group.

Darrell was excited to build a scarecrow with his team of gardeners. "You've got to plant the garden first," Ms. Stinson reminded him.

Melinda had a warning for her group. "I don't like bugs or worms or getting my hands dirty."

Sandra's group hardly noticed her. She sat quietly, with a book open on her lap. On a piece of paper, she sketched creepy crawly bugs.

The children spent an entire month researching gardening. Finally, they were ready for action, and on a crisp fall day they planted their garden. Most everyone came dressed in old jeans and T-shirts that they could get dirty. They got down on their hands and knees in the dirt.

"Yuck!" cried Melinda when she got dirt on her knee. "I'm going to mess up my clothes!"

Ms. Stinson asked Sandra to get materials from the classroom to make the reflectors. When Sandra came back, she demonstrated how to make a reflector. She cut a square of foil and poked a hole at its middle. Then she placed the hole gently over one of the plants, slid the foil down, and pressed it flat to the ground. The class did the same to the rest of the zucchini plants.

For the next week, Ms. Stinson led the class outside to check the garden. Each day was the same—no more borers! Finally, Ms. Stinson made an announcement. "I think all the bugs are finally gone!"

The kids crowded around Sandra with cries of "Good job!" and "You saved the zucchini!"

As they walked back to the classroom, Cal hurried to catch up with Sandra. "That was so neat," he said. "Could you show me how you figured that out?"

"Sure," Sandra said with a big smile. "I'll show you the book, and you can even borrow it from me if you'd like."

Then a small voice spoke up. "I've got an idea," said Sandra. Everyone turned to look at her, eager to hear what she had to say.

"I got this idea from a book I was reading . . ." Sandra's voice trailed off.

"Please tell us more about it, Sandra," said Ms. Stinson. Melinda looked at Sandra and gave her a smile of encouragement.

So Sandra told them about making reflectors from aluminum foil. For some reason, the reflectors often kept borers away from plants. "Maybe they don't like the sunlight shining off the foil," Sandra guessed.

In the garden, Cal busily yanked up weeds. Sandra seemed to be fascinated with a roly-poly bug. Despite Darrell's silliness—pretending to be a cow eating grass—the class had soon cleared the area. Ms. Stinson turned the dirt over with a shovel while adding peat moss to make the soil richer for plants to grow. The students used their hands to smooth out the soil. Then they took a step back and admired their work.

The next time the class visited the garden, Sandra raised her hand. "What do we do now? It's starting to get cold, and we can't plant anything. I hope we didn't do all this work in vain!"

"We had to prepare the garden so it will be ready for planting next spring," explained Ms. Stinson.

The class eyed the schoolyard. The trees looked almost bare, a gray sky spread above their heads, and the grass was turning brown. It hardly seemed like a season to care about gardening. Could Sandra be right?

Chapter 2 The Garden in Winter

A few days later, Ms. Stinson gave her students a new assignment. She challenged them to find the answer to a question: What can you plant in the fall? The students came back with exciting results. Garlic! Chives! Freezing temperatures and overnight frosts would not kill these bulbs as they nestled underground.

"What about daffodils?" asked Melinda, remembering her research. When Ms. Stinson agreed, Melinda's face lit up. Soon the class got to work planting.

No matter what the class did, however, the zucchini plants didn't get better. One day, something terrible happened. One of the plants died. So the class continued to hunt for answers. Could insects be boring through the zucchini and eating the plants from the inside? The children examined the stems of the unhealthy plants and found several small holes!

"We're going to have to try to cut the borers out," said Ms. Stinson. She made a slit in the stem, and inside sat a fat white caterpillar, which she removed.

"Gross!" yelled Melinda.

Ms. Stinson repeated this process with the other sick plants. Then she placed a mound of dirt around the slit to keep the plant growing.

For the next few day the students eagerly ran outside to check on their bug-free zucchini plants, but to their surprise, a few of the plants failed to perk up. Then another plant died.

"Well, class," Ms. Stinson sighed, getting up from her knees in a garden. "I'm afraid there's nothing more we can do for the zucchini plants."

"Garlic spray!" cried Darrell, as he jumped up with the book still in his hand. He explained that a mixture, including water, garlic, onion, and red pepper, might be strong enough to keep the bugs away.

After making the mixture, the students poured it into spray bottles and squirted the zucchini plants, but the bugs didn't go away.

Cal thought maybe beetles were attacking the plants, so the kids took turns sitting next to the young plants. When they found a bug, they picked it off, and even Melinda took her turn.

Even in the cold, snow, and ice of winter the students visited the garden. Bundled up, they gathered together to talk about the garden.

"What do you think our plants are doing right now?" Ms. Stinson asked.

"They are sleeping through the winter so they can be strong in the spring," said Cal.

"Yes," Darrell exclaimed. "They're kind of like bears that hibernate in the winter."

"Well, I think they are cold down there in the ground," said Sandra. "Just like I am. This garden isn't any fun."

"Oh, Sandra," Melinda cried. "I know we will have fun together in the spring picking the beautiful daffodils!"

Sandra shrugged. It was hard coming to a new school, but maybe she could find a friend in Melinda.

There wasn't much to do in the garden during the winter, so the class got ready for the coming spring. Each group had to decide what to plant.

At first, Cal wanted to plant cucumbers, but when he realized that everyone else in his group wanted carrots, he agreed. Melinda's group decided to plant cherry tomatoes.

Sandra's group decided on acorn and butternut squash. "They won't be ready until next fall," said Ms. Stinson.

"It'll be just in time to decorate the Thanksgiving table," offered Sandra quietly. She smiled when her whole group nodded and smiled back at her.

Darrell's group selected zucchini squash. "We are going to try to grow a zucchini as big as a baseball bat!" Darrell exclaimed.

Chapter 4 Disaster Strikes!

But one day, Darrell noticed that the leaves and stems of one of the zucchini plants were wilting. The students gave the plant extra water because they thought it was thirsty, but when they went out to check the next day, the plant didn't seem any better. Then another zucchini stalk started to wilt.

Ms. Stinson knelt down to inspect the sick plants, and when she stood up, the class could tell from the look on her face that it was serious. "Some kind of bug is eating our plants. Let's try and figure out a way to make the bug go away." The students jumped quickly into their research.

After planting day, the students visited the garden regularly. They kept the soil damp and free of any weeds.

Each group had different problems to solve. The tomatoes started to slump over, so the students put wooden stakes into the ground and tied up the plants with twine. The carrots were growing too close together, and the students had to thin out the rows by pulling some of the tiny seedlings out of the ground.

And how all the plants grew! The green carrot tops developed into lacy leaves, and the squash plants began to spread along the ground. And the students discovered that tiny green tomatoes liked to hide underneath the plants' leaves.

Chapter 3 Spring Arrives!

Spring had almost arrived. The weather turned warmer, and the class checked the garden every day. Soon, the children could see that the plants were growing!

The tips of the garlic and the onions they had also decided to plant poked through the ground. The green shoots of the chives stretched toward the sky, and the daffodils grew thick, dark-green stalks. On the day the daffodils bloomed into frilly yellow flowers, Melinda and Sandra picked a small bouquet for the classroom. Ms. Stinson said it was finally time to plant the rest of the garden.

On planting day the students, including Melinda, came to school dressed in their old jeans and T-shirts. Each group picked out a planting spot in the garden.

Cal and his group dug several shallow holes with their fingers. The carrot seeds were tiny, no bigger than the heads of pins! The group sprinkled in the seeds and then took turns making sure all the seeds had enough space.

Unlike the carrot seeds, the zucchini seeds needed to be bunched together without touching. Darrell took charge because he really wanted to grow a zucchini big enough to set a world record.

The acorn and butternut squash group drew circles in the soil as big as dinner plates. Everyone gathered around and took turns poking one seed into the ground at the center of each circle.

The tomato group did not plant seeds, since Melinda's grandmother's gardening club had donated some seedlings for them to use. They placed the small tomato plants into holes they had dug in the ground, and gently piled up dirt around the roots.

Then the children raced to fill up their watering cans. They stood over the rows and let the water sink deep into the ground.

Suggested levels for Guided Reading, DRA,™ Lexile,® and Reading Recovery™ are provided in the Pearson Scott Foresman Leveling Guide.

Life Science

Birds of Flight

by Lillian Duggan

Genre	Comprehension Skill and Strategy	Text Features
Nonfiction	• Fact and Opinion • Graphic Organizers	• Map • Diagram • Captions • Glossary

Scott Foresman Reading Street 4.3.2

scottforesman.com

ISBN 0-328-13447-3

9 780328 134472

Reader Response

1. Birds save energy when they fly in a V formation. Is this statement a fact or an opinion? How do you know? Find two other facts and two other opinions in this book.

2. Name some of the different ways that birds are able to navigate while migrating. Use a graphic organizer like the one below to order your thoughts.

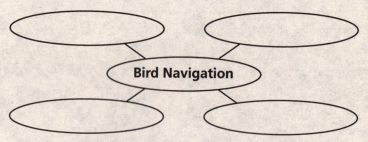

3. Read the following sentence: "The students flock to the cafeteria at lunchtime." Compare the meaning of flock in the sentence with the glossary word flock.

4. How does the diagram on page 13 help you understand how a vortex works?

Glossary

conservationists *n.* people who try to help living things survive.

endangered species *n.* an animal that is in danger of becoming extinct.

flock *n.* a group of birds traveling together.

flyways *n.* routes traveled often by migratory birds.

migrate *v.* to go from one region to another with the change in the seasons.

navigating *v.* moving to find a position or place.

thermals *n.* rising currents of air.

vortex *n.* a mass of air that moves in a circular motion and surrounds a vacuum.

Birds of Flight

by Lillian Duggan

Editorial Offices: Glenview, Illinois • Parsippany, New Jersey • New York, New York
Sales Offices: Needham, Massachusetts • Duluth, Georgia • Glenview, Illinois
Coppell, Texas • Ontario, California • Mesa, Arizona

Here's How to Do It!

1. Fill one bottle three-quarters full of water.

2. Using the duct tape, tape the washer to the top of the bottle filled with water. Make sure you don't tape over the hole in the washer.

3. Place the empty bottle upside down on top of the washer. Tape the two bottles together.

4. Turn the bottles over so the one with the water is on top. Quickly swirl the bottles in a circular motion a few times, then place the bottom bottle on a table. Watch the water closely. What does it look like?

5. Think about the kind of vortex that birds make when they flap their wings. How do you think this water vortex is similar to that kind? How do you think it's different?

Now Try This

Water Vortex

When birds flap their wings, they create a vortex of air. Another air vortex you may have seen (hopefully, not in person) is a tornado. A vortex can also be made from liquid. Think about the funnel of water that whirls down your bathtub drain when you unplug it. That's a liquid vortex.

What You Will Need

Ask an adult to help you find these things:
- two empty one-liter soda bottles with labels removed
- a rubber or steel washer that is the same width as the tops of the bottles
- a roll of duct tape
- water

Mysterious Migration

Have you ever looked up into the sky and noticed a giant letter *V* soaring high above you? The V is probably made up of migrating birds, such as geese, ducks, and others. Migrating birds can be found throughout the world, from the Arctic Circle in the north to Antarctica in the south.

Migrating birds have their own unique migration behaviors, or habits. For example, they may **migrate** at different times of the year or in different patterns. Some even have special ways of getting to their destination.

For hundreds of years, scientists and others have been curious about the migration habits of birds. Why do birds migrate? Where do they go? Is there a reason some birds fly in a V formation when they migrate? How do they navigate?

Scientists have studied the V flight formation of birds for years.

Why Birds Migrate

Birds generally migrate when the seasons begin to change. When cold winter weather arrives, many birds that spend the spring in the north travel south. Later, when warmer spring weather returns, these birds head back north again.

People often think that birds leave places that become cold because they cannot survive freezing temperatures, but this is not actually the case. Warmer places have more sunlight and plants, which means there are more insects and fruit—the birds' food.

Hummingbird

NASA hopes that one day passenger airplanes will fly as a group in a formation similar to birds. Then air traffic controllers will be able to manage these planes as if they were a single plane.

Perhaps someday people will travel the same way that geese, double-crested cormorants, canvasback ducks, and whooping cranes do. These birds follow the flyways in search of the right spot to bring their young into the world. And they do this in such a fascinating way!

These two jets are performing test flights for NASA. The plane in back is flying in the vortex made by the plane in front.

Airplanes in a V Formation

For many centuries, humans have tried to join birds and take to the skies. Begining with inventor Leonardo da Vinci in the fifteenth century, on to the Wright brothers in the nineteenth century, many people have studied the flight of birds.

Scientists today are still studying bird flight in hopes of improving the performance of airplanes. At the National Aeronautics and Space Administration (NASA), scientists have been trying to mimic birds by flying airplanes in a V formation. NASA has flown several test flights with two fighter jets, where one jet flies in the vortex of the other.

NASA scientists think that someday airplanes can save energy the same way geese and other birds do. When airplanes save energy, they use less fuel. This is helpful because not only is fuel expensive, but burning it is hazardous to the environment as well.

NASA's project has had great results because airplanes flying in a V formation have reduced their fuel usage by 15 to 30 percent. If passenger planes could fly this way, airlines could save millions of dollars in fuel costs, and planes would release less pollution into the environment.

Birds return home once the trees and flowers bloom again in the spring. Spring is a great time of year for birds to find food for their young, as well as gather materials for nest building. In the spring the birds return home to breed, lay eggs, and nest.

Many species of hummingbirds are migratory. They migrate from the northern United States and Canada to Mexico or Central America. Hummingbirds return north each spring when the flowers they eat are in bloom.

This mother hummingbird is feeding her young. Hummingbirds breed sometime between March and August.

Migration Routes

When North American birds migrate, they follow four general routes, known as **flyways.** These are the Atlantic flyway, the Pacific flyway, the Mississippi flyway, and the Central flyway.

Birds travel along these four flyways for several reasons. First, the flyways follow major land formations, such as the Atlantic and Pacific coasts, the Mississippi River valley, and the Sierra Nevada and Rocky and Appalachian Mountains. Each of these land formations lies in a north-to-south direction, so birds can follow the formations and use them as a guide.

Another reason birds travel along flyways is the same as their motivation to migrate—food. Coastal areas offer an abundant supply of food for migrating shorebirds, and birds traveling inland can find plenty to eat along the Mississippi River valley.

Finally, some birds can travel faster by flying over mountains. Above mountain ranges, warm air moves upward over the high slopes, and this movement of air creates rising air currents called **thermals.** Birds, such as eagles, vultures, and hawks, use thermals to help them save energy when they are flying.

Conservationists are people who try to protect living things that are in danger of extinction. In the past, to help prevent the extinction of the whooping crane, conservationists made efforts to change their migration routes so they would breed in healthy environments. That effort failed, but overall, conservationists have been successful because, by late 2003, the whooping crane population reached 426 birds.

Whooping cranes perform an exciting dance when they find a mate. They flap their wings, bob up and down, and leap into the air.

Whooping Cranes

Whooping cranes live in North America. With their necks stretched out in front, cranes fly long distances when they migrate.

Like eagles, vultures, and hawks, cranes will sometimes coast along thermals. But, before they take flight, cranes need to get a running start along the ground.

Whooping cranes live in grassy wetland areas. They spend the spring in the northern United States and Canada, and they winter between the southern United States and Central America.

The migratory range of whooping cranes is quite small because the whooping crane population is also very small, though **conservationists** are trying to help protect them. Whooping cranes are an **endangered species.** Endangered species are animals that are in danger of becoming extinct, or no longer existing. In 1850 the total whooping crane population in North America was fifteen hundred birds, but by 1941 it had dropped to just sixteen birds.

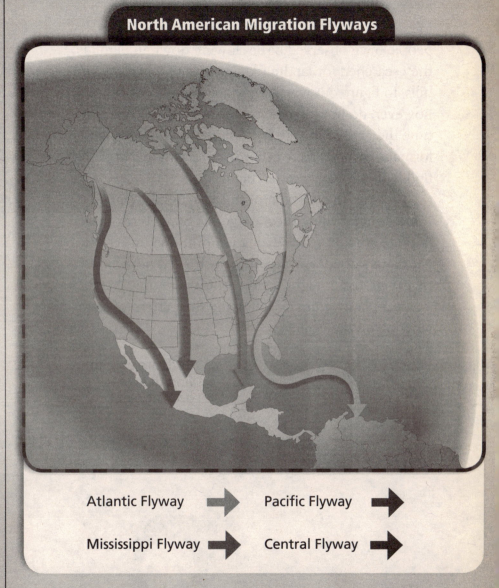

North American Migration Flyways

Atlantic Flyway →   Pacific Flyway →

Mississippi Flyway →   Central Flyway →

How Birds Navigate

As you've read, North American birds tend to follow the four flyways when they migrate. In fact, people have observed birds slowing down in flight as they searched for landmarks, such as river valleys and hills, to figure out where they are located. Most birds, however, do not follow land formations the entire time they are in the air. In addition to following land formations, birds have other ways of **navigating,** or finding their way when in flight.

Birds use the position of the Sun and the stars to determine where they are going. Some birds that migrate at night use the location of the setting Sun to get them started. An experiment showed how birds that migrated at night figured out where they were inside a planetarium by following the pattern of stars glowing on the ceiling.

Birds are able to find their way, even at night.

Canvasback Duck

Canvasback ducks are known for being fast and high fliers. They often travel in a V formation, but sometimes they travel in a line.

Canvasbacks normally breed in western Canada and the northwestern United States in summertime. They build their nests in the shallow marshes of prairie regions. Occasionally, a major drought in the northern Great Plains of the United States will force them to move farther north, and some migrate as far as Alaska.

In winter, the ducks head to Mexico and the Atlantic and Gulf coasts of the United States, where they live mostly in saltwater bays.

Similar to double-crested cormorants, canvasbacks dive for their food. They eat the roots of underwater plants, as well as some small animals.

Large flocks of canvasback ducks can be found along the Mississippi River and in Chesapeake Bay by the middle of November.

Double-crested Cormorant

Another North American bird that flies in a V formation is the double-crested cormorant. These birds spend the winter in the southern United States and the summer on the northern Pacific and Atlantic coasts. Double-crested cormorants live in lakes, rivers, swamps, and along coastlines.

Some double-crested cormorants do not migrate. Instead, they live year-round along the Pacific coast and in Alaska.

A double-crested cormorant looks similar to a duck, but it is actually a close relative of the pelican, as evidenced by the fact that both birds have webbed feet.

Watching double-crested cormorants eat is entertaining because of the way these birds dive underwater to catch a fish, return to the surface, flip the fish in the air, and swallow it head first.

The double-crested cormorant does not have waterproof feathers. It dries its wings by spreading them out.

Birds also have extraordinary senses of sight and hearing that help them figure out where they are as they fly. They can see ultraviolet light emitted from the Sun, and they can hear the sound of ocean waves and wind blowing over mountains thousands of miles away. Birds use their senses, along with their keen sense of the environment, to reach their destination. These navigators continue to get where they need to go, and many live to do so year, after year, after year.

Scientists studying European robins learned that birds may be able to see Earth's magnetic field.

Flocks

Different species of birds make the long journey between their winter and summer homes in different ways. For example, some species travel alone, and others travel in groups. A group of birds traveling together is called a **flock,** and a single flock might be made up of hundreds of birds.

You have probably seen flocks of birds flying above your neighborhood. Some flocks fly in an unorganized group, while others move in a pattern, or formation.

The three types of formations are clusters, lines, and compound, or combination, lines. Cluster formations are the most common, and some birds form flat clusters, while others fly in vertical stacks.

Line formations are the simplest, which are how some ducks fly–in long straight lines. Other birds form compound line formations when they combine lines to form shapes, such as a J, U, or V.

These birds fly as a flock.

Snow geese also fly in a V formation. Snow geese spend their winters in the southern United States and Mexico, but in June, they fly thousands of miles north to the Arctic tundra of northern Canada.

For most of the year, the Arctic tundra is frozen and nearly lifeless, so very few animal species live there year-round. This makes the tundra an ideal place for snow geese to breed because they have little competition for food. In the spring, when the tundra thaws and comes back to life, snow geese flock there by the thousands.

Snow geese nest in large groups. As many as twelve hundred nests can be found in one square mile.

North American V Flyers

The pelicans studied by the French scientists were great white pelicans. These pelicans live in Europe, Asia, and Africa. Many other bird species that fly in a V formation live in North America. These include Canada and snow geese, double-crested cormorants, canvasback ducks, and whooping cranes.

Geese

The honk that you may hear high above your head in the springtime is likely to be a flock of Canada geese flying in a V formation.

Canada geese live all over the United States and in most of Canada. Some migrate from northern Canada and Alaska to the southern United States and Mexico. Some Canada geese begin migrating back north in January or February, but others wait until March to begin their journey.

Canada geese live anywhere near water. You may have seen some where you live since they can be found in city parks, on golf courses, and near rivers and lakes.

Flocks in a V Formation

Many birds, including geese, pelicans, and cranes, fly in a V formation. For years, scientists have tried to learn why these birds fly in this manner. Many believed that the birds saved energy this way, but they were unable to prove their theory, or educated guess.

In 2001 a team of French scientists developed a way to test this theory on pelicans. They attached heart-rate monitors to a group of pelicans, and then the scientists measured the pelicans' heart rates when they flew solo and when they flew in a V. After the scientists collected their data, they compared the heart rates.

The scientists learned that the birds' heart rates were higher when they flew solo than when they flew in formation. The higher a bird's heart rate, the more energy the bird uses. So the French scientists' hunch was correct—pelicans do use less energy when they fly in a V formation!

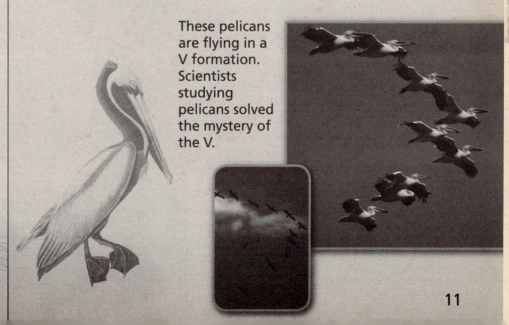

These pelicans are flying in a V formation. Scientists studying pelicans solved the mystery of the V.

Saving Energy

Why did the pelicans in the study save energy when they flew in a V formation? The answer, the scientists found, is that the pelicans could glide more often when flying with a group. Gliding requires little energy because the birds don't have to flap their wings.

A bird flying in a V formation can glide part of the time because the bird in front of it creates a **vortex** when it flaps its wings. A vortex is a mass of air that moves in a circular motion. Inside the circle of moving air is an empty space called a vacuum, which has a force that pulls objects toward it. That force helps the bird, which is flying behind, to move along, allowing it to glide for a period of time.

Many examples of vortexes can be found in nature, but perhaps the most familiar one is a tornado. A tornado is a funnel-shaped cloud that spins violently, creating whirling winds that are powerful enough to destroy buildings and uproot trees.

When birds fly in a V formation, they save a great deal of energy. They can use this energy to travel farther during migration.

This diagram shows how a bird's wing beat creates a vortex that makes flying easier for birds behind it in a V formation.

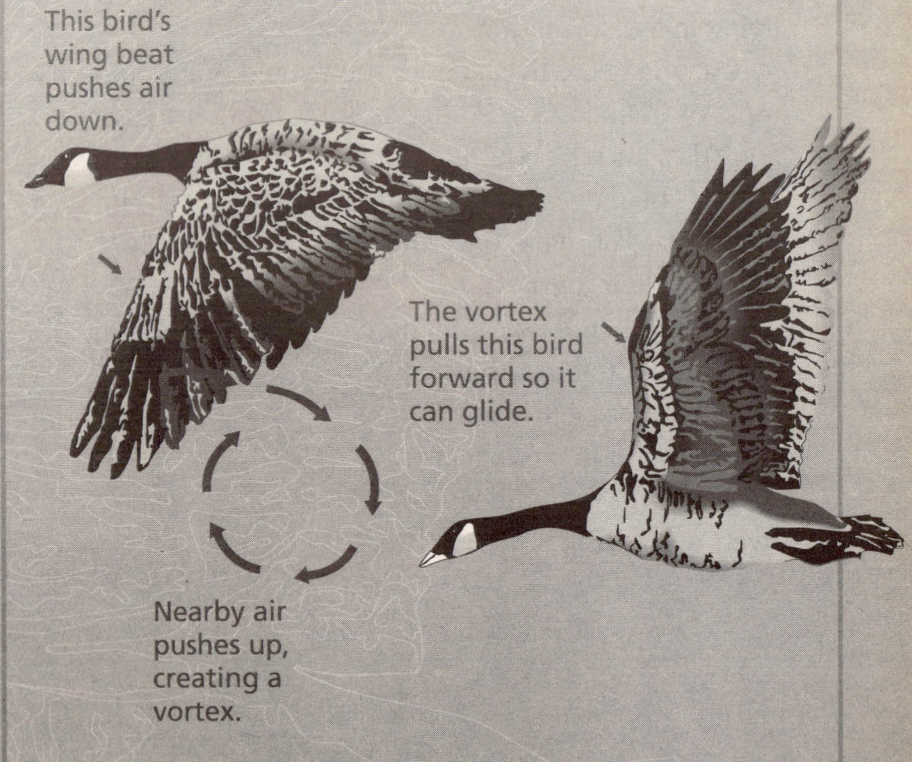

This bird's wing beat pushes air down.

The vortex pulls this bird forward so it can glide.

Nearby air pushes up, creating a vortex.

© Pearson Education, Inc.

Earth Science

Orbiting the Sun

by Donna Latham

Suggested levels for Guided Reading, DRA,™ Lexile® and Reading Recovery™ are provided in the Pearson Scott Foresman Leveling Guide.

Genre	Comprehension Skill and Strategy	Text Features
Nonfiction	• Generalize • Visualize	• Captions • Heads • Diagrams • Glossary

Scott Foresman Reading Street 4.3.3

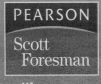

scottforesman.com

ISBN 0-328-13450-3

Reader Response

1. Galileo used his telescope to observe the Moon. Write a general statement about Galileo's observations.

2. Reread pages 4 and 5. Suppose you are a person who lived long ago. Visualize what you see in the sky. How do you explain it?

3. Look back through the book to find at least two words that were unfamiliar to you. Then reread the sections of text in which you found the words, and write a definition using context clues. Use the Glossary or a dictionary to check your definitions.

Word	Definition

4. Review the diagrams on pages 9 and 11. How did they help you understand Aristotle's and Copernicus's beliefs?

Glossary

brilliant *adj.* shining brightly; sparkling.

chorus *n.* anything spoken or sung by many people at once.

coward *n.* a person who lacks courage or is easily made afraid.

gleamed *v.* flashed or beamed with light.

satellites *n.* astronomical objects that revolve around a planet.

shimmering *adj.* gleaming faintly.

Orbiting the Sun

by Donna Latham

Editorial Offices: Glenview, Illinois • Parsippany, New Jersey • New York, New York
Sales Offices: Needham, Massachusetts • Duluth, Georgia • Glenview, Illinois
Coppell, Texas • Ontario, California • Mesa, Arizona

Here's How to Do It!

Create your own diagram of the solar system. Use print and online sources to find examples. You might look in nonfiction books about the solar system or check an encyclopedia for more information. You can also find online images to help you.

Draw and color your diagram, or try using poster paper and paint. You might want to use craft supplies to make your diagram three-dimensional, or maybe you will create a mobile to hang.

Include all of the planets in your diagram. Don't forget to add the three outer ones missing from the diagrams you have seen in this book! Label each planet. Share your completed diagram with your class.

Now Try This

Your Own Solar System

You have learned about some astronomers who had theories about the solar system, and you have had the chance to study diagrams showing those ideas. You have learned that when Aristotle and Copernicus studied the sky, the three outer planets, Uranus, Neptune, and Pluto, had not been discovered. Through chance observations and mathematical analysis, astronomers discovered the locations of these planets and their orbit around the Sun.

The Earth, the eight other planets, and the Moon all orbit the Sun.

Earth's Journey

Do you realize that right now you are moving at the incredible speed of 107,000 kilometers per hour (67,000 miles per hour)? It's true. You can't feel it, but at this very moment Earth is orbiting, or moving in a circle, around the Sun. Earth is not alone in this journey. In fact, eight other spherical, or ball-shaped, planets circle the Sun too.

You probably know that the Sun, Earth, and other planets make up our solar system. Smaller orbiting objects—such as comets, meteors, and asteroids—are parts of the solar system too.

You're also probably familiar with Earth's orbit, or path, around the Sun. But people were not always aware of Earth's journey. It was only through the work of early astronomers from long ago that people learned about the true nature of the solar system. Let's explore their discoveries.

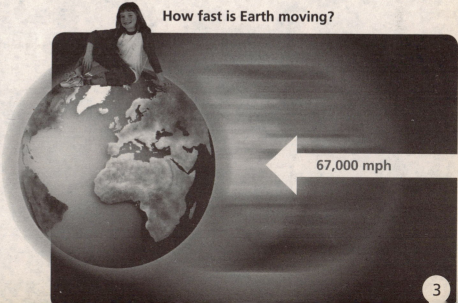

How fast is Earth moving?

67,000 mph

Astronomy

Astronomy is the study of planets, stars, and other objects in space. This science began in ancient times. In fact, many old tales from around the world are stories about space. Greek and Roman mythology tell of the planets and stars.

People in ancient times relied on myths to explain the natural world. Such stories offered an explanation for mysteries such as why the Sun seemed to move. Other stories explained constellations. They explained why **brilliant** stars were arranged in certain patterns.

Ancient people used characters to represent or symbolize objects in the sky. For example, ancient Greeks named the god of the Sun Helios. According to their myths, Helios drove a golden chariot of fire through the sky.

Ancient Greek temple

These images of the Galilean Satellites were taken by the Hubble Telescope. The Hubble Telescope, which is 595 kilometers (370 miles) above Earth, produces images that are remarkably clear and detailed.

Using his own small homemade telescope, Galileo had discovered these satellites about four hundred years ago. How do you think Galileo might respond if he could view these striking images today?

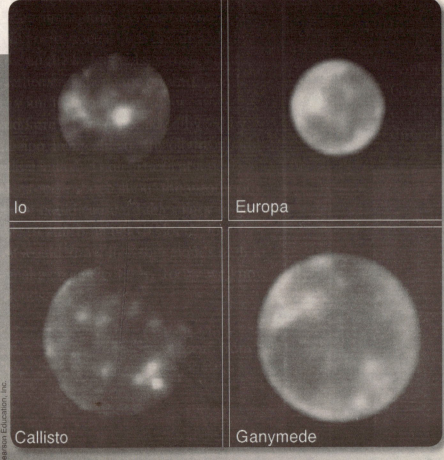

NASA images of the Galilean Satellites

The Moons of Jupiter

In January of 1610, Galileo made another discovery. Observing Jupiter, the largest planet, he saw what he thought were three stars around it. He continued watching the planet for a week, and when another star appeared one night, he was puzzled. He wondered if they were stars at all, but rather other planets, or satellites. Galileo's persistent questions got him closer to proving his ideas about the solar system. Today, we call these four satellites the Galilean Satellites. These four large moons are known as Io, Europa, Ganymede, and Callisto.

We now know that Jupiter has sixteen major satellites, along with many smaller ones. And that's not all we know. We are certain that Copernicus and Galileo were right—the Moon, Earth, and the other planets do revolve around the Sun.

We have Galileo to thank for paving the path to our knowledge of the solar system. His use of the telescope cleared the way for continuing discoveries and technologies. We greatly value his discoveries about the solar system, and we remember his strong beliefs in science and its use in testing ideas.

Some Native American stories told of the Sun and Moon. In them, the Sun and Moon were brother and sister.

The ancient Romans believed there was a Moon goddess named Luna. Did you know that the word *lunar*, which means "having to do with the Moon," comes from Luna's name?

Through their tales and stories, ancient people tried to make sense of the world around them. Because ancient people did not have the knowledge we have about space, they depended on these tales and stories. Through their tellings, they were able to offer ideas of what **shimmering** stars were. Or why the Moon that **gleamed** above them did not look the same every night.

But in time, ancient astronomers began to form new ideas based on scientific observations. Let's look at the sky through their eyes!

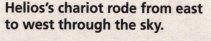

Helios's chariot rode from east to west through the sky.

Ancient Astronomers

An astronomer is someone who studies space and its heavenly bodies. Today, astronomers depend on high-tech tools to do their jobs. Space probes visit other planets to collect and bring back data for astronomers on Earth to study.

Satellite images from space help astronomers too. Powerful telescopes allow them to see what can't be seen with the eye alone. In ancient times, however, these scientific tools were not available. Without the high-tech tools available today, how did ancient astronomers study space? With the amazing tools available at that time—their eyes!

The next time you look at the night sky with just your eyes, remember that you are like an astronomer of long ago.

With that move, it became the first spacecraft to join in Saturn's orbit around the Sun. During its exploration, Cassini studied Saturn's atmosphere and discovered more about Saturn's rings. Cassini also sent back wonderful images for study on Earth.

Image of Saturn taken by the Cassini spacecraft

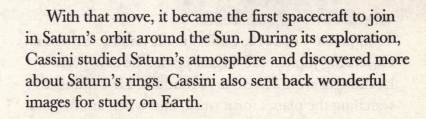

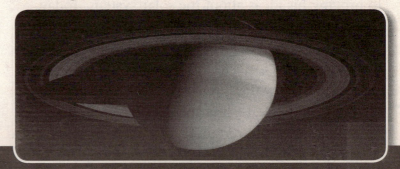

Saturn's Rings

With his telescope, Galileo also observed Saturn, the second largest planet. Earlier in the year 1610, he discovered Saturn's rings, but Galileo was not certain what the rings were. Using only a small telescope, he couldn't see them very well. At first, he called them ears. He thought they might be **satellites,** or objects that revolve around a planet.

Today, we know that there are seven rings around Saturn, and that they are made of billions of pieces of rock, dust, and ice. Orbiting at Saturn's equator, the rings make Saturn one of the most breathtaking sights in the night sky.

The Cassini Spacecraft

Science has come a long way since the discovery of Saturn and its rings. We have sent astronauts into space and, in 1969, astronauts landed on the Moon. Scientists' fascination with Saturn, however, has remained. On October 15, 1997, the National Aeronautics and Space Administration (NASA) sent the Cassini spacecraft into space. Cassini traveled an incredible 1.5 billion kilometers (934 million miles) to reach its destination. Finally, in the summer of 2004, Cassini began to travel around Saturn, in an opening in the icy rings.

This is a computer-generated image of the Cassini spacecraft on its mission.

By watching the sky, ancient people recognized that the Sun, Moon, and planets move. With the facts we have available today, we know this takes place because Earth and the other planets orbit the Sun, and the Moon orbits Earth. A scientist named Isaac Newton discovered three rules, or laws of motion, about how and why objects move. Today scientists are aware of these laws of motion, and they know that everything in the universe is always moving. Remember, Earth is moving right now, as it orbits the Sun.

Today's scientists are also aware of the force of gravity. As you might know, this force causes the planets to move. In the past, people did not know the importance of gravity. So they came up with guesses to explain why there was movement in the sky. Have you ever guessed before? Then you probably know that guesses are not always correct!

Astronomers today use data from satellites orbiting in space to study distant galaxies.

Earth-Centered Ideas
Pythagoras (582?–500? B.C.)

Pythagoras lived in ancient Greece. A mathematician and thinker, he was convinced that Earth was round and at the center of the universe. Pythagoras believed that the Sun, Moon, and other planets, as well as Earth, moved.

Aristotle (384–322 B.C.)

Aristotle, an important thinker, teacher, and scientist, also lived in ancient Greece. He studied science, collecting valuable information about plant and animal life. He came up with the idea that the universe was shaped like a circle. In the very center, he claimed, was Earth. He believed that Earth was stationary, or did not move. It would be a very long time before Aristotle's ideas were challenged. In fact, they would not be checked until the 1600s.

Ptolemy (A.D. 100?–165?)

The ancient Greek astronomer Ptolemy developed his own ideas. He believed that Earth was round but did not move. Instead, the Sun, Moon, and stars all moved around Earth. Each moved in a little circle, which he called an epicycle, around a bigger circle.

The changes in the Moon's appearance are called the phases of the Moon. Over the course of a month, the Moon appears to change shape. Its form ranges from a very narrow slice, or crescent, to a full sphere.

During its orbit, the Moon reflects different amounts of sunlight. Depending on how much of that reflection we see on Earth, we see a different part of the Moon. Thus the illusion that the Moon changes shape.

Phases of the Moon

The Surface of the Moon

Galileo made a major discovery about the Moon in November of 1609. By studying the Moon through his telescope, he learned that Aristotle and Ptolemy were not correct—the Moon was not smooth, as they had claimed. Instead, its surface was pitted and full of craters. The surface of the Moon also had flatlands, valleys, and mountains like Earth.

For over two weeks, Galileo studied the Moon, drawing sketches of its changes. During his observations, he noted that its light parts seemed to point away from the Sun, and its dark parts seemed to point toward it. He believed that the dark sections were really shadows. As the Sun fell on mountains and valleys, small shadows were cast that did not have the same appearance every night.

What did this mean? Galileo believed it meant that the Moon was moving around the Sun. As the Moon moved, its position toward the Sun changed causing the shadows to look different. Today we know that the Moon actually revolves around Earth.

People did not approve of Galileo's views at the time, but he stood his ground and paved the way for future theories.

Aristotle's Universe

This diagram shows the universe as Aristotle envisioned it. Notice that it is round. In the center of the universe is Earth. Around it are the planets that can be seen with the eye alone. These are Mercury, Venus, Mars, Jupiter, and Saturn.

Where are Uranus, Neptune, and Pluto? Those are the outer planets, which can only be seen through a telescope. They had not been discovered yet.

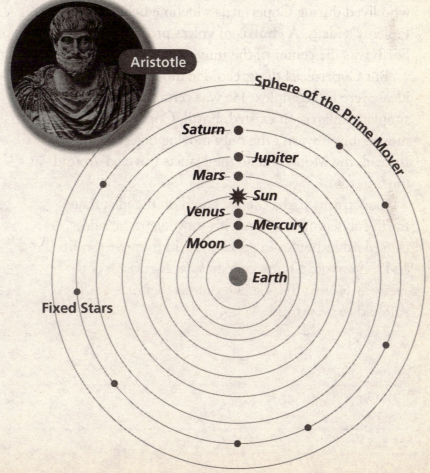

Sun-Centered Ideas

You have read about several ancient Greek astronomers' beliefs. They each had different ideas about whether Earth moved, but all viewed Earth as the center of the universe. It was not until almost fourteen hundred years later that a new thinker challenged those ideas, switching the places of Earth and the Sun.

Copernicus (1473–1543)

Today, we consider the Polish astronomer Nicolaus Copernicus to be the father of astronomy. Most people who lived during Copernicus's lifetime believed Ptolemy's ideas. A chorus of voices proclaimed that Earth was the center of the universe and did not move.

But Copernicus disagreed. He thought Ptolemy's ideas were too complex. He was certain that a much simpler explanation existed. Earth, Copernicus claimed, moved, but it wasn't the only moving object in the sky. Instead, the Moon and all the planets traveled around the Sun too.

Copernicus had a theory based on the idea that Earth rotated on an axis. This movement, he said, caused other bodies in space to seem to move too. In 1543, he wrote a book called *On the Revolutions of the Heavenly Spheres*. In it he laid out his theories, but they still had to be proved.

10

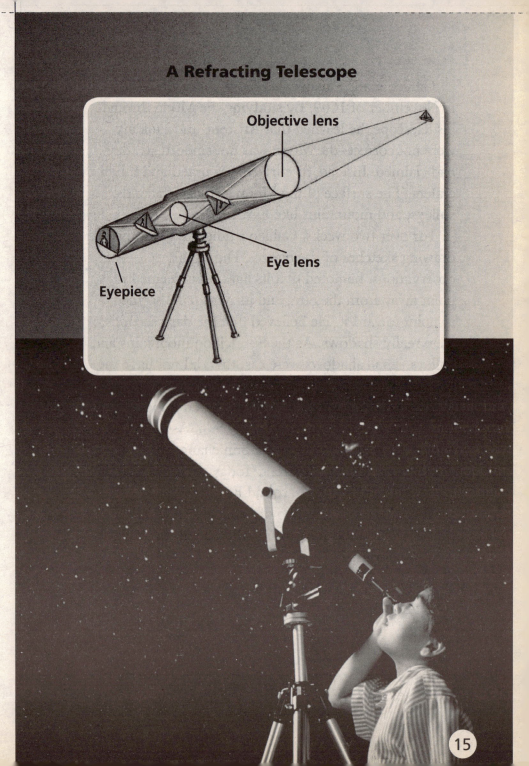

A Refracting Telescope

Objective lens

Eye lens

Eyepiece

15

How Does a Telescope Work?

Have you ever looked at the night sky through a telescope? As you probably know, a telescope is a tool used to make distant objects appear closer and larger. It allows us to view faraway objects in space that cannot be seen with our eyes alone.

While telescopes today can be enormous and high-tech, Galileo's was hand-held and homemade. To examine the skies, he used a refracting telescope.

A refracting telescope has two lenses. One lens is called the objective lens. The other, at the eyepiece, is called the eye lens. Though both lenses magnify, more is done by the larger objective lens, as it takes in and focuses light. A refracting telescope magnifies the object being viewed, making it many times larger for close examination.

Both Aristotle and Ptolemy believed that the Moon had a smooth surface. Remember, they had only seen the Moon with their eyes. Now, with the telescope, Galileo had a tool that had not existed in ancient Greece. He would be the first to use it to get a better view of the Moon.

The diagram below depicts the universe as Copernicus visualized it. Earth is no longer at the center. Copernicus's ideas were heliocentric, or Sun-centered. Compare this diagram with Aristotle's, and note how the Sun and Earth have switched places.

In Copernicus's universe, Uranus, Neptune, and Pluto are still missing. Even fourteen hundred years after Aristotle, these distant planets remained unknown.

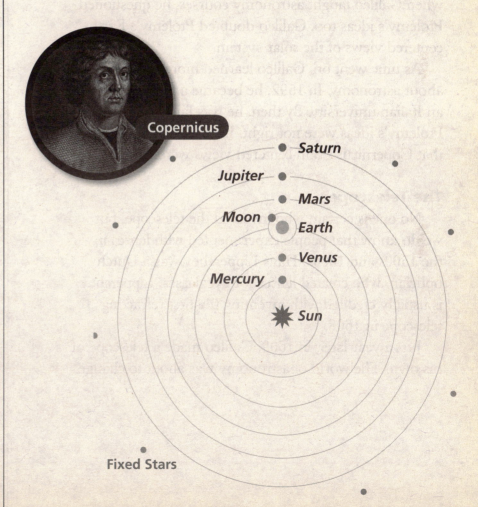

Galileo (1564–1642)

Galileo's Ideas

Galileo Galilei, now simply known as Galileo, was born in Pisa, Italy. With a gift for mathematics, he worked first as a tutor and then as a professor. As Galileo planned the lessons that would help his students learn, he kept learning himself. Galileo studied Aristotle and questioned his ideas about space. Later, when Galileo taught astronomy courses, he questioned Ptolemy's ideas too. Galileo doubted Ptolemy's Earth-centered views of the solar system.

As time went on, Galileo learned more and more about astronomy. In 1592, he became a professor at an Italian university. By then, he was fairly certain that Ptolemy's ideas were not right. Instead, Galileo believed that Copernicus's Sun-centered views were correct.

The Telescope

No one is certain who invented the telescope, but we do know that people experimented with lenses in the 1500s and 1600s. Hans Lippershey was a Dutch optician, who created lenses for eyeglasses. Lippershey is usually credited with inventing the first refracting telescope in 1608.

Just a year later, in 1609, Galileo made a telescope of his own. The world of astronomy was about to change.

Galileo's Telescope

Once Galileo had his homemade telescope, he aimed it at the sky. Now he was able to test Aristotle's and Ptolemy's ideas. He proved that they were incorrect.

Galileo wasn't always easy to get along with. Known for both his biting sense of humor and his strong opinions, he was no coward. Though his ideas were not always popular, he was never afraid to voice them.

Galileo was not the first person to invent a telescope, but he was the first to use it to observe the sky.

Suggested levels for Guided Reading, DRA,™ Lexile,® and Reading Recovery™ are provided in the Pearson Scott Foresman Leveling Guide.

Science

Science

Earth Science

Wild Weather

by C. A. Barnhart

Genre	Comprehension Skill and Strategy	Text Features
Nonfiction	• Graphic Sources • Predict	• Captions • Labels • Heads • Glossary

Scott Foresman Reading Street 4.3.4

PEARSON

Scott Foresman

ISBN 0-328-13453-8

9 780328 134533

90000

Reader Response

1. Using a chart similar to the one below, write the title of this book at the center. Write facts that you learned from the book's captions and pictures in the ovals around the center.

2. Predict what might happen if you saw stratus clouds in the sky.

3. Write the words *hurricane, blizzard,* and *dust storm* at the top of a three-column chart. Under each, write adjectives that a writer might use to describe each storm.

4. What information did you learn from a caption that wasn't in the main text?

Glossary

category *n.* (used with numbers 1–5) a classification of the severity of hurricanes.

cirrus *n.* a high cloud formation that is thin and feathery in appearance.

cumulus *n.* a puffy cloud formation that is round at the top and flat on the bottom.

drought *n.* a long period of too little rainfall.

dust storms *n.* windstorms that carry small particles of dirt from a dry area.

erode *v.* to wear away.

meteorology *n.* the science or study of weather.

radar *n.* a machine or system for measuring the distance, direction, speed, etc., of unseen objects by the reflection of microwave radio patterns.

stratus *n.* a flat, gray sheet of clouds that spreads over a large area.

surge *n.* a sudden or violent rushing wave of water.

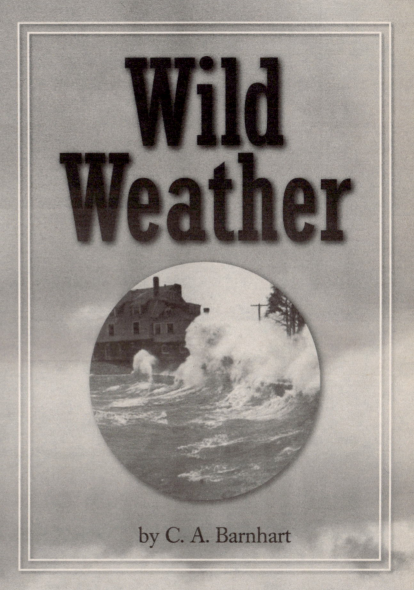

Wild Weather

by C. A. Barnhart

PEARSON
Scott Foresman

Editorial Offices: Glenview, Illinois • Parsippany, New Jersey • New York, New York
Sales Offices: Needham, Massachusetts • Duluth, Georgia • Glenview, Illinois
Coppell, Texas • Ontario, California • Mesa, Arizona

Here's How to Do It!

1. Keep a weather diary where you describe the weather each day. Be sure to write about interesting changes in the weather. Include how you reacted, what you felt, or what you noticed about the weather on a particular day.

2. Write a history of storms where you live. Your local paper should have articles from the past about storm events. Ask older people in your community if they remember an especially serious weather event. Record their stories in your diary.

3. Look for pictures of past storms and include them in your diary or history. Add pictures of places that still show signs of earlier storm damage, such as a photo of a building, a stand of trees, or a beach area.

4. Once you've collected some weather history, decorate your notebook. Make sure that you've included pictures showing the effects of big storms. Share your weather history with classmates, and learn more from their reports about the weather where you live.

Now Try This

Be a Weather Historian

Do you like rainy days? Does snow make you happy? Do you like days that are sunny and clear? No matter how you feel about the weather, you cannot do anything to change it, but you can find out more about the weather by being a weather historian.

The Great White Hurricane of 1888

Weather

If you were an astronaut gazing at Earth from your spacecraft, Earth and the space around it would look very clear, like a multicolored ball hanging in front of a dark backdrop. What if you looked at a picture of Earth taken from a satellite? A satellite orbits Earth at a lower level than the astronaut. It would show only one part of Earth at a time. From this point of view, Earth looks as if it is shrouded in a veil, the atmosphere. As your space camera approaches Earth, you can see clouds and clear spaces which make up the large swirling masses that determine the weather we experience on the ground.

People always want to know what the weather will be. Sailors and farmers are especially affected by weather, and long ago, being able to "read" the clouds, winds, and sky was a valuable skill. These practical weathermen understood enough about the weather to recognize winds that could cause trouble. They might not have been able to attach names to clouds, for example, but they would know that thin clouds high in the sky would signal a change coming. Today we know these as **cirrus** clouds.

Earth as seen from space

The name **cumulus** might not have meant anything to our practical weathermen, but when they saw cumulus clouds floating up in the sky like cotton balls, they knew they could expect fair weather. If cumulus clouds became darker in color and piled up in the sky, a thunderstorm was brewing. **Stratus** clouds, which look like flat, wrinkled gray sheets lying across the sky, can indicate snow in cold weather or rain in warmer weather. A wind from a certain direction could bring a storm.

The difficulty for our early practical forecasters, however, was that they based their forecasts on what they could see at that moment. They did not have much time to prepare for either good weather or dangerous storms. Farmers and sailors, in particular, recognized which cloud formations signaled a simple a change in weather or an approaching storm. But the advance warning they got from "reading" the clouds would have only given them several hours' notice. Today **meteorology,** the science of weather, has been helped a great deal by advances in technology.

As you can see, the forces of nature can be fierce, and it is important to be prepared when severe weather is expected. Hurricanes, blizzards, and dust storms have destroyed homes and communities, as well as taken lives. The damage caused by strong winds, crashing waves, blinding snow, or whirling dust may have been repaired over time, but people who have lived through severe weather will never forget their experiences. Technology has helped meteorologists predict storms so that people can be prepared before danger strikes. That is why being able to view Earth from above the clouds is so important.

Extreme weather conditions and events make good stories. While storms can be as exciting as frightening movies, they are real, and they are uncontrollable. Through technology, we have been able to predict when wild weather is on its way. As we learn more about our weather, we can reduce the amount of destruction that great weather events can cause.

Hurricane

Blizzard

Dust storm

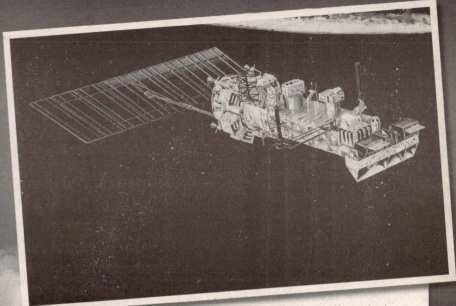

Weather satellites help meteorologists make forecasts.

Meteorologists rely on **radar** images, or images sent from weather satellites, to observe masses of air, the high and low pressure areas that create the weather we experience on Earth. Meteorologists send up weather balloons to measure temperature, pressure, and wind levels high in the atmosphere. By collecting this data, meteorologists can estimate the kind of weather that is likely to affect a large or small area of Earth for a whole season, not just the next few days.

By recording weather information in computer databases, meteorologists can compare it with data collected from the past. This means that weather forecasts are based on actual temperature, wind, humidity, and pressure readings taken from both high in the atmosphere and closer to the ground. Forecasters can also study weather occurring one place in the atmosphere that may eventually affect weather in another distant place.

Space technology has also helped with forecasting the weather. Long ago, a scientist might have wished to fly high above the weather to see what it looked like before it reached a certain place on Earth. Through space technology, meteorologists observe air masses in the atmosphere, which means that meteorologists can look at the weather from above the clouds.

Clouds of dirt in a dust storm

These houses in Texas are about to get hit by a dust storm.

Dust Storms of the 1930s

But what can anyone do about a kind of storm that lasts for nearly ten years?

More than seventy years ago, severe **drought** struck five states in the mid and southwest. There was little rainfall, so the soil became very dry and blew away in high winds. The drought lasted for nearly ten years and caused thousands of farmers to leave the area. When too little rain falls on unplanted, unprotected land, blowing wind can create **dust storms.**

During a dust storm, particles of dirt are carried by the wind, and sometimes the wind carries so much dust that people are blinded and choked by the whirling particles. The sky darkens, and the blowing dust enters a house or barn through any little crack or opening. During this period of drought and dust storms, Dust Bowl farmers lost their farms, animals, and all their savings.

Today, farmers plant lines of trees to break up the winds so they are less likely to **erode** the soil. Today, instead of planting crops in the dust bowl, farmers use it as grassland and pasture for cattle.

Understanding and planning for weather is important to everyone. Airlines need to know if the weather will cause problems with the flights they have scheduled, and a ship's captain must know what the weather will be like in order to plot a safe course across an ocean. Local and state governments need to know when a serious storm is approaching so that people can be warned and protect themselves from its effects. Families also want to know what the weather is going to be like when they are planning a picnic or hoping to attend a baseball game.

Technology helps meteorologists forecast the weather.

The Hurricane of 1938

Planes used to drop hurricane warnings to fishermen in their boats.

Even long ago, before forecasters had radar, satellites, and computers to help them predict the direction and force of a storm, people who lived along the southeastern coast would expect hurricanes between June and November. However, where hurricanes were rare, it was a very different situation. In 1938, toward the end of September, a hurricane raced up the eastern coast of the United States, tore across Long Island, New York, and then went straight north into New England.

People on their way to work climb over piles of ice and snow.

Every large airport on the east coast was shut down. High winds and fallen trees downed power lines, and heavy snow collected on rooftops which caused some buildings to collapse. Millions of people were without electricity, which meant that they did not have heat.

Sophisticated computers helped meteorologists recognize that this was not an ordinary storm. Meteorologists issued storm warnings to all the areas likely to be in the path of the Storm of the Century. In most cases, people stayed in the safety of their own homes. Since most people were warned about the storm, they were able to prepare for it.

These serious storms are exciting to read about, and, if you are in a safe place, they are exciting to witness. For those who are injured, or who have lost their homes, a storm is something they will never forget.

The Storm of the Century (1993)

More than one hundred years later, in 1993, the eastern United States experienced another blizzard. Some people called it the "Storm of the Century." This storm hit the entire eastern part of the United States, from Maine to Florida, and almost half of the country was snowed in.

Heavy snow fell on parts of the southeast, an area that rarely receives even a light dusting of snow. In Tennessee, fifty-six inches fell in one place, while Birmingham, Alabama, measured six-foot snowdrifts. In northern Florida, several inches of snow fell, and high winds caused damage similar to the kind caused by a hurricane.

A woman digs out her snowed-in car.

It is not often that hurricanes travel to the northeastern part of the United States. Usually, hurricanes lose their force before they reach New England, and before they can bring strong, gusty winds and high tides, which can cause some flooding and damage. Most of the time, storms in New England are not considered life threatening weather events, unlike major hurricanes.

The United States Weather Bureau knew about the hurricane of 1938 before it was supposed to hit the western coast of Florida. Because of weather conditions in the southern part of the country, however, the storm turned eastward and seemed to be heading out into the Atlantic Ocean. Since forecasters knew that the last major hurricane to hit New England was in 1869, it seemed unlikely that this hurricane would travel inland.

The destruction caused by hurricanes can take many lives.

This couple sits in what is left of their home after the hurricane of 1938.

A high-pressure air mass stationed over the Atlantic Ocean was blocking the storm from moving out to sea. The conditions were just right for the hurricane to be drawn along the east coast, across Long Island, and inland through New England. The storm kept moving north at more than fifty miles per hour!

The hurricane of 1938 was the most powerful storm that New Englanders had ever experienced. It was a **Category** 3 hurricane with winds gusting over 180 miles per hour. Hurricanes are classified from 1 to 5 according to severity—5 being the most severe. The hurricane downed power lines. Trees were uprooted, roads were washed out, and bridges were destroyed. Since people did not know the hurricane of 1938 was coming, there was not enough time for them to evacuate, and hundreds of people were killed.

The blizzard of '88 caused much damage and loss of life.

Trains, taxis, and ferry boats were unable to run. In fact, the storm stopped trains from going in and out of Grand Central Station. New York City, one of the busiest cities in the world, came to a halt, and it took many days for the city to get back on its feet. One result of the Great White Hurricane was that New York City decided to build a subway system so that the city would never again be paralyzed by a storm.

The Great White Hurricane of 1888

Because it lies next to the ocean, the eastern coast of the United States gets many heavy snow and rain storms. As a storm system moves across water, it picks up moisture and becomes stronger. If such a storm happens along with very cold temperatures, the result is a huge snowstorm. Storms that have heavy snowfall, strong winds, and cold temperatures are called blizzards, and they can last two or more days.

The Great White Hurricane was one such historic blizzard. It occurred in March 1888 and affected the entire east coast of the United States from Maryland to Maine. It lasted for three days, unleashing more than four feet of snow on New York City, and nearly five feet of snow on New England. Winds caused the snow to blow into tall drifts, with some drifts reaching as high as second-story windows!

The blizzard of '88 came on so quickly that New Yorkers were caught unprepared. The storm began late on a Sunday night in March. The weather had been warm, and residents thought that the storm would pass. On Monday morning, many people left their homes to go to work, but the storm got worse and worse. Some people were stranded at work, while others tried to walk home through the blinding snow.

People who survived the hurricane of 1938 were grateful, and some people wrote articles or letters about what they saw and felt while the storm raged around them. Some people survived the storm by clinging to the roofs of their houses. Some people watched as their homes were blown apart and carried off by the **surge** of water that came ashore with the hurricane. No one ever wanted to get caught in a storm like that again!

Young girls rummage through the hurricane-damaged remains of their home.

Hurricane Charley (2004)

If you lived in Florida in the summer of 2004, you will remember Hurricane Charley. Meteorologists spotted Hurricane Charley in the South Atlantic long before it reached Florida. Their warnings stated that Charley would be at least a Category 3 hurricane, striking with heavy rain and winds of up to 130 miles per hour.

Another danger was that Charley might create a great storm surge, which would cause flooding in many coastal areas. Many people packed bags and left their homes, while others made plans to stay in emergency shelters where they would be safe. Anyone living close to the water was forced to leave. Shopkeepers had to board up windows so they would not be shattered by Charley's strong winds.

As things turned out, Charley was a Category 4 hurricane with winds as powerful as 155 miles per hour! It struck Florida's west coast and sped across the state, causing great damage. The hurricane uprooted trees and snapped them in two, smashed mobile homes, and flooding buildings.

Hurricane Charley blew roofs off homes, collapsed walls, and shattered windows. In some places the electricity went out, and there was no running water. Hurricane Charley tossed cars into the air as if they were toys. As bad as Charley was, though, there was less destruction and loss of life than if there hadn't been weather predictions, as in the hurricane of 1938. Because they were warned, people expected Hurricane Charley and had time to prepare.

Hurricane Charley near the southern tip of Florida (above) and the destruction it caused (left)

Suggested levels for Guided Reading, DRA,™
Lexile,® and Reading Recovery™ are provided
in the Pearson Scott Foresman Leveling Guide.

Social Studies

Genre	Comprehension Skill and Strategy	Text Features
Nonfiction	• Generalize • Text Structure	• Captions • Heads • Summary

Scott Foresman Reading Street 4.3.5

PEARSON

Scott
Foresman

scottforesman.com

ISBN 0-328-13456-2

90000

9 780328 134564

The PRICE *of a* PIPELINE

BY BENJAMIN LAZARUS

Reader Response

1. Based on what you have just read, would you say the Trans-Alaska Pipeline was a simple project or a complicated project? Give reasons for your answer.

2. How does the early section on "Alaska's Environment" prepare you for the later sections on the impacts of the pipeline?

3. Find the word *interconnected* on page 6. What does it mean? Find other words in a dictionary that use the prefix *inter-*. What does *inter-* mean?

4. Look at the two food chains on page 15. How does each one show that plants and animals are interconnected?

Glossary

canopy *n.* a cover formed by the leafy upper branches of trees in a forest.

fragrant *adj.* having a pleasant scent.

environment *n.* the area in which something exists or lives.

lichens *n.* a plant that is a combination of algae and fungus, usually found in crusty patches on rocks or ground.

permafrost *n.* a permanently frozen layer of soil.

pollen *n.* the fertilizing element of flowering plants.

pollinate *v.* to convey pollen from flower to flower.

thermokarst *n.* a landscape where many small pits are formed by the melting of ground ice, or permafrost.

tundra *n.* a treeless plain typical of the arctic and subarctic regions.

wondrous *adj.* wonderful, remarkable.

The Price of a Pipeline

BY BENJAMIN LAZARUS

Editorial Offices: Glenview, Illinois • Parsippany, New Jersey • New York, New York
Sales Offices: Needham, Massachusetts • Duluth, Georgia • Glenview, Illinois
Coppell, Texas • Ontario, California • Mesa, Arizona

Here's How To Do It!

1. Research your topic to get another part of the pipeline story. Write down 10 key points on the information you found. Then consider this: How has the presence of the pipeline affected what you researched? For instance, did it cause an improvement? Did it cause a harmful change? Did it inspire more work done in the field?

2. Take your findings and your research and consider what you learned in this book. Now it's time to make a general decision and then write.

3. Write two paragraphs:
   In the first paragraph, write your decision: What do you think about the pipeline? Did you decide it was a good idea? a bad idea? a mixed idea?
   In the second paragraph, write about how your research helped you come to your decision. Did your research support your first impression? Or did it change your mind?

23

Now Try This

Go to the library or use the Internet to learn more about Alaska. You may want to have a parent or teacher help you find the best websites or materials. Then, pick a topic related to Alaska and the pipeline. It can be:

- Native American tribes in Alaska
- Wildlife conservation in Alaska
- Climate change in Alaska
- Finding new sources of energy besides oil

Oil!

Without oil, we could not live as we do. Oil fuels most cars, trucks, buses, boats, trains and planes. It fuels machines in factories. It heats homes, offices, and schools. Oil is used to make products like ink, crayons, bubble gum, dishwashing liquids, ammonia, deodorant, eyeglasses, records and tires.

In 2003, the United States used 375.3 million gallons of oil a day for transportation and .468 million gallons of oil a day for other purposes. But the United States produces only 44% of the oil it uses. The rest is imported from other countries.

Importing oil from other countries is expensive. It's also risky. If there are problems in an oil-producing region, oil supplies can shrink and prices can climb. So American oil companies are always looking for ways to supply their own oil. They set up drilling sites all over the country to look for this valuable resource.

The pipeline promised to solve American's oil problem.

The Exxon Valdez Disaster

On March 24, an oil tanker called the *Exxon Valdez* began its journey out of port. The new ship was 987 feet long, with 11 cargo tanks and a crew of 19. It was carrying a full load of oil. A little after midnight, it ran into an underwater reef. The impact ripped into the hull. Eight cargo tanks were torn open. Within hours, 11 million gallons of oil spilled into Prince William Sound. Within two months, 500 miles of Alaskan coastline was covered in oil.

Immediately, many thousands of fish, sea birds, and sea mammals began to die. In the weeks, and months to come, deaths increased. Emergency crews from around the world raced to save the oil-coated wildlife. Hospitals were set up to clean creatures as big as whales and as small as sparrows.

The accident showed how unprepared Exxon was for such a major spill. It actually took three years before intensive clean-up began. In 1994, a jury ordered Exxon to pay $5 billion in fines. The tragedy proved that the pipeline project was indeed full of risk.

Ten years later, the effects of the disaster are still being felt. Prince William Sound may never fully recover. Of the dozens of species of wildlife that suffered damage, some are still weakened. Populations have shrunk. In some species, the young have crippling birth defects. But other species are recovering.

ACCIDENTS

The environmental damage caused by thermokarst can be repaired. But experts say it will take at least a billion dollars. Billions of dollars have also been spent dealing with another effect of the pipeline, accidents.

Accidents in the pipeline cause oil to spill into the environment. Oil, a harsh pollutant, harms living things all the way up the food chain. If ingested, oil is poisonous. But even contact with it can kill an organism. Oil in the water can suffocate fish by clogging their gills. It coats whales' and porpoises' blowholes, making it impossible for them to breathe. On land, it can coat birds, mammals, and their food and homes.

No one could promise that there would be no accidents on the pipeline. In fact, there were many. But some accidents made front-page news. In February 1979, an explosion in a pipe caused a spill of over 16,000 barrels of oil. In 2001, a hunter shot a bullet into a pipe's connecting weld, causing another leak. But back in 1989, an accident took place that turned into a major environmental tragedy.

The Exxon Valdez oil spill took place in 1989.

In 1968, oil companies discovered an enormous field of oil at Prudhoe Bay, on the northern coast of Alaska. Prudhoe Bay is above the Arctic Circle. It's far too remote for most forms of transportation. How would the oil companies get the oil to the rest of the United States?

THE PIPELINE

The answer was a pipeline. It would have to transport the oil 800 miles, to the port of Valdez. Valdez, though far south in the Gulf of Alaska, was the nearest ice-free port. There, oil could be loaded onto tankers and shipped to the rest of the United States.

Oil companies rushed to create a plan. They faced many challenges: They had to construct a pipe system to withstand the dramatic Alaskan climate, as well as Alaska's earthquakes. Oil would need to flow freely through the pipe. Since oil comes out of the ground hot, the heat generated in the pipe would need to be spread out. Heated pipes could harm the **permafrost**—a permanently frozen layer just below the surface of the ground. The oil companies were worried that if the permafrost melted, it could cause the pipe to sink and possibly break. The port of Valdez also had to be turned into a major shipping zone, capable of handling giant oil tankers.

Environmental Risks

But the idea of a pipeline crossing Alaska raised many questions. Some scientists and wildlife experts were concerned about the **environment**. They disagreed with the oil companies, and felt that the impact of melted permafrost on a pipe was not the point. For them, the point was the danger of damaging the permafrost itself. Alaska's environment is fragile and interconnected. It sustains many forms of life. These, in turn, support and sustain each other. So harming one part of the environment could cause major damage to other parts.

Some environmental experts asked, what will happen to this special world if there is an accident? What would an oil spill do? What about the effects of roads and trucks? Some people believed the enormous construction project was simply too much for the Alaskan environment.

Landslides in Alaska happen when the solid layer of ice on the ground melts. The condition is called thermokarst.

Thermokarst

The roads have had another effect across much of the entire surface of Alaska. They have created a condition called **thermokarst**.

Thermokarst means that the solid layer of ice on the ground has melted. This can happen because of melting snow on the pipeline roads. When the snow melts on the roads, it leaks into the ground and melts the ice beneath the surface. When this ice melts, the ground caves in. Ruts, tunnels, mounds and valleys form.

Under the wheels of tractors and construction vehicles, thermokarst gets worse. When the roads were built or repaired, heavy-tired vehicles created deeper holes and valleys in the fragile ground. Along the coast, thermokarst eroded the shoreline, causing the sea level to rise. That has damaged nesting and breeding sites of some migratory birds.

Thermokarst has a clear cost to humans as well. As the land becomes more unstable, landslides result. In one case, a landslide destroyed an entire Native American village. In another, it swallowed up runways at the airport in the city of Fairbanks.

Roads were constructed across the fields where herds of caribou had fed for generations. The roads reduced the food supply by damaging the soil. As a result, the caribou herds could not get enough to eat.

A third effect involves the chemicals used to build the roads. During the rainy season, those chemicals were washed from the roadbed into the soil. Once in the soil, they spread out. Plants were killed when they came into contact with these chemicals. Minerals the plants use for nutrition were damaged by the chemicals, which also harmed the plants. As groundwater flowed into streams, the chemicals in the ground flowed into those streams as well. Fish were affected. Animals that ate the fish were also affected.

Others, however, believed the pipeline was a terrific idea with little risk. They argued that the pipe would be well constructed and the chance of accidents would be extremely low. They believed that the effects of roads and trucks on the land would be minor. Finally, they argued that the tremendous benefits to the entire country greatly outweighed any possible risks.

In 1970, people fought to halt the project with a series of lawsuits. They argued that the pipeline would have lasting effects on Alaska's environment. They requested that the oil companies find less destructive ways to transport the oil.

But the oil companies insisted that they could make sure the pipeline was harmless. They argued that every day spent trying to halt the pipeline was costing the United States millions in foreign oil payments.

The environmentalists lost. In 1973, President Richard M. Nixon signed the Trans-Alaska Pipeline Authorization Act. By 1974, construction was underway.

Construction

When it was built, the pipeline was the most expensive, privately funded project of its kind. It cost 8 billion dollars. Creating a marine terminal at the port of Valdez cost $1.4 billion. Creating the pipeline required five separate contracting companies and a crew of 21,000 people. Twenty-nine temporary camps were built. Three million tons of material were shipped to the construction sites. Fourteen airfields were built to transport crew and materials.

The pipe itself is steel, and measures 48-inches in diameter. It is built in six separate sections that, when connected, run 799 miles from northern to southern Alaska. It crosses three mountain ranges and more than 800 rivers and streams. Some parts are buried underground.

Engineers worked to find solutions to the challenges of placing the pipeline in the Alaskan climate. The pipeline is built in a zig-zag so it can naturally expand and contract, depending on outside temperatures. To keep oil moving, 12 pump stations were built along the pipeline. To help prevent the oil's heat from melting the permafrost, radiators were installed.

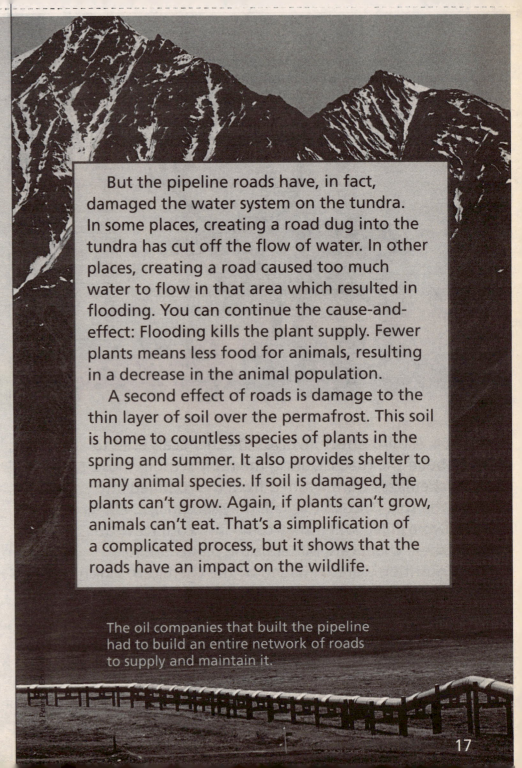

But the pipeline roads have, in fact, damaged the water system on the tundra. In some places, creating a road dug into the tundra has cut off the flow of water. In other places, creating a road caused too much water to flow in that area which resulted in flooding. You can continue the cause-and-effect: Flooding kills the plant supply. Fewer plants means less food for animals, resulting in a decrease in the animal population.

A second effect of roads is damage to the thin layer of soil over the permafrost. This soil is home to countless species of plants in the spring and summer. It also provides shelter to many animal species. If soil is damaged, the plants can't grow. Again, if plants can't grow, animals can't eat. That's a simplification of a complicated process, but it shows that the roads have an impact on the wildlife.

The oil companies that built the pipeline had to build an entire network of roads to supply and maintain it.

The Pipeline's Impact

Has any aspect of the Trans-Alaska Pipeline damaged Alaska's environment? Have there been any accidents? Has the pipeline been running normally? Let's take a closer look at one important part of the working pipeline system: roads.

The Impact of Roads

Hundreds of miles of roads had to be built in Alaska to transport crews and materials to the pipeline project. To create the roads, parts of the landscape had to be plowed and graded.

Part of this landscape includes miles and miles of Alaskan tundra. When thawed, this tundra works like a giant system of tiny water channels. Water flows freely through these channels. It fills watering holes for animals, and provides plants with vital nutrients. Additionally, the plants provide food for some of these animals. These grazing animals provide food for other animals.

The pipeline was finally completed in June 1977. That August, oil began to flow. The first tanker to ship pipeline oil from the port of Valdez was the *ARCO Juneau*. Since then, some 16,000 tankers have been filled at Valdez, and more than 13 billion barrels of oil have traveled through the pipeline. Daily, the pipeline can transport up to 2.1 million barrels. That's a lot of oil.

But were the oil companies right? Has the pipeline been a success with minimal damage to the environment? Or were the environmentalists right? Were Alaska's landscape and wildlife harmed? Was the Alaskan environment changed forever?

What would the pipeline do to the untouched beauty of the Alaskan tundra?

Winters on the Alaskan tundra are long and summers are short. But animals that live there have adapted to its environment. In fact, it would be harder for them if conditions change.

Alaska's Environment

To understand the relationship between the pipeline and the Alaskan environment, it's important to understand what makes Alaska so unique.

Alaska is an enormous state. At its widest points, it measures 1400 miles from north to south and 2400 miles from east to west. Its landscape includes mountain ranges, glaciers, fjords, bays, streams and rivers, island chains, and vast stretches of land. It has many different regions and climates. Some regions are covered with snow and ice most of the time. Other regions are heavily forested, with a dense **canopy** high over the forest floor. Still others are a combination of mountains, sloping fields and flat lands.

An Underwater Food Chain

Imagine one aspect of the food web, in the water along the Alaskan coast:

1. The cold, unpolluted arctic waters provide an ideal home for healthy marine organisms, such as plankton and algae.
2. Tiny fish feed on the organisms.
3. Larger fish feed on the smaller fish.
4. Seals feed on the larger fish.
5. Whales and polar bears feed on the seals.

A Food Chain on Land

Now let's take a close look at life on the tundra of northern Alaska. Here's how one link of the food chain affects another:

1. Summer's warming temperatures create vast fields of wildflowers, grasses and shrubs across the tundra.
2. The plant life provides homes and food for insects, such as flies and bees.
3. Nesting and breeding birds feed on the plentiful supply of insects.
4. The birds, with enough food to thrive, reproduce and lay their eggs.
5. Some of the eggs provide food for predators, such as foxes and bears.
6. The predators, with enough food to thrive, reproduce and give birth to the next generation.

Nature's Food Chains

An environment is like a system of balances. It involves a series of food chains, in which the smallest creature is related to the largest. Scientists call the series of food chains a food web, since each species may eat more than one kind of food, and is dependent on at least one other species. You can see, in a food web, that something as minor as dropping a cup of gasoline into a lake could actually make bears sick, or worse.

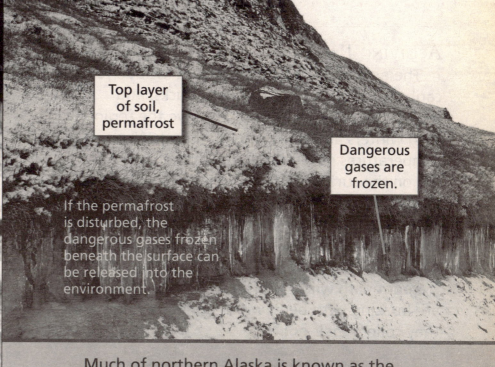

Top layer of soil, permafrost

Dangerous gases are frozen.

If the permafrost is disturbed, the dangerous gases frozen beneath the surface can be released into the environment.

Much of northern Alaska is known as the tundra. The **tundra** may look like a frozen wasteland, but it's not. It's a **wondrous** system of seasonal freezing and thawing that supports hundreds of different species of wildlife and plants. The tundra includes a surface layer of soil that can be as deep as six inches. Below that is the permafrost layer.

The permafrost is an extremely important part of the tundra, for many reasons. It keeps the ground in place and makes it stable. It keeps dangerous gases frozen beneath the surface, so they are not released into the air, water, or soil. These gases include carbon dioxide and methane. The permafrost also helps rain drain into rivers and streams, keeping waterways full of fresh water.

A LIVING PARADISE

The animals living on the tundra include fox, caribou, grizzly and polar bears, ducks, and snowy owls. They are able to survive the region's long winters and short, cool summers. When temperatures rise in the summer, the layer of soil on the surface of the tundra bursts into life. **Lichens** dapple once-bare rocks. Valleys fill with flowering plants, mosses, and shrubs. Those plants depend on seasonal freezes in order to come back to life every spring. Then, the air is **fragrant** with wildflowers. Fields of wildflowers are buzzing with bees, which **pollinate** flowers as they collect their **pollen**.

Wildlife you'll find in different regions of Alaska includes salmon, moose, black-tailed deer, caribou, mountain goats, wild sheep, bears, wolves, harbor seals, porpoises, dolphins, humpback and minke whales, sea lions, sea otters, and walruses. Alaska is also home to more than 400 species of birds, from the tiny sparrow to the great bald eagle. In addition, thousands of migratory birds come to Alaska each spring.

Alaska's plant life changes depending on the region. Alaska is home to 33 native tree species, including the Sitka spruce, western hemlock, alder, white spruce, cottonwood, and paper birch. The mosses, wildflowers, and other plants (some underwater), that grow in various regions provide vital food for fish, birds, and animals.

A polar bear crosses the ice.

Suggested levels for Guided Reading, DRA™, Lexile®, and Reading Recovery™ are provided in the Pearson Scott Foresman Leveling Guide.

Science

Science

Tricking the Eye

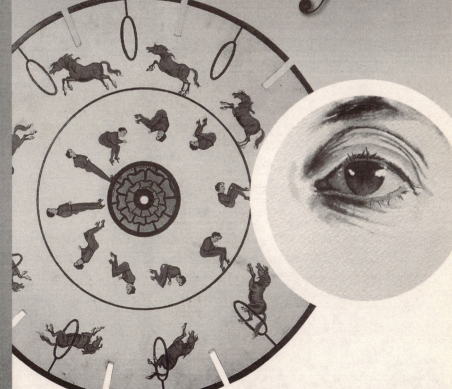

Genre	Comprehension Skill and Strategy	Text Features
Nonfiction	• Compare and Contrast • Predict	• Table of Contents • Diagrams • Call Outs • Glossary

Scott Foresman Reading Street 4.4.1

PEARSON
Scott Foresman

scottforesman.com

ISBN 0-328-13459-7

9 780328 134595

90000

by Stephanie Wilder

Reader Response

1. Using a chart similar to the one below, write *computer-assisted* and *computer-generated* in the top box. How are computer-assisted animation and computer-generated animation alike? How are they different? What can you conclude?

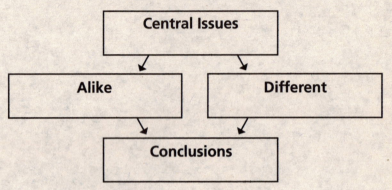

2. Predict what will happen when you see an optical illusion.

3. How did context clues help you understand what *concave* means?

4. How do the labels on the diagrams help you to understand better what you are looking at?

Glossary

accommodation *n.* the automatic adjustment of the lens of the eye to see objects at various distances.

animate *v.* to make lively.

cerebral cortex *n.* part of the brain that receives signals from the senses.

computer-assisted animation *n.* two-dimensional computer animation; a series of still computer images put together to create movement.

computer-generated animation *n.* the process by which a computer uses models and formulas to make a still image move in lifelike ways, often in three dimensions.

concave *adj.* curved inward.

frames *n.* individual still images that make up a cartoon.

illusion *n.* something that appears to be different from what it actually is.

optical illusion *n.* illusion having to do with sight or seeing.

perception *n.* the brain's understanding of something.

Tricking the Eye

by Stephanie Wilder

Editorial Offices: Glenview, Illinois • Parsippany, New Jersey • New York, New York
Sales Offices: Needham, Massachusetts • Duluth, Georgia • Glenview, Illinois
Coppell, Texas • Ontario, California • Mesa, Arizona

Here's How to Do It!

1. First, you need to gather your materials. The easiest way to get started is to find a small, empty notebook. (If you don't have one, don't worry. Take several pieces of blank paper and cut them into equal-sized pieces. Next, staple them together on the left-hand side to make a book.) You will also need markers, crayons, or pencils to draw your cartoon.

2. Begin by drawing a picture on the first page of your notebook. This can be a picture of anything that you would like to see moving, such as an animal, person, robot, or boat.

3. Next, draw the same picture on the second page. This time make a very small change in the direction of the movement you want to create.

4. Continue drawing the picture, changing it just a little bit each time, until the movement is complete. The more pictures you draw, the longer your cartoon will be.

5. Finally, after you have finished each drawing, hold the book with your left hand and flip through it very fast with your right hand. Watch as your drawings come to life!

Now Try This

Make a Flip Book

As we have already learned, the first cartoons were made by putting a series of still images together to make them look as if they were moving. Now it is your turn to make your own cartoon. The flip book was one of the first kinds of cartoon. Making a flip book is easy and fun.

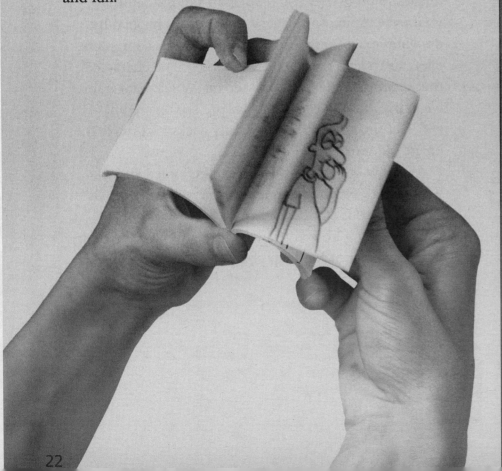

CONTENTS

CHAPTER 1	4
Illusions and Animation	
CHAPTER 2	8
Your Eyes and How You See	
CHAPTER 3	14
Computer Animation	
CHAPTER 4	18
Optical Illusions	
Conclusion	21
NOW TRY THIS	22
Make a Flip Book	
Glossary	24

Chapter 1 *Illusions and Animation*

What do you see in this picture?

Look again. Are your eyes playing a trick on you? How can one picture really be two pictures at the same time?

You are looking at an **optical illusion.** Optical illusions like this one make you wonder if your eyes are really seeing the things you think you see. Is that a picture of an old woman, or is it a young woman with her face turned away? As strange as it may seem, it is both!

Magicians use these types of tricks in their acts, but playing tricks on the eye is not just for magic shows. We may not realize it, but illusions are a big part of the cartoons we can see every day.

Conclusion

The creation of cartoons has come a long way. So has our understanding of our own brain.

Long ago, it was discovered that a group of still images put together could appear to move before your eyes. Animators started making this happen by drawing images on pieces of paper. Today, computers allow us to take this simple idea and create characters that seem to come to life on-screen. When we see this, we know that the characters we are seeing are not real. But the animators have many tricks that make the image seem real.

We now know that the eye can be fooled and that what you think you see might not be what is actually in front of you. Optical illusions are everywhere. Understanding how your eyes work and how the brain perceives images can help you to tell illusion from reality.

Cartoons are animated stories. We can see them everywhere. Some are drawn by hand, some are made using puppets and clay, and others are made using computers. But no matter how they are made, they are all based on the same idea. They all trick the eye.

In most animation a group of still images, called **frames,** is put together to create the **illusion** of movement. Each still picture is just a little bit different from the one before. When they are filmed all together it looks like the characters are actually moving. But it takes a lot of these still pictures to make a whole movie. It takes twenty-four different frames to make up only one second of a movie!

Early examples of animation

In the early days of cartoons, the many still pictures that make a cartoon had to be drawn by hand, and this took a lot of work. So animators came up with a few tricks to make their jobs easier.

Instead of drawing a whole new picture for every frame, they decided to draw only the parts of the picture that needed to move. Usually this meant making one background drawing. The characters were drawn on clear plastic sheets and laid over the

Cartoon animation uses two-dimensional drawings.

still background. The characters would change and look like they were moving, but only one background drawing was made. This method is called cel animation.

Another old trick is called the slash-and-tear system. Here the moving characters are drawn on regular paper, but then they are cut out. This way the different images of the moving characters can be placed on top of the background drawing. Either way, what you think you see is the characters coming to life.

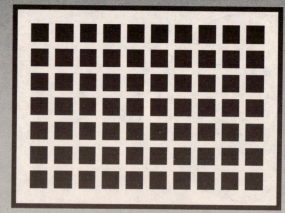

Hermann Grid

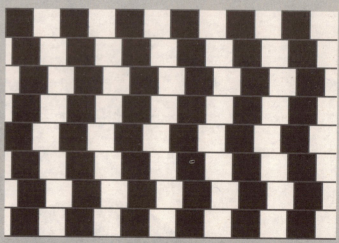

Optical Curve Illusion

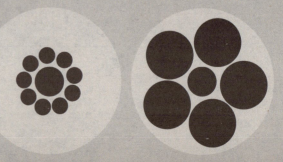

Van Ebbinghaus-Titchner Illusion

Chapter 4 Optical Illusions

Take a look at some of these optical illusions. Do any of these images seem to move? Is your **perception** of each of these pictures the truth? In the first optical illusion, do you see gray dots that appear and disappear where the white lines intersect? Are they really there? In the second optical illusion, do the black lines look wavy or straight? In the third optical illusion, which of the center dots do you think is bigger? It is funny how your eyes can play tricks on your brain, isn't it?

Optical illusions, like the ones here and the one earlier in this book, can trick your brain into seeing something very different from what is actually drawn on the page. This type of illusion is the basic idea behind all of the cartoons we watch. Putting still images together and simply changing one or two details can make them appear to move. Computers can create the illusion of a substantial or living object. Other types of optical illusions can play the same tricks.

There are many other ways to **animate.** One very simple way is stop-motion animation. With this method, clay models or puppets are photographed. Then they are moved just a little bit and photographed again. They are photographed at each stage of their action. The stills are then placed together in sequence, and it appears to the person watching that the models or puppets are moving on their own.

This trick is also used in movies with live actors. Before computers, special effects were done through simple camera tricks. If directors wanted to make something disappear, they would first film the scene with the object in it. Then they would stop the camera and remove the object. When the film started rolling again, it would appear as if the object had just vanished, like magic.

Stop-motion animation uses three-dimensional models instead of drawings.

Chapter 2 *Your Eyes and How You See*

So why do these simple tricks work? They are optical illusions. Your eyes are looking at an object, but your brain interprets it as something completely different.

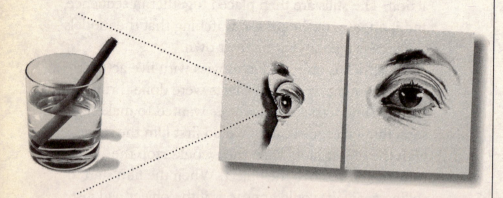

Actually, your eyes do not see at all. They just detect light and reflect it to your brain. Your brain does the seeing for you. Your brain takes the information that your eyes send, and it turns that information into something you can understand. Your brain can play some pretty funny tricks on you!

Your eye has three layers. The first layer is the sclera (SKLIR-uh). This layer is the outside part of your eye. It is a protective layer. The middle layer is the choroid (KOR-oid). This layer contains the muscles that help you focus. The last layer is the retina. Your retina contains cells called rods and cones. These are light-sensitive. Your retina is also the part of your eye that gives information to your brain.

When you see a character made by the computer in three dimensions, it seems to move smoothly. It looks real and substantial on screen, as though it were a solid, living, breathing creature. It also gives the appearance that it is part of its background and not separated from it. A computer-assisted character sometimes looks less substantial and less real than a computer-generated character. It does not necessarily look like a living creature. It is not part of the background, since it is only in two dimensions. It seems to float in front of its surroundings.

The eye and the brain often do not perceive computer-assisted images as real. But computer-generated characters are more easily perceived as real. The illusion is complete when the artist convinces the viewer of this reality.

This animation was based on data taken from the rover's onboard sensors.

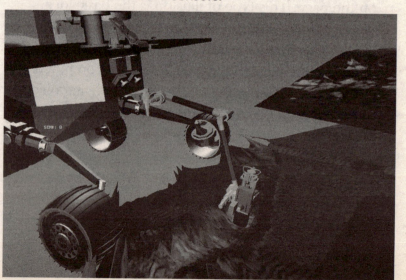

Computer-generated animation of the Mars rover from NASA

Another kind of computer animation is **computer-generated animation.** Here the computer creates an entire motion picture rather than a series of still pictures.

Computer-generated animation can produce the illusion of a three-dimensional world. Animators make digital models of their characters and backgrounds. They then give the computer the information needed to make these models move on screen.

This type of animation is much more difficult for the computer, but it is very real for the viewer. It makes the world that the computer images have created seem to come alive.

The part of your eye that has color is called the iris. The pupil is the opening in the center of the iris. The iris adjusts the size of the pupil to let in the right amount of light. When it is dark, your iris shrinks, causing the pupil to expand. This lets in as much light as possible. When it is bright, your iris expands, making the pupil shrink. This prevents too much light from coming into your eye. The iris is in the choroid layer, just behind the cornea. The cornea is a clear layer over the iris and pupil.

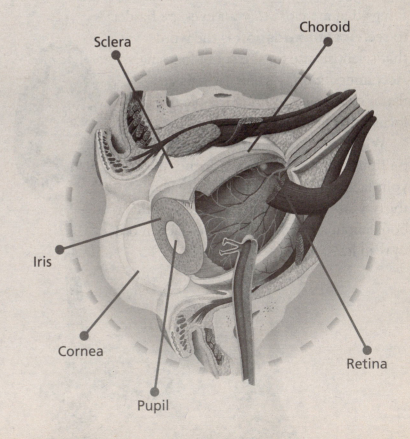

Animators use the camera to make you see just what they want you to see. The camera makes it seem as though still images are turning into moving ones. Your eye, in some ways, works just like a camera. It essentially takes a picture of what is in front of you and gives it to your brain. Your brain's job is to figure out what image your eye has just given it.

Your eye turns light into images. Then it sends the information as nerve signals to your brain. It then displays them on your retina. Things that are far away are easy for your eyes to focus on, while things that are close to your eyes are harder to see. **Accommodation** is the word that scientists use for the act of focusing. Accommodation is when the lens gets flatter or rounder to bring the picture into focus on your retina.

When you were born, you could focus on things that were only 2½ inches from your face. But by the time you are about thirty years old, you will have to hold this book about six inches from your face in order to read it.

Computer-assisted animation was the first form of computer animation. Artists use the computer to create still images and to make them come to life. This is two-dimensional computer animation. The computer is used to make a group of still images that begin to move only when they are put together. This uses the same principle that hand-drawn cartoons use. In this case the images are created on a computer screen instead of on a piece of paper. Each time the artists create an image, they make sure the new image looks slightly different from the image that came before it. This is how they make it seem like the character is moving.

A woman works in digital animation at Studio Ghibli in Tokyo. Studio Ghibli has produced such films as the Academy Award–winning *Spirited Away*.

The picture that appears on your retina is actually upside down. It is your brain that takes that picture and turns it right side up. All this happens without you ever knowing about it.

Have you ever looked at the reflection of your face in the top of a spoon? It is upside down. The spoon reflects light in the same way that your eye does. This is because the shape of the spoon is **concave,** or bent inward, just like the shape of your eye. A concave lens curves inward. It disperses light rays. This means that when light rays strike a concave lens, the light spreads out and goes in many directions. Your eye's concave lens is what inverts images, or turns them upside down.

Just as the concave shape of the spoon inverts the image, so does the eye's concave lens.

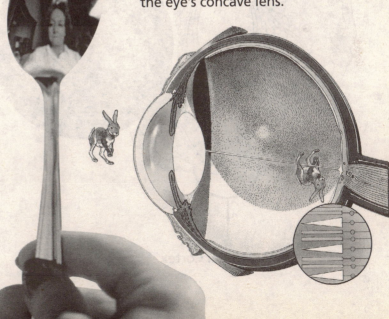

Chapter 3 *Computer Animation*

Cartoons from long ago used the tricks you read about earlier to make it seem as if still drawings were moving. Some cartoon creators of today still use these tricks, but many of them use the computer to help them create the illusion of movement.

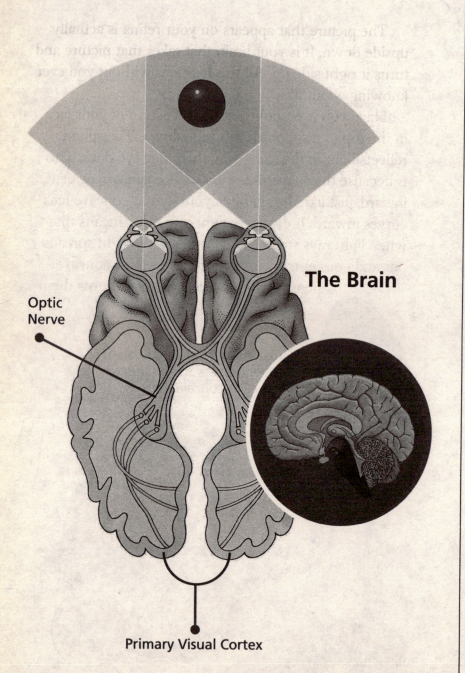

The Brain

Optic Nerve

Primary Visual Cortex

When you see anything, the image you are seeing is light being reflected off the object. Light bounces off objects and travels though your eye. An upside-down image appears on your retina. Then the image is turned into an electrical signal that travels to your cerebral cortex.

The **cerebral cortex** is the part of your brain that receives signals from all your senses. The cerebral cortex has many parts, and interpreting electrical signals sent from the eye is just one of many jobs that this part of the brain does. The cerebral cortex recieves the signals that the eye sends to it and interprets them. When the signals arrive in the cerebral cortex, they are interpreted right side up. Your brain has turned the signal into an image that you can understand.

The ability of your brain to turn electrical signals into images that you can understand is what allows you to see things such as cartoons and magicians. But the tricks of the animators and magicians make the things you see seem real.

Suggested levels for Guided Reading, DRA,™ Lexile,® and Reading Recovery™ are provided in the Pearson Scott Foresman Leveling Guide.

Life Science

Science

Genre	Comprehension Skill and Strategy	Text Features
Nonfiction	• Compare and Contrast • Visualize	• Captions • Call Outs • Diagrams • Glossary

Scott Foresman Reading Street 4.4.2

scottforesman.com

ISBN 0-328-13462-7

9 780328 134625

Echolocation:
Animals Making Sound Waves

by Laura Johnson

Reader Response

1. Using a chart similar to the one below, compare and contrast the echolocation methods of dolphins and bats. How are they similar? How are they different?

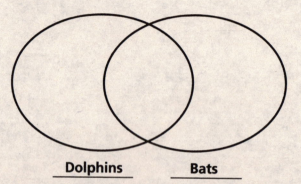

2. What details from the book help you visualize how dolphins use echolocation?

3. What other meaning might the word *hammer* have? How do you know which meaning it has in this book?

4. Do the captions help you understand the topic of this book better? How?

Glossary

anvil *n.* the central bone of three tiny bones in the middle ear.

cochlea *n.* a spiral-shaped tube in the inner ear.

echolocation *n.* a method of finding objects by using sound waves and vibrations.

hammer *n.* the outermost bone of three tiny bones in the middle ear.

larynx *n.* voice box.

lymph *n.* the fluid in the cochlea.

melon *n.* the fat-filled area in the front of a dolphin's head that focuses the echolocation clicks as they leave the dolphin's head.

nose leaves *n.* the flaps of skin on a bat's nose that direct sound forward.

pinna *n.* the skin-covered outer part of an ear.

stirrup *n.* the innermost of three tiny bones in the middle ear.

Echolocation:
Animals Making Sound Waves

by Laura Johnson

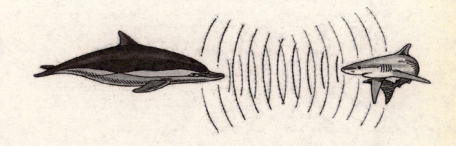

Editorial Offices: Glenview, Illinois • Parsippany, New Jersey • New York, New York
Sales Offices: Needham, Massachusetts • Duluth, Georgia • Glenview, Illinois
Coppell, Texas • Ontario, California • Mesa, Arizona

Here's How to Do It!

1. Gather several glasses of the same size and line them up on a table. Starting with the glass on the right, fill it with about half an inch of water. Move down the line filling each glass with a little more water. You should be able to see that each glass has more water in it than the glass to its right.

2. With a piece of silverware, lightly tap the glass to hear a sound. As you move down the line tapping each glass, notice how the pitch of the sound changes. Does the pitch sound high or low? Does that mean that the sound wave is short and fast or long and slow?

3. Think about the vibrations you and a friend can create with a rope. On a piece of paper, draw a line showing what the sound wave coming from each glass might look like. Do the waves in your lines get longer or shorter as the pitch gets lower?

23

Now Try This

EXPERIMENT WITH SOUND!

As you have read, dolphins make sound waves. They use echolocation clicks to navigate and to find food. As you also know, dolphins make and receive other sounds, such as whistles, that sound like squeaks to our ears.

High sounds have fast vibrations, and low sounds have slow vibrations. You and a friend can demonstrate this with a piece of rope. If you hold one end of the rope and a friend holds the other, you can practice making fast and slow waves, or vibrations. With a flick of your wrist, you can make a long, slow wave. If you move your hand faster, you can make shorter, faster waves. Short, fast sound waves make higher sounds, or pitches, than longer, slower sound waves.

Try experimenting with sound waves by making high and low pitches!

Moving your hand slower makes longer waves.

Moving your hand faster makes shorter waves.

Human Ears

What body parts do people and animals use to hear? If you answered *ears*, you would be correct about people and most animals—but not all animals. Instead of ears, some use their . . .

Well, let's not begin there. Let's begin by understanding how our own ears work to hear sounds.

The human ear has three parts: the outer ear, the middle ear, and the inner ear. The part of your outer ear that is on the side of your head is called the **pinna**. The pinna catches sound waves, almost as if it were a catcher's mitt. It sends sound waves into the auditory canal and along to the eardrum. Sound waves vibrate, or move quickly, off the walls of the auditory canal. The vibrating action makes some sounds become louder than they were when they first entered the canal.

The eardrum is a thin flap of skin that stretches across the end of the auditory canal. It separates the outer ear and the middle ear. Inside the middle ear are the three smallest bones in our bodies: the **hammer,** the **anvil,** and the **stirrup.** When sound waves make the eardrum vibrate, the vibrations make these bones move. When these bones vibrate, the sound waves are passed on to another thin flap of skin called the oval window. The oval window separates the middle ear and the inner ear.

The middle ear is connected to the back of the throat by the Eustachian tube, which lets air in and out of the middle ear. When you "pop" your ears, this tube suddenly opens.

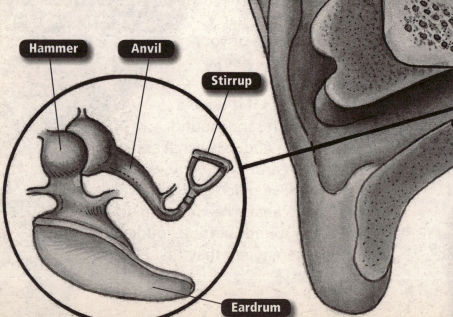

Not many animals have the ability to echolocate. The shrew, a mouse-like mammal, is one of the few other animals that echolocate to discover information about its surroundings. Its method of echolocation is not nearly as advanced as that of the dolphin or the bat. Like dolphins, some species of shrews emit clicks. Their clicks help them find worms and insects in the dark.

Next time you are riding in a car or on the school bus, close your eyes and try to imagine that you are a dolphin swimming in a dark ocean or a bat flying through a forest at midnight. Try to "see" a mental picture of your surroundings, using only your sense of sound. What are you passing on your right? On your left? Is something in front of you? Is something coming toward you?

Wouldn't echolocation clicks come in handy?

Shrews are very small and weigh about as much as a nickel.

Not all the sounds that bats make are for echolocating. Some sounds are made just for communicating with each other. Bats make sounds to defend their own territory and to communicate with their babies. Baby bats live in "nursery caves" with thousands or even millions of other baby bats. Mother bats can locate their own babies by their unique voices.

Many people are afraid of bats. They have heard stories about bats attacking people, but most of these stories are not true. Bats are gentle and shy animals, unless they feel they are being threatened. Bats do a lot of good things for the environment and for us. They spread seeds and pollinate fruits and flowers. They also eat millions of mosquitoes.

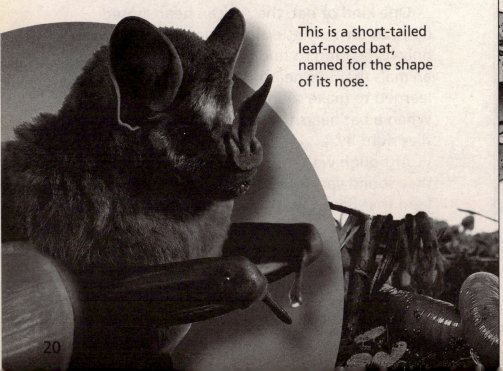

This is a short-tailed leaf-nosed bat, named for the shape of its nose.

In the inner ear is a tube called the **cochlea** (KAHK-lee-uh). It's about the size of your fingertip, and it has the shape of a snail. The cochlea is filled with fluid called **lymph.** In the middle of the lymph there is a thin strip of skin that is covered by over two million tiny hairs. Each tiny hair reacts to a particular vibration. When sound waves pass into the inner ear through the oval window, they cause tiny waves, or ripples, in the lymph. When the lymph ripples, these tiny hairs bend. There are nerves along the bottom of these hairs. When the hairs bend, these nerves send messages about sound vibrations to your brain. In a fraction of a second, your brain figures out what the vibrations mean and lets you know what you are hearing. By the time you are an adult, your brain will be able to recognize almost half a million different sounds!

Knowing how people hear will help you understand how some animals hear without using their ears. It all has to do with sound waves and vibrations.

Dolphins

Deep in the ocean, dolphins live in an underwater environment that is often dark and cloudy. Because they cannot depend on their eyesight in these conditions, dolphins have developed an ability to "see" with sound. This ability is called **echolocation**. The first part of the word *echolocation* is *echo*. Can you guess why?

Using echolocation, dolphins use their jaws—not their ears—to feel vibrations. Dolphins have six air sacs underneath their blowholes. By tightening the openings to the air sacs and forcing air through them, dolphins make sounds called echolocation clicks. These clicks are short sound waves.

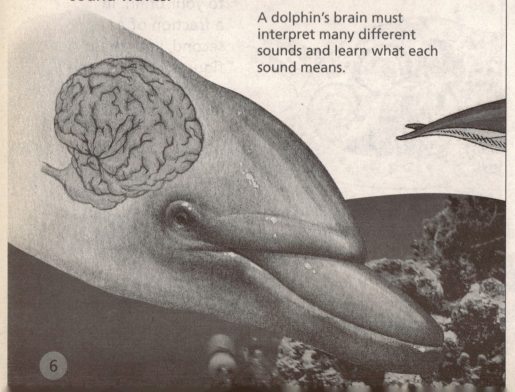

A dolphin's brain must interpret many different sounds and learn what each sound means.

One kind of bat, the African heart-nosed bat, can turn off its echolocation pulses and use only its hearing to find prey so it will not warn animals that it is nearby. Other moths have learned to make sounds that imitate bat noises. When a bat hears this noise, it gets confused and flies right by.

Although we cannot hear most bat pulses, they sound very loud to bats. In fact, they are so loud that bats have to protect themselves from their own sounds. When a bat makes sound pulses, its ear blocks out the noise. As soon as the sound ends, the ear is ready to listen for the returning echo.

Groups of bats often spend their days sleeping in caves.

Many bats love to eat moths! In fact, that's all that some bats will eat. In response to this danger, some kinds of moths have developed their own natural "anti-bat" protection. They have grown fuzzy wings that bats' echolocation pulses won't bounce off of. How effective!

But some bats have found a way around this. They have developed a different kind of echo that can detect fuzzy wings! Maybe fuzzy wings are not so effective after all.

Other moths have ears and are able to hear bats' echolocation pulses. When they hear the pulses, they are warned that a bat is nearby. This warning gives them some time to hide.

The fat-filled area in the front of a dolphin's head is called the melon. The melon focuses, or directs, the clicks as they leave the dolphin's head. The clicks travel out through the water. Some of the clicks echo, or bounce, off objects in the water. (That's where the echo part of the word comes from.) The echoes bounce back toward the dolphin and hit its jaw.

The vibrations travel through the dolphin's lower jaw to its inner ear. Then the vibrations are passed on to the hearing center in the brain.

The dolphin can sense the location of the shark through echolocation.

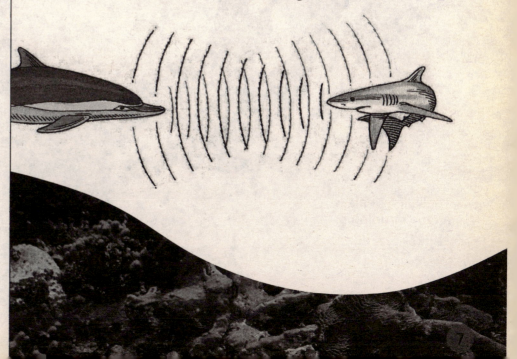

Using echolocation to sense their environments, dolphins create a mental picture of what is in the water around them. They can tell how far away an object is, depending on how quickly or slowly echoes come back. If echoes come back quickly, an object is near. If it takes a while for them to come back, an object is farther away.

Besides figuring out how near or close an object is, echolocation clicks can tell the direction an object is traveling. They can also tell the object's speed, size, and shape.

The killer whale is a type of dolphin.

How Bats Use Echolocation

At night when a bat is hunting, it sends out sound pulses.

The sound pulses bounce off the insect.

The echo of the sound pulses help the bat catch its prey.

Have you ever heard the expression "You're as blind as a bat!"? Actually, the expression is misleading because some bats have excellent vision. Bats that eat fruit instead of insects have large, bulging eyes that see very well.

Bats that eat insects need to use echolocation because they hunt at night. At night there is less competition for food and therefore less chance that other animals will hunt the bats themselves! The echolocation method that bats use is very similar to that which dolphins use. As bats cruise through the night sky, they emit, or send out, sound pulses. When the sounds echo back from an object that seems like it might be something to eat, the bat flies in that general direction.

As it flies toward the prey, the bat sends out very short sound pulses—as many as 170 in a second. This is called a feeding buzz. These short sound pulses can detect very tiny objects, such as mosquitoes, moths, or gnats. The pulses also tell how fast and in what direction the objects are moving. A bat's echolocation is precise enough to find even a single strand of hair!

Dolphins can make hundreds of echolocation clicks in a split second. They can also send out sounds that are powerful enough to stun, or temporarily paralyze, fish. Huge killer whales (which are actually dolphins, not whales) can even stun penguins. This certainly makes food easier to catch!

Humans cannot hear individual echolocation clicks, but we may be able to feel them. If you are ever lucky enough to be in the water with a dolphin that is echolocating, it might be possible for you to feel these clicks passing through the water.

Scientists have done experiments with dolphins to learn about echolocation. They have placed covers over dolphins' eyes and found that the dolphins were still able to find their way to an underwater target. When scientists put soundproof covers over the dolphins' lower jaw, the dolphins were not able to echolocate very successfully.

Even though these studies show that dolphins' eyes are not as important for finding things as their jaws, dolphins actually have very good eyesight. Their eyes move independently, which means that each eye can look at something different at the same time. This ability helps them look out for predators around them. But it is also a problem. Since their eyes are on the sides of their heads, dolphins have trouble seeing things that are straight ahead of them. Echolocation solves that problem.

Just behind their eyes, dolphins have tiny ear holes. Many scientists believe that these ears are only useful for hearing sounds above the surface of the water, and not under it.

Most bats eat insects, but some eat fruit. Usually the insect-eating bats use echolocation. They are the bats with large ears.

Do you remember that our outer ears catch the sound waves around us? Bats' large ears do the same thing—but even better! Our outer ears do not move, but theirs do. Many bats' ears can rotate to catch sound coming from different directions. When they catch sound waves, they direct them to sound-sensitive cells inside their ears. These cells pass along signals to the brain.

As its name indicates, the Egyptian fruit bat (above) eats fruit. Its ears are small because it does not echolocate. The long-eared bat (left) eats insects. Look at the size of its ears!

Bats

Like dolphins, most bats use echolocation to catch food and to get information about their surroundings. But there are some differences. Bats produce their sound pulses differently than dolphins receive echoes.

Dolphins produce sound in their nasal passages. Bats have a **larynx** (LA-rinks), or voice box, that produces sound. Some bats send their sounds out of their mouths. Others snort their sound out of their noses. Bats that "call" through their noses have flaps of skin around their noses called **nose leaves**. Nose leaves push the sound waves forward. Nose leaves are handy for bats that carry food in their mouths because they are able to eat and echolocate at the same time! Each kind of bat makes a unique echolocating sound. Just as humans cannot hear dolphins' clicks, we cannot hear most bat sounds.

Dolphins do use their eyes and ears, but it is really their jaws that are most important. Dolphins make and receive other sounds besides clicks. They are very social animals that live in groups called herds. To communicate with members of their own herds, dolphins whistle and make noises. To our ears, these noises sound like squeaks, squeals, and groans. But to other dolphins each sound is a different and important message. Researchers have learned that dolphins can pass along information to other dolphins, such as "I need help" and "There is food here."

Dolphin trainers use whistles and hand signals to communicate with dolphins. The skilled mammals can be trained to leap high out of the water and to do tricks.

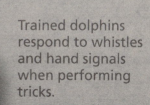

Trained dolphins respond to whistles and hand signals when performing tricks.

Dolphins actually call each other by name. Soon after giving birth, a mother dolphin whistles over and over again to her calf. She does this so the calf can find her in a group. The calf's first whistle may be just one long note. The whistle gradually becomes more complicated until it turns into a unique whistle. This new whistle is called a signature whistle. It becomes the dolphin's "name" for the rest of its life.

A dolphin's brain is much larger than the brains of other mammals. Scientists believe that they need large brains to communicate so well and to use complicated echolocation skills.

As you now know, dolphins "hear" very well with body parts other than their ears. Next, you will read about bats. They have huge ears, but they still use echolocation!

Some dolphins communicate through whistles.

Biography

Social Studies

Alexander Graham Bell, Teacher of the Deaf

by Juna Loch
illustrated by Don Dyen

Genre	Comprehension Skill and Strategy
Historical Fiction	• Literary Elements: Character and Setting • Monitor and Fix Up

Scott Foresman Reading Street 4.4.3

Suggested levels for Guided Reading, DRA,™ Lexile,® and Reading Recovery™ are provided in the Pearson Scott Foresman Leveling Guide.

ISBN 0-328-13465-1

scottforesman.com

Reader Response

1. The person telling the story is called the narrator. Who is the narrator of this story? On a separate piece of paper, explain how the narrator feels about Alexander Graham Bell. Give examples° from the story to support your view.

2. Think back to a part of the story that was confusing to you. How did you make sense of it as you were reading? Write about something you thought was confusing, and explain what you did to figure it out.

3. Look at the word "apparatus" on page 6. Using context clues, what do you think "apparatus" means? On a separate piece of paper, write your own definition and a sentence using the word.

4. Bell's dog says that his master's interest in everything was what made him a great inventor. Do you agree or disagree? On a separate piece of paper, explain your position. Give an example from the book to support your point of view.

The Failure That Worked

In 1888, to the nation's horror, someone shot two bullets into President James Garfield. Amazingly, the president lived for weeks afterwards. A team of doctors tried to remove the bullets.

No one had x-rays back then, so no one knew where the bullets were. Alexander Graham Bell believed that he could help his president. Since the bullet was made of metal, he thought he could use a magnet to find it! He was sure the bullet would make a sound as the magnet pulled it near. He rushed down to Washington to try and save Garfield. After several passes, Bell said he located the bullet deep inside Garfield's body.

Later, Bell learned that his wasn't the only new invention in the president's bedroom that day. The president had been lying on a new steel-springed mattress. The steel springs were what Bell's magnet had found!

Alexander Graham Bell, Teacher of the Deaf

Editorial Offices: Glenview, Illinois • Parsippany, New Jersey • New York, New York
Sales Offices: Needham, Massachusetts • Duluth, Georgia • Glenview, Illinois
Coppell, Texas • Ontario, California • Mesa, Arizona

Chapter 4
The Incredible Bell

In 2001, the U.S. Congress voted to give the credit for the first telephone to Antonio Meucci, an Italian-American who discovered the principle of the telephone in 1849, but could not afford to patent his idea. Bell had the first patent.

Bell still helped make the 20th century incredible in many ways. He invented something called an iron lung, which helps sick people breathe. He improved the phonograph and he invented a machine called an audiometer to test hearing. Guess what? When we measure sound, we measure it in units called bels or decibels. They are named after Bell!

Bell remained, to the end, a man interested in everything. Along with inventing and teaching, he was also the first president of the National Geographic Society. He made the magazine into something colorful and fun for everyone to enjoy.

Three years after he invented the telephone, my master created a phone that worked by sending sound on beams of light! He called this a "photophone." Of course, dogs don't use phones, but it made humans very excited.

Now my master was famous and very rich. But he still spent his time and his money finding ways to better people's lives. Whenever people asked him what he did for work, he always said, "I'm a teacher of the deaf." Helen Keller, who was deaf and blind and couldn't speak, wrote a book and dedicated it to him. He was very proud. So was I, even though she didn't mention my name in the book.

CONTENTS

CHAPTER 1   4
Can a Dog Talk?

CHAPTER 2   8
Teaching the Deaf to Talk

CHAPTER 3   14
Teaching Electricity to Talk

CHAPTER 4   23
The Incredible Bell

Chapter 1
Can a Dog Talk?

This story may seem like it's about the invention of the telephone, but it's really about a great man who did great things to help his fellow human beings. This is also a story of me, a dog. I am a Skye terrier, which is a handsome kind of dog. My master, Alexander Graham Bell, or Aleck, taught me to talk. Some people say this is only a myth, but you can trust me. Dogs don't lie.

Now, before we get to the telephone, we have to go back to Scotland. This is where my master, Aleck Bell, was born. He was always interested in how things work.

My master was very interested in vibrations. There was a big piano in his living room. Aleck spent most of his time looking inside the piano. He noticed that different strings would buzz when he played different notes. He tried to interest me in it too, but I am a dog. I am more interested in rabbits.

© Pearson Education, Inc.

The telephone my master patented had two parts. There was a transmitter, which turns your voice into an electrical current. There was also a receiver. This receives the current and turns it into air waves. The transmitter was made of a small capsule filled with carbon grains. It was covered with a thin aluminum skin or membrane. When my master spoke into it, the membrane vibrated. When he spoke loudly, the grains of carbon moved close together. When he spoke softly, they were loose. Because the grains moved around, they created the different currents my master said he needed.

Inventing a telephone was exciting. I was ready to take a break and chase cats, but my master couldn't stop working. He was still interested in everything!

Aleck was also curious about how our mouths let us talk. He even made an apparatus that was a model of the human mouth.

One day my master started moving my mouth, so that I made the sounds "Ow-ah-oo, Ga-ma-ma." He called in the family to hear.

Once again, my master moved my mouth so that I said "Ow-ah-oo, Ga-ma-ma."

"The dog asked 'How are you, Grandmama?'" my master said.

We stared at him in amazement. When Watson had plucked at the reed, my master had *heard* its sound, rather than the signal it made. What's more, he knew exactly what it was. If he had not been a musician, he would have missed it.

He also knew what it meant. Something as small as that plucked reed could carry a sound. That proved that the human voice could send sound over a wire, too! By the following spring, Watson and my master had made a working telephone! He rushed to get a patent. A patent gives you ownership rights to an idea. He got there an hour before another scientist, Elisha Gray, who claimed to have invented the telephone, too.

Hold on because things are about to get really exciting. On June 2, a mistake allowed my master to see a miracle.

On that day, my master was in one room and Watson was in another. Watson was fiddling with the Harmonic Telegraph. I lay by his feet hoping he would scratch my head.

Suddenly, my master came flying out of the other room! He was breathless with excitement.

"What did you do, Watson?" he cried. "Wait—don't touch anything!"

Here I must set the record straight. I don't want you getting the wrong idea. I was not really asking the ancient granny how she was feeling. Dogs do not make that kind of small talk.

My master made me make those sounds because he was interested in how the throat and mouth make human sounds. He wanted to put that knowledge to an important use. He wanted to teach deaf people how to speak. When he was only 24, he got his chance. That year, he arrived in Boston, Massachusetts, and took a job teaching deaf people. From then on, he always described it as his life's work.

Chapter 2
Teaching the Deaf to Talk

My master used a system his father invented to teach deaf children to talk. It was called "Visible Speech."

If something is visible, it can be seen. Visible Speech showed you where to put your teeth and tongue to make any sound! My master and his father showed this system to professors at many colleges.

I knew that a human voice could make me move to run after a ball! If it could do that, maybe there was hope for my master and his experiments.

My master did not know how to make electricity speak. So he got a helper—a man named James Watson.

One day, they were working on the Harmonic Telegraph. "I want to make a speaking telegraph," my master told Watson.

"The voice isn't strong," Watson said. "How will we get it to move through the wires?"

"The tiny eardrum is as thin as tissue paper," my master said. "But it can move the bones of the inner ear. When that happens, we can hear." My master sighed. "If a tiny eardrum can move sound, surely we can find some way to do it too!"

Now, my master Aleck thought if hearing people could use Visible Speech, then deaf people could, too.

He showed his deaf students how to make all the different sounds. He taught them to move their tongues to the back of their throats so they could make a "K" sound. He showed them how to open their mouths to say an "A" sound and how to put their tongues to the backs of their teeth to say "T." There you have it, my least favorite word! Cat. His students could not hear that they had done it right, but they could all say "Cat."

"What does this have to do with the telephone?" I hear you asking. This is part of the reason why my master, Alexander Graham Bell, invented the telephone.

I want you to know my master like I do. He did not think the most important thing he ever did was to invent the telephone. He thought teaching the deaf was more important.

My master wanted to find an even better way to help his deaf students than with Visible Speech. He built another human mouth. This time, the mouth measured the vibrations from speech.

Students could now measure the sounds they were making. My master also built a model of the ear. He worked like a dog, and I do not use that term lightly. But he still had questions.

"Do you know how the voice works, my dear dog?" my master asked me one cold March day.

"When a person talks," my master explained, "the sound is made by air. You breathe in air. The air passes through a muscle called the voice box. The voice box vibrates. It pushes the air together, creating little waves of sound. These sound waves travel through the air until they reach an ear. There, they strike the thin skin of what's called your eardrum. The eardrum tells your brain what it hears. Then, you hear it! Isn't that wonderful?"

I nuzzled his hand. "If we could only make electricity talk!" he said. I didn't really understand. These things are complicated for dogs.

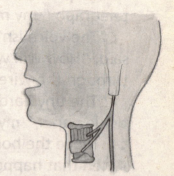

Air coursing through our voice box creates sound.

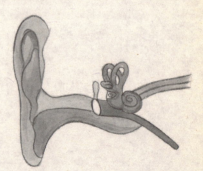

Sound waves reach the ear.

Chapter 3
Teaching Electricity to Talk

Now if my master Aleck had not experimented with his piano as a boy, he would not have known about vibrations. If he had not known about vibrations, he would not have tried to make the Harmonic Telegraph. And if he had not been working on the Harmonic Telegraph, he could not have made the mistake that led to the telephone.

It's all tied up together, you understand. And if my master Aleck had not been so interested in everything, he would not have starting thinking about a *speaking* telegraph!

Back in 1871, if you wanted to communicate with someone far away, you could only send a message along a wire with a kind of code on a machine called a telegraph.

By the 1870s, people knew that sound is made by vibration. If you strike an object in any way, it vibrates. The amount an object vibrates is called its "natural frequency." Some objects vibrate a lot. Other objects vibrate a little. If you put two objects that vibrate the same amount near each other, and strike one, the other object will vibrate, too! My master thought these vibrations might be the key to making a telephone.

How would this help Aleck make a telegraph that could send more than one message at a time? My master did an experiment. He attached thin pieces of metal, or "reeds," with different vibrations to a telegraph. Each reed could carry one message.

Could that message be picked up by another reed on the other end of the wire? My master thought so. He thought that the messages from the different reeds would travel together on the same wire. Each message would be picked up by a reed with the same natural frequency on the other end of the wire! My master called this idea the "Harmonic Telegraph." Harmonic has to do with harmony, which means "together."

Suggested levels for Guided Reading, DRA™, Lexile,® and Reading Recovery™ are provided in the Pearson Scott Foresman Leveling Guide.

Social Studies

THE CODE TALKERS

Genre	Comprehension Skill and Strategy	Text Features
Nonfiction	• Graphic Sources • Ask Questions	• Captions • Chart • Heads • Glossary

Scott Foresman Reading Street 4.4.4

PEARSON
Scott Foresman

ISBN 0-328-13468-6

9 780328 134687

BY GRETCHEN MCBRIDE

Reader Response

1. Using the Code Talkers' Dictionary on page 15, what is the literal translation for fighter plane? Why do you think the Code Talkers used that word? Use a three-column chart similar to the one below to write your response.

English Term	Literal Translation	Why?
fighter plane		

2. If you interviewed some Code Talkers, what questions would you ask them? Where can you go to find more information about the Code Talkers?

3. *Cryptography* means "the art or process of creating or figuring out secret codes." The suffix *–graphy* means "the process of recording, writing, or drawing." List three other words with the same suffix and write their definitions.

4. Under what section heading could you find information on an ancient Diné ceremony? Why would it be included there?

Glossary

ancient *adj.* very old or of times long past.

ceremony *n.* a formal act or set of acts performed according to tradition for a special purpose.

cryptography *n.* the art or process of creating or figuring out secret codes.

decipher *v.* to make out the meaning of something that is puzzling or not clear.

fluently *adv.* smoothly, easily.

recruit *v.* to sign up persons, especially for military service.

reservation *n.* land set aside by the government for a special use, especially for the use of a Native American nation.

scholars *n.* people who have much knowledge.

tonal *adj.* of or relating to the high or low pitch of a sound.

translated *v.* changed from one language into another.

The Code Talkers

BY GRETCHEN MCBRIDE

Editorial Offices: Glenview, Illinois • Parsippany, New Jersey • New York, New York
Sales Offices: Needham, Massachusetts • Duluth, Georgia • Glenview, Illinois
Coppell, Texas • Ontario, California • Mesa, Arizona

Here's How to Do It!

1. With a partner, write down our twenty-six-letter alphabet and decide on a symbol—it could be another letter or a number—to stand for each letter.

2. Now, you and your partner can decide what kinds of messages you are likely to send each other. Perhaps you would like to talk about your favorite afterschool activities. Come up with a list of words that you are likely to need for your messages. Now decide on the list of code words to use instead. For instance, perhaps your code word for "basketball" could be "Sun." (A basketball is round like the Sun.) The alphabet and code word lists will be the two keys you use for decoding messages.

3. Write a four-line message to your partner. If any words in your message have code words, use the code words. Next, use your alphabet list to change your message into code. Then exchange messages with your partner. Using your decoding keys, see how quickly and accurately you can decode your partner's message.

4. Exchange your keys with another team, and see if you can write and decode messages in their secret code.

5. Here is the biggest challenge: Exchange messages with another team without exchanging the code word keys. Can you break their code?

Now Try This

SEND CODED MESSAGES

See if you could be a cryptographer! The Code Talkers used a spoken code and used entire Diné words to stand for single letters. Let's see if you can make up a written code using just a letter, number, or symbol for each letter.

A	B	C	D	E	F	G	H	I	J	K	L	M	N	O
1	Z	Y	X	2	J	V	T	3	B	S	P	W	C

Create your own code using letters and numbers.

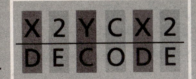

Try to break the codes of another team.

Their Story

For many years the story of the Code Talkers could not be told. Their extraordinary service to the United States during a time of war remained a secret.

The Code Talkers were a special group of soldiers who served our country during World War II. Until 1968 our government kept the mission of the Code Talkers top secret. The people who served as Code Talkers could not tell anyone—not even their families—about the work they did in the war, but now their story can be told. It begins with the Diné people.

The Diné now live primarily in the southwestern part of the United States, but how they came to be there is not known. Since the language of the Diné is somewhat like the languages of Native American groups living in the northwestern part of the United States and Canada, it is thought they may have migrated from the north some time in the distant past to the land that is now their home.

A Diné man (1910) and woman with child (1930s)

Diné: The People

The name *Diné* means "The People." The Diné are also known as the Navajo, a name given to the nation by outsiders. Some **scholars** believe *Navajo* comes from a Native American language and means "large area of cultivated land." No matter how others refer to them, the Diné maintain a strong sense of their own identity.

The land the Diné have farmed for centuries in what we know today as Colorado, New Mexico, Utah, and Arizona is sacred to them. As settlers moved from the eastern United States to the west in the middle of the nineteenth century, the Diné and other Native American people had to struggle to keep their traditional homelands.

A Diné Code Talker receives the Congressional Gold Medal from President G. W. Bush in 2001.

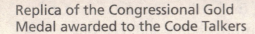

Replica of the Congressional Gold Medal awarded to the Code Talkers

Returning Home

As many as 420 Diné served as Code Talkers during World War II. These heroes had served their country in an important way, but there could be no special recognition for them when they returned home. The Code Talkers were sworn to secrecy. They could tell no one of the special code they had created, and they upheld their vow of secrecy. The code was such a success in communicating wartime information that it was kept secret for years after the end of World War II.

Like the other returning Diné soldiers, the Code Talkers were honored by their community. Their families performed traditional cleansing ceremonies to help them recover from their experiences in battle. Many veterans would become leaders of their people.

Finally, after the order for secrecy was lifted, the Code Talkers could receive the official honors of their country. In 1982 President Reagan honored them by declaring August 14 to be National Code Talkers Day. In July 2001 President George Herbert Walker Bush bestowed the Congressional Gold Medal on the twenty-nine original Code Talkers. The other Code Talkers received the Congressional Silver Medal of Honor. The code created by the Code Talkers remains the only code never to be broken by an opponent.

Monument Valley, in Arizona and Utah, is part of the Diné homeland.

The Diné faced a difficult time in 1864. They were forced by the United States government to walk three hundred miles to Fort Sumner in New Mexico because the government wanted to claim Diné land and use it for its own purposes. At Fort Sumner the Diné people were held against their will until 1868. For people who were so attached to a land they believed to be their natural and sacred homeland, this was a terrible hardship.

Finally, in 1868, a treaty was signed that allowed the Diné to return to their land. Because of the bad treatment they received at the hand of the government, many Diné remained distrustful of the United States government for many years. In spite of this, the Diné came to the defense of the United States during World War I and World War II. They fought for the United States and for their own Diné people.

Traditional Ways

Many people or groups of people have traditions that are special to them and make them unique. The Diné are no different. They are a deeply spiritual people, practicing their **ancient** religious traditions along with other religious traditions brought to them by missionaries.

Just as the land they call their home is special and sacred to them, so are the ceremonies that the Diné practice. These ceremonies make up their culture and are a way of life for them. The sacred ceremonies of the Diné teach them about their history, about human responsibilities, or about the world around them. Ceremonies also are used to bless a new home, care for the sick, or bring goodwill to the community.

Some ceremonies involve drypainting, which is made with grains of colored sand. The images created are often symbols of strength for Diné people in need. The drypainting is swept away to end the **ceremony.**

The Blessing Way is an ancient and sacred ceremony of the Diné. During this ceremony, the people may sing special songs, have a ritual bath, and say prayers. The ceremony is meant to protect the people at a time of change and challenges. The Blessing Way would be important for many of the Diné Code Talkers upon entering World War II.

The Diné practice drypainting inside a mud hogan (top). A close-up of a drypainting shows color and delicate details (bottom).

The Code Talkers were important to many of the operations of the American military in the Pacific, but perhaps the most important battle was the battle of Iwo Jima. During the battle of Iwo Jima, the Code Talkers worked nonstop sending and receiving hundreds of messages. Their work was flawless.

The tiny island of Iwo Jima, barren and lacking drinkable water, was held firmly by the Japanese. The United States wanted the island because of its strategic location. It would serve as a landing strip for disabled planes as they traveled between aircraft carriers and major Japanese cities. It took an entire month to secure the island, and the cost in lives—both American and Japanese—was tragically high. Almost twenty thousand Americans were wounded, and more than sixty-eight hundred were killed. Almost all of the Japanese soldiers on the island died. The American victory, though costly, would prove to be crucial in winning the war.

American Marines raise the U.S. flag over the Pacific island of Iwo Jima.

U.S. Navy Corsair

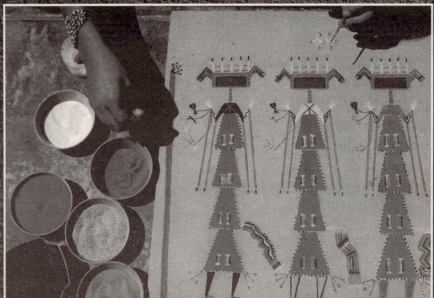

World War II

When the United States entered World War II in 1941, many Diné men enlisted in the armed services. Diné women also volunteered and became part of the Women's Army Corps. For many of these men and women, it would be the first time they would leave the Diné **reservation.** Although life in the military was strange to them, the Diné soldiers excelled in tests of physical endurance. An outdoor life in a harsh environment had prepared them well for this new challenge.

By the end of the war, thirty-six hundred Diné would serve in the armed forces. Of these, more than four hundred would come to be called Code Talkers. They would perform an extraordinary service for their country and their people.

U.S. Marine Code Talkers relay a message with a field radio.

Code Talkers in Battle

The Code Talkers had to memorize the expanded alphabet and long list of code words. They tried to choose code words that would be easy for them to remember. Nothing could be written down in the field, and their transmissions had to be fast and accurate. The lives of American soldiers depended on them.

Philip Johnston's idea proved to be a good one. The Marines continued to recruit Diné who met the requirements for the special program. Code Talkers went through the rigors of basic training with the other recruits and were required to meet strict English and Diné language standards as well. Johnston, although too old to fight in World War II, rejoined the military and trained Code Talkers.

The first Code Talkers reported for combat duty to General Alexander Vandegrift's First Marine Division on Guadalcanal in August 1942. With bravery and skill, the Code Talkers played a part in every important battle in the Pacific. By speaking their secretly coded language over radio, they transmitted crucial battlefield information. Their commitment to their job and their diligent work helped America greatly.

U.S. Marine Code Talkers Corporal Henry Bahe, Jr., and Private First Class George H. Kirk in the jungles of New Guinea, December 1943

Japan used secret codes before attacking Pearl Harbor.

One of the challenges in any war is communication. Military headquarters must be able to get messages to the soldiers fighting in the field, and the soldiers must be able to report back to headquarters. If an army is to be successful, it is crucial that these communications be kept secret from the other side.

During World War I, the United States set up its first office especially for **cryptography,** the art or process of creating or figuring out secret codes. Even when the nation was not officially at war, this office worked to break the secret codes being used by foreign nations. They were usually successful, but on December 4, 1941, the code that the Japanese had been using suddenly changed. The United States code readers could no longer **decipher** it. This may be one reason the United States Navy was not ready for the attack by the Japanese on Pearl Harbor on December 7, 1941. Clearly, cryptography would be vitally important in World War II.

The Language of the Diné

World War I veteran Philip Johnston knew that being able to send secret messages in an unbreakable code would be important for the United States to win World War II. He also knew that American Indian languages had been used with some success for communications during World War I.

Johnston was the son of missionary parents. While Johnston was growing up, his family lived on a Diné reservation. From the age of four, he had played with the Diné children and had learned to speak their language. The Diné language became almost as familiar to him as the English he spoke with his parents.

As an adult, Philip Johnston realized that the Diné language he had learned as a child was a complicated one, and that not many people outside of the Diné community could speak the language or even understand it when they heard it.

This earthen hogan can be found on a Diné reservation.

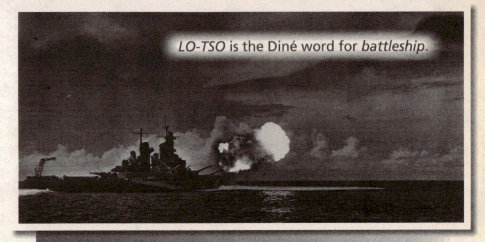

LO-TSO is the Diné word for *battleship*.

Code Talkers' Dictionary

English Term	Diné Word	Literal Translation
America	NE-HE-MAH	our mother
dive bomber	GINI	chicken hawk
fighter plane	DA-HE-TIH-HI	hummingbird
battleship	LO-TSO	whale
destroyer	CA-LO	shark
amphibious	CHAL	frog
anti	WOL-LA-CHEE-TSIN	ant ice
bomb	A-YE-SHI	eggs
bulldozer	DOLA-ALTH-WHOSH	bull sleep
creek	TOH-NIL-TSANH	very little water
farm	MAI-BE-HE-AHGAN	fox arm
not	NI-DAH-THAN-ZIE	no turkey
river	TOH-YIL-KAL	much water

The Code

It would not be enough to speak Diné over the radio in the field. There were other Diné serving in the military who would understand the language. The military could not risk having those men captured and forced to translate messages.

The Code Talkers first developed a twenty-six-letter alphabet with whole Diné words standing for letters. They would use this to "spell" over the radio. But the vocabulary of the Diné language did not have the words for the military terms that would be used over and over again. For a term such as "tank," the Code Talkers thought of something that reminded them of a tank. They thought of the word "turtle." Other words had some connection to what they stood for; for example, "potato" stood for hand grenade because of the objects' similar shapes.

The Code Talkers started with a simple twenty-six-letter alphabet, but they expanded it to more than four hundred letters to make the code harder to break. If the same word stood for the same letter in every message, an expert could break the code by noticing which words occurred most often in the code. In English, for instance, the letter *e* is the most frequently used letter. It would be easy to figure out which symbol stood for *e*, in a code that used only one symbol for it.

Window Rock, in Arizona, is a landmark of the Diné.

Traditionally, Diné is an oral language without a system of writing. Scholars from outside the Diné community who wanted to learn the language tried to write it down the way they heard it, but this was very difficult.

The language of the Diné is not like any of the European languages. The sounds are very different. People who have not grown up speaking it find it difficult to hear the difference between some of the sounds. Like Chinese, Diné is a **tonal** language. This means that making a sound higher or lower in pitch can give the sound a different meaning. The grammar of Diné is also complicated and different from English and other European languages.

Philip Johnston knew that he was one of the few people outside the Diné nation who could speak Diné well. And even he, who had learned the language as a child, could not speak or understand it perfectly. For these reasons, he thought that the Diné language might be a good basis for a secret code.

The Experiment

Philip Johnston thought his idea for a secret code might help his country. Johnston traveled to Camp Elliot in San Diego where he met with Colonel James E. Jones, the Signal Corps' communications officer for the U.S. Marines. Colonel Jones listened to Johnston speak the Diné language, and he was amazed. He had never heard anything like the sounds Johnston made. Colonel Jones agreed to set up a test of Johnston's idea.

On February 28, 1942, Johnston brought with him to Camp Elliot four Diné who **fluently** spoke both their native language and English. One pair of Diné was given a military message in English. They **translated** the message into Diné and transmitted it by radio to the other pair of Diné in another room. The second pair translated the message back into English. Their work was quick and accurate.

The Marines were impressed and gave Johnston permission to **recruit** Diné men who could speak both Diné and English for the project. The recruits would also have to meet the strict physical requirements for the Marines, and they could be told only that they were to be "specialists." These Diné would come to be known as Code Talkers.

Diné veterans march in a parade.

Suggested levels for Guided Reading, DRA,™ Lexile,® and Reading Recovery™ are provided in the Pearson Scott Foresman Leveling Guide.

Genre	Comprehension Skill and Strategy
Fiction	• Plot • Prior Knowledge

Scott Foresman Reading Street 4.4.5

scottforesman.com

ISBN 0-328-13471-6

Professor Science
AND THE SALAMANDER STUMPER

by Donna Latham

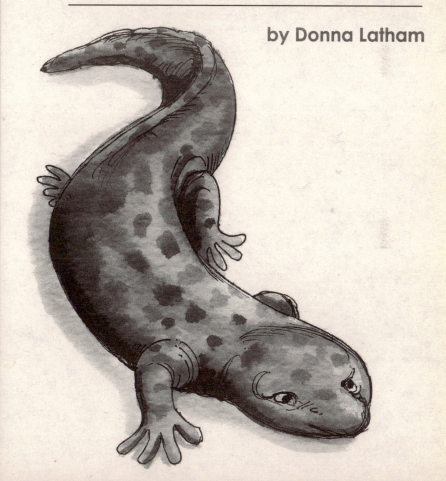

illustrated by Bill Petersen

Reader Response

1. The plot is what happens in a story. In this story, Doug, the narrator, mostly shared events in the order in which they occurred. Skim the story to find the one place that Doug stopped telling you events in the order they happened to discuss something that had happened in the past. How did this help the story?

2. Use what you already know about mystery stories to explain why Nicole considered Todd a suspect.

3. Reread pages 10 and 14. Using a chart similar to the one below, use context clues to define the word *grotto*.

Word	Context Clues	Definition

4. Why do you think Todd went straight to Doug when a giant load of fish food was missing at the Dolphin Exploratorium?

Endangered! The Japanese Giant Salamander

You've read about the ways Dr. Fernandez tried to build a great habitat for the Japanese giant salamander, but what is the state of its habitat in the wild?

As Dr. Fernandez explained, the giant Japanese salamander is an endangered animal. That means that it is at risk of becoming extinct. How did it become at risk? In the same unfortunate way that other animals have become endangered. Its habitat is being destroyed. Dams have been built across the rivers where the salamander makes its home in Japan. In order to make the dams, people have cleared away the rocky areas where the salamander lays its eggs.

What is being done to make sure that the salamander will have a place to lay its eggs? One idea is to build dams out of stone. That way, the nooks and crannies the salamander needs will be available. It is a solution Dr. Fernandez would like!

Professor Science
AND THE SALAMANDER STUMPER

by Donna Latham
illustrated by Bill Petersen

PEARSON

Scott Foresman

Editorial Offices: Glenview, Illinois • Parsippany, New Jersey • New York, New York
Sales Offices: Needham, Massachusetts • Duluth, Georgia • Glenview, Illinois
Coppell, Texas • Ontario, California • Mesa, Arizona

23

"I want to fill up my notebook too," said Sophie excitedly, and she held up a little notepad Mom had given her. "I can't write yet," Sophie said, "but I can draw."

"That's a great way to start recording your observations," said Mom.

"Yes, some scientists use sketches and pictures along with written notes to show details about what they are researching," said Dr. Fernandez. Sophie beamed and flashed a big smile.

"I can't wait to start!" she exclaimed.

"It will be nice to have illustrations to match up with the facts that I record too," I added.

Suddenly, Todd burst into the room. His hair was sticking out all over his head, and he looked flushed and upset.

"Professor Science," he called, out of breath. "I need your help at the Dolphin Exploratorium! A giant load of fish food is missing."

"Let's go, Sophie," I said. "This sounds like a mystery you can help me with."

My mom has one of the wildest jobs in the world. It is conveniently located just a few blocks away from my school. Every day after middle school lets out, my big sister, Nicole, walks over to pick up my younger sister, Sophie, and me at Robert Frost Elementary School. Then we rush over to Mom's work. You never know what we'll discover—a lion with a sore tooth or baboons having a ball.

Like I said, Mom's job is wild! She's the zookeeper at Lakemoor Zoo. When I grow up, I want to be a scientist, like Mom. I love to hang around the zoo and learn all kinds of scientific stuff. I have a special notebook Mom gave me to record all my observations. I never go anywhere without it.

When Nicole came to pick us up today, she was waving a note Mom had tucked into her lunch.

"Doug! Sophie!" she called. "Mom has some exciting news to tell us when we get to the zoo."

"I wonder what it is," said Sophie. "Maybe some little koala babies were born, or the dolphins learned some new tricks."

"I'll bet a new animal's arriving at the Herpetology House," I said. Herpetology is the study of reptiles and amphibians, and the Herpetology House is my very favorite place in the whole zoo.

"There's been a major ruckus there lately. Haven't you noticed that one area in the back that's all boarded up?" I said. "There must be something huge going on back there. I've heard pounding and drilling and sawing for weeks."

"You don't think it's a new dolphin act?" asked Sophie, disappointed. Dolphins are her favorite animals. I take her to the Dolphin Exploratorium every single time we visit Mom. She can't get enough of their big smiles and talented tricks.

Todd, the dolphin trainer, is proud of the exhibit, and it is the most popular one in the whole zoo. Todd is really knowledgeable about dolphins, and he teaches them to do great tricks, like jumping through hoops. He lets Sophie feed the dolphins.

"This exhibit is great, Mom," said Nicole a few weeks later when we joined Kaneesha and Dr. Fernandez to have a look.

The exhibit was finally about to open. The art students went back to the drawing board. This time, they used water to keep the concrete moist as it dried. The heat lamps were removed, and the concrete held tight.

The rock grotto was perfect. It had ledges the salamander could rest on, and it had a great big opening where the giant salamander was hiding right now.

"I wish we could see him!" said Sophie.

"Keep watching. He'll come out," Mom promised. "Well, Doug, I guess we have you to thank for helping this exhibit get built again, the right way!"

"Yes," said Kaneesha. "When this opens to the public tomorrow, it's going to make a lot of people happy, especially me!"

"Oh, thanks," I said. "You know, Soph, I hope the salamander comes out too! I'm dying to fill up my notebook with facts about him!"

© Pearson Education, Inc.

"Sorry, Soph! Maybe it'll be a gigantic python for the Herpetology House," I said hopefully. "How cool would it be to have a thirty-foot python there?"

"Pretty cool, Professor Science!" said Nicole. She always calls me that. I like my nickname because learning about science is my hobby.

The Herpetology House is another popular exhibit at the zoo, and I'm not the only one who is wild about it. Kaneesha, the animal handler there, is always busy directing tours or caring for the animals. She knows everything about all the animals there and about the habitat, which is the place where animals live.

"Well done, Doug!" said Mom, smiling. "I'm proud of the way you used what you know about science to figure out the mystery. Thank goodness the salamander hasn't arrived from Japan yet. But now that we know how to avoid this crash in the future, what can we do about the present?"

"What are we waiting for?" asked Kaneesha. "Let's get everyone back on the job and get this exhibit off the ground!"

"It was the combination of the heat lamps and the concrete that made this exhibit come tumbling down," I explained. "Remember what Rob did to keep the concrete moist?"

"Sure," said Nicole. "He carefully covered the foundation with water and the wet burlap."

"Very observant," I said. "That moisture kept the foundation from cracking."

"So I guess that's why the foundation is still in place," said Kaneesha.

"But I guess the students weren't aware of the way to use concrete, since they brought in heat lamps to dry it." I went on. "It got way too hot in here, and heat causes water to evaporate. Because the water evaporated, the concrete became more and more dry, and it shrank. The concrete shrank until it cracked."

"And those cracks made the crash?" asked Sophie.

"You'll be my assistant in no time, Soph! Yes, the cracks caused the crash."

"Doug, you rock!" said Nicole with a smile. "Get it?" she laughed. "I guess I was wrong to blame Todd for the crash. It was really all about science."

Just last night, Sophie and I looked at my science notebook. Thanks to Todd and Kaneesha, I've filled up my science notebook with tons of animal information, and Sophie always begs me to read it to her at bedtime.

"Sophie, did you know that the largest group of reptiles is formed by lizards and snakes? There are about thirty-eight hundred species, or kinds, of lizards and around twenty-seven hundred snake species. Most lizards prefer warm or hot habitats. So do snakes, although one type lives in Finland and Sweden, above the Arctic Circle."

"Doug," asked Sophie, "what are amphibian habitats like?"

"I know it's in here somewhere," I said, as I rustled around in my notebook. "Aha! Amphibians spend part of their lives on water and part on land, so their habitats are moist places, such as lakes, streams, and ponds."

"Doug, do you think I can be your helper when you become a scientist?" asked Sophie.

"Do you want to be an animal handler like Kaneesha or a trainer like Todd?"

"Either one—or else a superstar," she yawned. I laughed and closed my notebook.

I remember that conversation as if it were yesterday. Oh, that's right, it *was* yesterday!

"I thought we'd never get here," said Sophie as we arrived at the zoo. "Let's hurry and find Mom. I can't wait to hear her news."

"Still holding out for dolphin tricks?" Nicole asked.

"You never know!" laughed Sophie.

As we arrived at the zoo, we saw Mom walking with a tall, gangly man we had never seen before.

"Kids, I want you to meet Dr. Fernandez, he's a herpetologist, and he's designing a fantastic new exhibit for the zoo." We all introduced ourselves.

"Is a new animal coming to the zoo?' asked Sophie.

"Yes," said Mom. "I couldn't wait to break this news to you. Remember the Japanese giant salamander we saw at the Wauconda Zoo last year?"

"How could we forget?" asked Nicole.

"That thing was enormous!" I added.

"I'm glad it left such a lasting impression," laughed Dr. Fernandez. "At more than five feet long and one of the largest salamanders in the world, it is an unforgettable sight, and now Lakemoor Zoo is getting its own Japanese giant salamander."

"Well, Professor Science," said Nicole. "What are we waiting for? Let's start looking for clues to solve this mystery!" She turned her head slowly as she scanned the room.

"I don't think that will be necessary, Nicole," I said confidently. "I think I have this salamander stumper all figured out!" Everyone stared at me, and Sophie crossed her fingers. "I think I have some notes about . . . ," I said, my voice trailing off as I rustled through my notebook. "Let me just look something up."

We all clustered around Kaneesha as she heaved open the door. Waving us in, she stepped inside, and we eagerly followed.

Suddenly, we stopped short, our mouths opened in horror, and everyone gasped. "Oh, no!" cried Sophie.

The habitat was in shambles. Heat lamps had fallen down, shattering glass on the floor and knocking down plants around the pond. The plants looked limp and lifeless.

"What on earth . . . ?" said Dad.

"This is a crime scene!" shouted Kaneesha. "Someone has vandalized our exhibit!"

"Who would do a thing like that?" I asked in disbelief.

Mom pondered my question for a minute and said, "I have no idea—I'm baffled."

"I'm stumped too," began Nicole. "Wait a minute. Remember how Todd got irritated whenever we talked about the salamander? He wasn't exactly thrilled about it coming here, and he didn't want competition with the Dolphin Exploratorium."

"Let's not be so quick to draw conclusions," Mom cautioned us sternly. "We need to gather facts before we make any serious accusations like that."

I can't believe Mom managed to keep this a secret from us, but I guess we have been preoccupied with the dolphin exhibit a lot lately.

"I remember that these salamanders are endangered," I said.

"Yes," said Dr. Fernandez. "They're nearly extinct."

"It stinked?" asked Sophie, her nose wrinkled.

"Extinct," said Dr. Fernandez, smiling. "That means that they would all die out."

Because the Japanese giant salamander prefers to live in dark, cool, moist places, Dr. Fernandez explained that the new habitat would feature a pond and a cave. "We're going to create a rocky grotto for our new resident," he explained. "These salamanders like to hide in caves during the daytime and come out at night. You see, like many amphibians, they live on both water and land."

"What do they eat?" asked Nicole.

"Mostly insects, fish, and worms," said Dr. Fernandez. "In fact, they have sticky tongues that help them slurp up their prey!"

"Here goes Professor Science," laughed Nicole, as she noticed me busily jotting down notes.

"These are great facts!" I exclaimed.

"Here's a fact that might really intrigue you," said Dr. Fernandez. "The Japanese giant salamander has barely changed appearance in thirty million years." Dr. Fernandez invited all of us to return the next afternoon, when the concrete was going to be poured to make the foundation for the rock grotto.

When Saturday came, we zipped over to the zoo with Dad. Sometimes Mom worked in the morning on Saturdays, and we all liked to stroll around the zoo together in the afternoons. Sophie had gotten Dad excited about the salamander, and we were all eager to find out about the progress being made on the exhibit. With my hand itching to do some notetaking, I could not wait to see the exhibit. Walking up to the entrance of the zoo, Sophie pulled Dad's arm, urging him to move faster.

We found Kaneesha conducting a tour, and when her group thanked her and left, she joined up with our family.

"I think I can guess what you want to see," she teased. "I'll open the exhibit so we can all see how it's going—this is so exciting!" We put some special heat lamps in here overnight so the grotto would dry quickly. I haven't seen it since yesterday, but it was looking great then."

"Is concrete the same thing as cement?" I inquired the next day, as we watched the workers preparing the gray concoction.

"That's an excellent question," said Rob, one of the workers. "Cement gets mixed with other ingredients to make concrete."

"You mean like the ingredients we mix together when we make cookies?" asked Sophie.

"Well, kind of," said Rob. "Cement is a very fine, gray powder. See, here's some in the bag." We drew closer for a look. "It gets mixed with water, gravel, sand, and some crushed stone to make concrete. It can be formed into any shape. Then the mixture changes and hardens. It becomes superstrong."

"Hmmm," Todd grumbled. "Kaneesha told me all about it. The Dolphin Exploratorium has been the most popular exhibit at this zoo since I was a kid. Kaneesha is gloating like crazy! She thinks everyone will scramble to the Herpetology House to see the salamander." Todd looked unhappy.

"Don't worry, Todd," said Sophie. "This will always be my favorite place in the whole zoo."

"And I'm sure we'll keep bringing her here every single day," reassured Nicole sympathetically.

Each day after school, we took a glimpse of the progress on the exhibit. A group of art students from the college in town had volunteered to make the grotto. It would have all kinds of nooks and crannies for the salamander to explore. The students arranged boulders and sealed them together with concrete to create a cave. Other rocks and ledges framed the cave, so the habitat's new resident would have cool places to doze.

I rustled around in my notebook. "I knew I had some notes about cement. Dad told me all about it. The powder is made from clay and limestone, which is a sedimentary rock! When fragments from weathered rocks get compressed, they form sedimentary rock," I explained.

"That's right," said Rob, "and the ingredients we mix the powder with to make concrete are rocks too. In fact, many building materials are made from rock."

We watched as the workers dumped the thick, gray goop onto wooden planks that had been laid as supports. They used wooden spades to move the concrete right up against the planks and to press it into the corners. Then they smoothed the entire surface with a tool called a trowel.

"These will hold this foundation nice and tight," he said.

We watched as the workers covered the whole foundation with water.

"What's that for?" I wondered.

"It keeps the concrete moist so it won't crack." Rob then covered the foundation with a wet piece of burlap to keep it from drying too quickly. I wrote quickly, recording everything.

Since new workers were going to be busy building the grotto for the next week, we spent most of our time visiting Todd at the Dolphin Exploratorium, and Sophie chattered a million miles a minute.

"Todd, a new salamander is coming! It's coming all the way from Japan, and it's huge—taller than Doug."

Suggested levels for Guided Reading, DRA™, Lexile,® and Reading Recovery™ are provided in the Pearson Scott Foresman Leveling Guide.

Social Studies

The Incredible Journey of Thor Heyerdahl and the Kon-Tiki Raft

by Johanna Biviano

Genre	Comprehension Skill and Strategy	Text Features
Nonfiction	• Author's Purpose • Predict	• Captions • Heads • Maps

Scott Foresman Reading Street 4.5.1

ISBN 0-328-13474-0

9 780328 134748

Reader Response

1. Before the voyage of the *Kon Tiki*, where did people believe the first Polynesians came from? Does the author show you that one theory is stronger than another? Use examples to support your answer.

2. What was the author's purpose in writing this story? What clues did she give you that the raft would make the journey safely to Polynesia? Make a list of some of the clues.

3. Some words used in this text, such as *bow* are homonyms. You can tie a bow on your shoe, take a bow at the end of a performance, or sit in the bow of a boat. List all of the homonyms in this book. Give at least two meanings for each word.

4. The book you just read talks about history, biology, archaeology, and even meteorology. Look these words up in the dictionary and write down their meanings. Then find examples in the text. Make a chart to organize your examples.

Glossary

bow *n.* the forward part of a ship, boat, or air-craft.

cargo *n.* the items carried by a sea vessel.

celestial *adj.* of or about the sky or outer space.

conducted *v.* to have led or guided.

navigation *n.* the process of finding and keeping a ship's or aircraft's position on course.

quivered *v.* to have shaken or trembled.

stern *n.* the rear part of a ship or sea vessel.

The Incredible Journey of Thor Heyerdahl and the Kon-Tiki Raft

by Johanna Biviano

PEARSON
Scott Foresman

Editorial Offices: Glenview, Illinois • Parsippany, New Jersey • New York, New York
Sales Offices: Needham, Massachusetts • Duluth, Georgia • Glenview, Illinois
Coppell, Texas • Ontario, California • Mesa, Arizona

Here's How To Do It!

1. First, plan what to bring as your cargo. Make sure that two of your items are a notebook and pen. What else do you need? You may need hiking boots, a flashlight, and some trail mix, or you may need your glasses and a camera. List the things you need to bring. Then list the items you *want* to bring. Do you have the space to bring everything?
2. When you're ready to go, assign roles to the friends and family who come along. You will need a navigator to keep track of the directions. Are there other jobs that would help you get to your destination safely?
3. On to the adventure! Make sure to jot down the interesting things you see and do in your notebook; this will be your Captain's Log. For each entry, write down the time and your location. When you return, the Log will help you share your journey with friends.

Now Try This

Navigating Your World

Could you be the captain of your own adventure? Explore the world around you! Use your navigation skills to go on your own adventure.

Before starting out, think of a place near your home that you would like to see and explore. You could go to a state park, a museum, or a historical site that interests you. Like Thor Heyerdahl, do your research first! Find out how to get there and write down clear directions. Will you need a car, a bus, a bicycle, or just your own two feet? Check the weather reports so you can plan what to wear. Find out the main attractions of your destination and make note of what you want to see there. Estimate how long your trip will take. Invite friends and family to come along!

An Idea Is Born

A young man from Norway and his wife sit on the beach of Fatu Hiva, a tropical island in French Polynesia. They dig their feet into the cooling sand. The young man stares into the horizon. He feels the wind and watches the waves. Both always come here from the east. He wonders about the first people who came to this island. Suddenly, he gets a remarkable idea.

Thor Heyerdahl and his wife, Liv, first went to Fatu Hiva in 1936. They went to study and collect samples of wildlife. This branch of study is called zoology. While they were there, Thor also became interested in ancient rock carvings and the myths about them. These stories told how people first came to the island of Polynesia.

Thor was sure the accepted stories and myths about where the Polynesians came from were not correct. Now he had only to prove it.

A traditional Polynesian Tiki sculpture

Where Did the Polynesians Come from?

There were lots of different theories about where the Polynesians came from. Everyone seemed to have a different idea.

Some anthropologists thought that these people came from the West. They thought Polynesians came from India, China, Malaysia, even Germany or Scandinavia! Polynesians said that their ancestors arrived on the islands after a long journey over the sea.

The uninhabited island was named Kon-Tiki Island. Knut and Torstein contacted Tahiti by radio with the news that they were safe ashore.

A Journey's End

After spending several weeks in the islands, meeting the Polynesians living there, the crew of the *Kon-Tiki* finally headed home. Had Thor Heyerdahl proved his theory? Even after publishing a book and making a film of his travels, scientists still were not sure. Thor Heyerdahl, however, had made the journey and had survived for many more adventures!

Safe Arrival

After three long months, the crew saw the first flock of birds they had seen in months. The men knew that land must be nearby. On their ninety-seventh day at sea, the crew spotted land. They were overjoyed at the sight and couldn't wait to feel the soft island sand between their toes. The *Kon-Tiki* had made it!

The wind, however, turned against them. It pushed the *Kon-Tiki* back out to sea. Days later, they approached another island, Angatou. Two Polynesian men rowed a small canoe out of the dangerous coral reef to greet the boat, but there was no safe way to bring the *Kon-Tiki* to shore. They drifted out again in despair.

The raft now headed straight for a dangerous reef. With no way around it, the crew prepared to go over it. They knocked out the centerboards and lashed their cargo tight to the raft. The *Kon-Tiki* bumped up against the reef, and wave after wave smashed against it. The men hung on to the ropes and stays with all their strength. The mast quivered, broke into pieces, and smashed into the cabin roof.

Finally, they made it to shore safely. At last they could stand on the reef in shoes—shoes they hadn't worn for 101 days.

Thor Heyerdahl was among those who believed that Polynesians may have come from South America. Spanish conquistadores, explorers of the 15th and 16th centuries, had noted that the native people used small rafts to fish and travel up the coast of Peru in South America. If any group of people had traveled to Polynesia 1,000 years before then, they would have used small rafts such as these.

How could a tiny raft make a journey of more than over 4,000 miles? Everyone thought that a raft made of light balsa wood and handmade rope could never complete the journey.

Or could it? Thor Heyerdahl thought about how similar the pyramids and temples in Polynesia were to buildings found on the coast of Peru. Was there a connection? he wondered.

Tall Tales or Truth?

Heyerdahl also knew that the conquistadores had legends of a bearded, light-skinned people living in Peru, who were led by a man called Kon-Tiki, or the Son of the Sun. Legend had it that these people worshipped a sun god, and were later driven out of Peru by the Inca Indians.

Heyerdahl wrote about Spanish explorers finding the South Sea Islands and about how they were astonished to find people of lighter skin with long beards living there. These people said that Tiki had brought them to these islands. Could these people be the tribe who had been driven out of Peru?

Thor Heyerdahl thought so. He was sure he had put all of the clues together and had absolute proof that Polynesians came from South America. But no one would even read his paper or believe his idea! Heyerdahl studied the ocean currents and trade winds of the Pacific Ocean to prove the Polynesians made a 4,000 mile journey across that ocean.

Meeting and Greeting Ocean Fish

One night the crew noticed phosphorescent spots—light glowing beneath the ocean's surface. Often, different types of plankton would glow this way, but the spots seemed to cover one huge animal. In the morning, they saw the creature—a sixty-foot whale shark! The whale shark is the largest fish in the ocean, and its jaws can grow up to four feet wide. Although the shark swam around the raft for several hours, it never attacked the raft or the crew.

Smaller sharks, however, made the water dangerous for swimming. Once, while one sailor checked the bottom of the raft, a shark headed straight toward him! The men on board harpooned the shark to save Knut from a nasty bite. By the end of the trip, the crew knew sharks so well that they could catch them by their tails!

The crew had another surprising night visitor. They would wake up to find baby octopi as they **quivered** on the roof! At first they thought the octopi had crawled on board with their long tentacles. Then, one night, a strange thing landed on deck with a loud smack. An octopus had used its tentacles to jump through the water to escape a shark.

© Pearson Education, Inc.

The crew of the *Kon-Tiki* found that they were never bored during their three months at sea. The fish were curious about the raft and not afraid of it, as they might have been if it were a big ship.

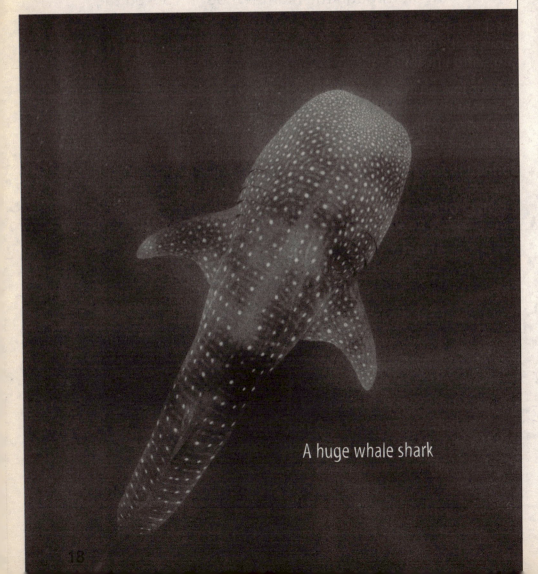

A huge whale shark

Currents in the Atlantic and Pacific Oceans

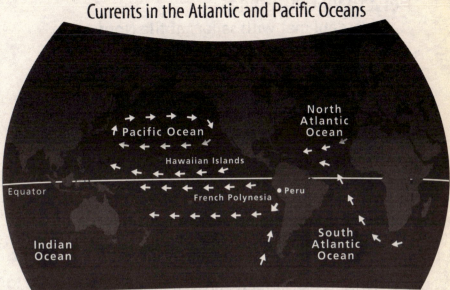

The Impossible Adventure

The cooler air and currents from the south flow toward the warmth of the equator. Heyerdahl imagined the mysterious bearded men of Peru floating on a current all the way to Easter Island, Fatu Hiva, and the other islands of Polynesia. He knew that if he could get help to build a raft, he could prove his theory by making the dangerous trip himself!

To make a trip over 4,000 miles of empty ocean, Heyerdahl needed money, supplies, shipmates, and lots of other support. He went to New York City, to try to convince **dignified** scholars, seamen, and members of the Explorers Club that his plan would work. Most discouraged him, but one man from the Explorers Club promised to raise money for the adventure.

Heryerdahl Gets Going

Heyerdahl met with sailors at the Norwegian Sailors' Home to get their opinions. Some thought a raft could make the journey easily, but no one wanted to join the adventure—not until Thor met an engineer named Herman Watzinger, the first man to sign up for the trip.

Herman and Thor worked as a team to solve problems. The first was finding a crew. They quickly hired Knut Haugland and Torstein Raaby, both Norwegian radio engineers. Erik Hesselberg, a navigator, and others soon followed.

Then the U.S. Armed Forces agreed to support the trip if Thor and his crew would do some experiments for them. They wanted to test food provisions, such as knives, forks, and spoons that floated in water, a small stove, and other items.

Along with military food provisions, the *Kon-Tiki* carried coconuts, tropical fruit, dried meats, and lots of sweet potatoes, just as the original travelers might have prepared. Thor and his crew quickly learned that fishing was the easiest way to eat. In fact, flying fish flopped on board the raft all through the night. Whoever cooked the next morning would gather all of the fish on deck and prepare them for a meal. They even had enough that they used some of their night visitors as bait for bigger fish!

One night, Torstein, who slept closest to the cabin door, got frustrated by the night steersmen stepping on his hair. He put a lamp by his head only to wake to the company of a snake mackerel!

Flying fish would "fly" onboard.

Can you imagine embarking on a sea voyage, knowing that you would not set foot on land for 100 days? The men aboard the *Kon-Tiki* thought carefully about what cargo they brought on board. First, they had to pack food, medical supplies, extra materials for the raft, and fishing gear. Those items took up most of the space on the raft.

Packing Their Bags

The men didn't need extra clothes in the tropical heat, but there were other things they wanted aboard. Torstein and Knut had to pack radio equipment and batteries. Erik brought paints, brushes, and a guitar! Another crew member packed his box of books. The raft also carried plenty of film for recording their adventure.

Thor Heyerdahl needed to make sure he could build and safely sail a raft in South America. So he asked important diplomats in New York City and Washington, D.C., who were from Peru and Ecuador, for help.

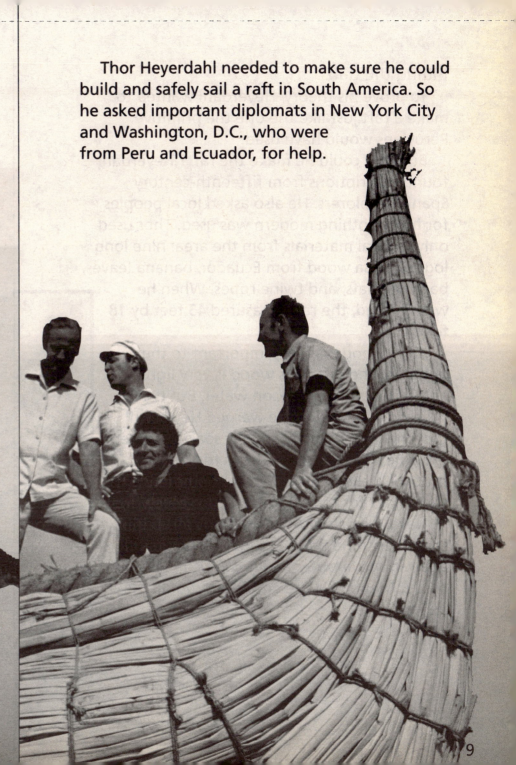

Riding the Raft

To prove his theory, Heyerdahl wanted to make a raft just like the one the primitive Peruvians would have used.

But how could he make the raft? Heyerdahl found descriptions from fifteenth-century Spanish explorers. He also asked local peoples for help. Nothing modern was used. Thor used only natural materials from the area: nine long logs of balsa wood from Ecuador, banana leaves, bamboo mats, and twine ropes. When he was finished, the raft measured 45 feet by 18 feet.

Balsa wood was very important to the design of the raft. This wood is very light, and it floats like a cork on water. But it does have drawbacks. People warned Heyerdahl that the logs would gradually soak up water, grow heavier, and sink. Thor's trip would probably take at least 97 days. Could the raft stay afloat for that long?

Naval experts also warned Heyerdahl that the ropes to tie the raft together would rub against one another and grow weak and break. Eventually, the entire raft would fall apart!

Following a Sky Map

At night, Hesselberg used his knowledge of the stars, just as the South Americans and Polynesians had in the past. Just as the Greeks depended on the North Star, Orion, and other constellations to chart their course, Hesselberg looked for a group of stars shaped like a parrot fish and used its position in the sky to calculate their progress on the seas. Hesselberg measured the distance and direction the raft traveled each day, and he marked the point on a map. According to his measurements, they traveled an average of 42 miles a day.

Don't Always Believe What You're Told!

The stormy seas lasted only for a few days, but they proved that the raft was seaworthy. They also proved that the *Kon-Tiki* was just the right size. If the raft had been larger, it may have been snapped in half by the waves lifting up the **bow** or the stern.

The twine ropes didn't fray as experts warned. Instead, during the worst storms, they were protected by the balsa wood as they pushed into it. The logs were were tied loosely enough to move independently, which helped the raft ride waves. It also allowed ocean water to flow through them, like soup through a fork.

Thor and his crew discovered that the raft was easy to steer because of the movable centerboards. By adjusting the depth and the angle of the centerboards, they **conducted** the raft steadily in any direction.

Making Star Tracks

Although many navigational tools and instruments were available to Heyerdahl and his crew, they chose to use **celestial navigation**. This means plotting a course by the sun and stars, just as the Peruvians would have. Erik Hesselberg, the navigator, kept track of the raft's progress day by day. Like the Peruvians, Hesselberg noted the position of the sun during the day.

Finding balsa wood wasn't easy. Balsa wood grew in the rain forest, but when Thor and Herman arrived in Ecuador, it was rainy season and no one wanted to go with them into the forest. The ground would be muddy and hard to walk on, so they would need a jeep. Luckily, the president of Ecuador got them one. Once in the rain forest, they found and cut the logs. Then they floated them down the Rio Guayas to the Pacific coast.

Strong winds caused trouble for the boat.

The Beginning of the Kon-Tiki Journey

Despite all of the terrible warnings, the six men began their journey on the morning of April 28, 1947. A tug boat pulled the *Kon-Tiki* out of the Callao harbor in Peru and left the raft to drift with the winds and the currents.

Immediately, the sail filled with the trade wind, and the raft picked up speed and headed northwest. The crew had a hard time controlling the raft on stormy seas. For the first three days, they struggled to control the oar they used to steer, which was at the raft's **stern**. The violent waves kept them rolling, and steering the raft required two men at a time using their full strength. The job was so tiring that they had to schedule one-hour shifts. The *Kon-Tiki's* crew worried that they would have to face this kind of work for the whole 97 days!

During these frightening first days, the crew made sure that the men steering were tied to the boat with ropes. The violent waves could easily sweep them overboard with little chance of rescue. The raft was so small that it would be hard for a plane or helicopter to see it on the ocean, much less send out a rescue party.

Suggested levels for Guided Reading, DRA,™ Lexile,® and Reading Recovery™ are provided in the Pearson Scott Foresman Leveling Guide.

Social Studies

Genre	Comprehension Skill and Strategy	Text Features
Nonfiction	• Compare and Contrast • Visualize	• Captions • Glossary • Map • Sidebars

Scott Foresman Reading Street 4.5.2

PEARSON
Scott Foresman

scottforesman.com

ISBN 0-328-13477-5

9 780328 134775

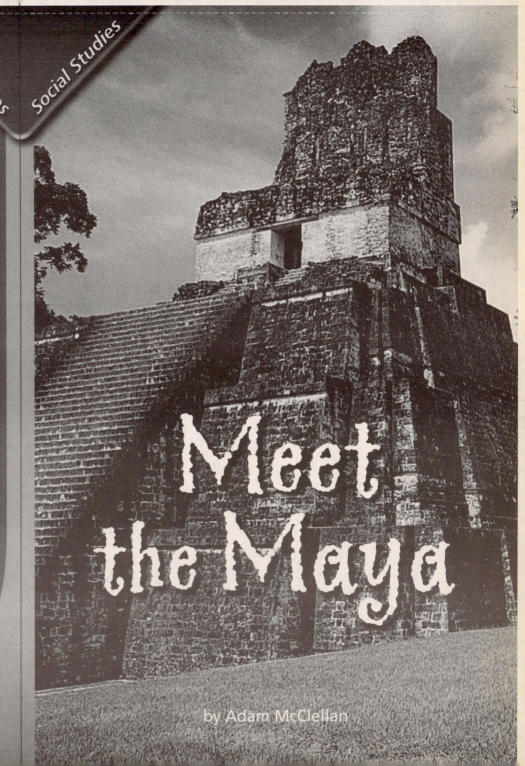

Meet the Maya

by Adam McClellan

Reader Response

1. How were the Mayan and Roman civilizations similar? How were they different? Make a Venn diagram to show their likenesses and differences.

2. On page 11, what words does the author use to help the reader visualize how early astronomers studied the planets?

3. The word astronomy contains the prefix *astro-* which means "stars" or "space." Make a list of other words that contain this prefix. Explain how each relates to stars or space.

4. Review the headings used to organize the book. Do they present the story of the Maya in chronological order or by topic? Explain your answer.

Glossary

abandoned *v.* left behind.

abruptly *adv.* very suddenly.

astronomy *n.* the study of outer space.

civilians *n.* people who are not soldiers.

glyphs *n.* written or carved symbols.

dialects *pl. n.* regional variations of a language distinguished by pronunciation, grammar, or vocabulary.

highlands *n.* a hilly or mountainous area

limestone *n.* a rock formed from shells or coral and used in building.

maize *n.* the corn plant or the grain it produces.

Mesoamerica *n.* an area that includes what is today southern Mexico and the western part of Central America.

reservoirs *n.* places for storing large amounts of water.

ruins *n.* what is left after a building, wall, etc. has fallen to pieces.

syllabograms *pl. n.* written or printed symbols that stand for single syllable.

terraced *adj.* rising in steplike fashion.

Meet the Maya

by Adam McClellan

Editorial Offices: Glenview, Illinois • Parsippany, New Jersey • New York, New York
Sales Offices: Needham, Massachusetts • Duluth, Georgia • Glenview, Illinois
Coppell, Texas • Ontario, California • Mesa, Arizona

Here's How To Do It!

1. Create a list of six English words that have more than one syllable. For example: *rooster, elephant, sundae*
2. Break the words down into syllables. For this exercise, you don't need to use a dictionary—just listen to how the words sound to you.
3. For each syllable, create a picture, or glyph, that represents the sound the syllable makes. Write each glyph next to its syllable so that you have a translation key.
4. Rewrite your original six words using your syllabograms. Then try using the syllables to make other English words.
5. Trade your words and your translation key with a classmate. See if you can decipher each other's writing.

Now Try This

Say It in Glyphs

Do you ever get tired of writing your words in plain old letters? Well, who says there's no other way to do it? Try taking a page from the Mayan book!

The Mayan writing system included a set of syllabograms, each of which represented a single syllable in the Mayan language. Now it's your turn to try creating syllabograms for English.

Maya King Bird-Jaguar

Long Ago in Central America

By the fourth and third centuries B.C., the once great Roman Empire had begun to decline. On the other side of the world, another civilization was on the rise.

In the jungles and highlands of Central America, the Mayan people were just beginning their golden age. Like the Romans, the Maya controlled a vast empire and had their own calendar, writing, and math systems.

The Maya lived in a large area ranging from Central America into southern Mexico. The area is known as **Mesoamerica**. Ancient Mayan lands are now part of the countries of Mexico, Belize, Guatemala, El Salvador, and Honduras.

Evidence of Maya life in Mesoamerica dates all the way back to 2000 B.C. In their early days, the Maya lived simply. Their culture was based on small-scale farming.

But by the first century B.C., the Maya's culture had developed. It peaked from A.D. 300 to 900. During that time, the Maya built hundreds of cities out of stone. Each city had glorious temples in its ceremonial center. The Maya also created their own math system, calendar, and system for understanding the stars.

The Maya Today

The Maya people are still with us today. In fact, there are about six million Mayan living in Mexico and Central America. The Maya language lives on, too. Different regions have developed their own **dialects**. In fact, there are now thirty-one different Mayan languages!

The Maya live in a modern world but they still hold on to many of their ancient beliefs. Some Maya are even learning their ancient writing system. In some villages, "day-keepers" follow the days of the original Mayan calendar.

People from all over the world are still fascinated by the amazing Maya and come to visit their incredible ancient cities. Perhaps, one day, you will too!

This woman is photographing an incredible Mayan ruin.

Young Maya girls today dress much the way they did hundreds of years ago.

The Maya traveled on foot or in canoes.

The World of the Maya

How do we know about the Maya? Like the ancient Romans and Greeks, the Maya left behind remarkable examples of their life and culture. From their art, writing, and architecture, we can tell that the Maya were an amazing civilization.

The ancient Maya lived in three main regions of Mesoamerica. In the north, there was dry, scrubby land, with soil that was not very good for farming. In the south, bordering the Pacific Ocean, there were high mountains. Here the soil was rich and good for farming. In the eastern and central regions there was a tropical rain forest. This was the heart of Mayan civilization.

Maya pyramid

Egyptian pyramid

Magnificent Temples

At its height, the Mayan civilization was the most powerful civilization for hundreds of miles in any direction.

The Maya built large structures out of **limestone**. The biggest of these were the temple-pyramids, which usually sat at the center of a city. Rising as high as 212 feet, they were centers for the Maya religion. Traveling Maya also used these temples as landmarks, since their tops rose high above the trees.

A Spanish conquerer stands of the heads of two Maya.

Spanish Rule of the Maya

In the early 1500s, the Spanish arrived, looking for new lands to rule. The Maya fought hard against the Spanish, but the Spanish soldiers were too well armed for them. Plus, the Maya weren't unified. Instead of having one strong government to bring them together, they had just little independent city-states.

Eventually, Spain conquered the Maya. The Spanish brought with them new diseases such as measles and smallpox, which the Maya quickly caught. Within the first hundred years of Spanish rule, nearly ninety percent of the Maya died.

The Mystery of the Maya

How could such an amazing people simply leave their cities? There isn't one simple answer.

Some researchers think the Maya might have disappeared from their cities because of overcrowding. The Maya lived in the rain forest, which is a fragile place. As more and more of the rain forests were destroyed, the Maya found it harder to live and farm. In fact, researchers have found Mayan skeletons that show signs of malnutrition.

Another thing that may have hurt the Maya is the weather. Scientists have found that the years from A.D. 800 to A.D. 1000 were the driest in eight thousand years! There might have been a terrible drought. This could have dried up the Maya's water supply in the cities' **reservoirs**.

The Maya might have left their cities when water like this disappeared in a series of droughts

Pyramid of Kukulcan

Mayan Masterpieces

Today, people flock to the Mayan **ruins** to see these remarkable buildings firsthand. How the Maya built them is still a mystery. Unlike other civilizations, such as the ancient Romans, the Maya didn't use pack animals to carry materials and supplies.

Unlike the triangular pyramids of ancient Egypt, Mayan pyramids have four sides. Some are **terraced**, rising in smaller and smaller levels, much like steps. Up each side was a steep flight of stairs. At the top were altars used for religious ceremonies.

The Maya also built ceremonial platforms, with mythological figures carved into their sides. They built ball courts, and tall buildings that we now know were observatories.

The Maya believed that they were created out of corn flour by the gods. Most Mayan meals involved corn. *Tortillas* were made from corn meal. Mashed corn wrapped in corn husks made *tamales*. Ground corn mixed with hot water made a drink, *atole*.

The Maya abandoned their great cities, but they left behind many great monuments.

For hundreds of years Mayan warriors in rival cities fought small battles. At first, **civilians** were left out of the fighting. By the year A.D. 700, all that changed. Civilians now had to fight too. Worse, the fighting became more violent, and the Maya began to destroy one another's cities. It took a hundred and fifty years for the fighting to stop. When it did, nine-tenths of the Mayan population was gone.

The golden age of the Maya ran from A.D. 300 to A.D. 900. But then, it ended **abruptly**. Archaeologists have found evidence that suggests the Maya simply **abandoned** their great cities.

Ready, Set, Count!
Learning About Mayan Numbers

The Mayan counting system was so simple that most could learn to use it. All Mayan numbers were written using just three basic symbols. A dot stood for the number one. When there are five dots, it became a line. That line stood for five. You could write out any number from one to twenty by placing bars and dots on top of one another. Look at the example below:

```
••       =2
——       =5
——       =5
————
TOTAL 12    Add them all together
            and what do you have?
```

Mayan numbers differed from ours in two important ways. First, the Maya wrote their numbers from top to bottom instead of from left to right. Second, the Maya based their system on the number 20 instead of on the number 10.

```
20s      ••         40
place    (20)+(20)   +
—————————           
1s       •          6
place    (1)+(5)    ——
                    46
         Add them all together!
         20 + 20 +1 +5. You get 46!
```

The Maya knew the value of zero. Think of our own system. Without zero, we wouldn't be able to tell the difference between 20,004 and 24! The Mayan zero was a shell symbol.

Mayan Life

The Maya were successful farmers. They grew maize, or corn, squash, beans, and peppers. They developed expert farming techniques, including ways to provide crops with fresh water. Cities and villages had cenotes, or freshwater wells.

To farm the dense rain forests, the Maya practiced a method of clearing land called slash and burn. They cut and burned all wild plants in the area. They also rotated crops to keep the soil from being drained of all nutrients. And after two years of planting, a field was left alone for ten years.

The Maya also fished and hunted turkey, deer, and armadillo. They picked wild fruit and even had a form of chocolate.

Yet despite their magnificent temples, and their sophisticated farming methods, most Maya lived in small, simple houses. These were built with mud walls and thatched roofs supported by poles. A one-room house held a whole family.

A mud and thatch house in Ecuador

The ruins of an ancient Maya observatory at Chichen Itza, Mexico.

How Do You Read Glyphs?

Sometimes a single glyph stood for a whole word. There were 600 of these single glyphs, called logograms. Another set of 150 glyphs, called **syllabograms** stood for the different syllables of the Mayan language.

What did Mayan writing look like? If you were using syllabograms to make a word, you might organize them into one block. These shapes would be stacked on top of one another or placed side by side. To read them, you would start at the top left and work down to the bottom right.

In the 1950s, researchers began unraveling the mystery of Mayan writing. Today, we know the meaning of more than three-fourths of all glyphs!

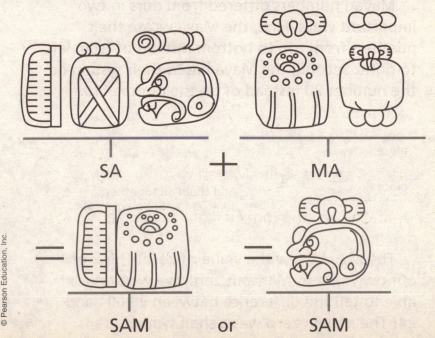

SA + MA

= SAM or = SAM

Maya writing looked like pictures, but every picture had a meaning.

The Mystery of Mayan Writing

We know a lot about the Maya because they invented their own system of writing. According to some experts, writing has been invented only one other time in human history!

Most Maya didn't know how to read and write. Instead, the Mayan rulers and priests kept this knowledge to themselves. Because of this, most of the surviving Mayan writing is about the rulers.

Mayan writing looked like pictures or symbols on a page. These symbols were called **glyphs**. Like Egyptian hieroglyphs, which were also pictures, many of the Mayan glyphs were drawings of objects from the Mayan world. Some glyphs are harder to understand than others.

Early Astronomers

In modern times, we have electricity to light up the night. In the time of the Maya, they had the stars. The Maya had a great curiosity about the movement of the planets and the sun. They believed the sky had a big influence on life on Earth. In some ways, they were right.

Without computers or telescopes, Mayan priests studied **astronomy**. As the planets moved, they used simple tools, such as a forked stick placed in the ground, to help them observe the positions of Venus, the Sun, the Moon, and the constellations. Windows or doors were placed so that sunlight or moonlight would hit them directly. Other buildings were aligned to mark the movement of planets, such as Venus.

The Maya based some religious ceremonies on important events in the solar year, such as the spring and fall equinoxes (when day and night are the same length). In addition, the Maya created entire calendars based on their understanding of the sky.

The Mayan Calendars

The Maya used three different calendars at the same time. The 260-day *Tzolkin* (divine) calendar was used in the Mayan religion. In everyday life, or civil life, the Maya followed the *Haab* calendar.

Mayan astronomers tracked the Sun's position and discovered that a year was a bit more than 365 days. The Haab divided that year into 18 months of 20 days each, followed by a five-day period at the end of the year. This end period, the *Uayeb,* was considered a time of bad luck.

20 x 18 +5?

Multiply 20 days by 18 months and add five more days. What do you get? 365. That's the same number of days as in a standard calendar year. (Ours is divided into 12 months, however.) The Maya valued accuracy. They calculated that a year was 365.242036 days long.

From Kin to Baktun

The Long Count calendar divided time into five different units:

- *kin* (one day)
- *uinal* (20 kin)
- *tun* (18 uinal—or about one year)
- *katun* (20 tun—about 20 years)
- *baktun* (20 katun—just under 400 years)

The third Mayan calendar is known as the Long Count. Like the *Tzolkin*, the Long Count was used in Mayan religion. It was used to count the time that had passed from the start of the Mayan era. According to the Long Count, the Mayan era began in 3114 B.C. The basic unit of the Long Count was the *kin* (day). A Long Count date was a complicated series that included five different units of time.

Suggested levels for Guided Reading, DRA,™ Lexile,® and Reading Recovery™ are provided in the Pearson Scott Foresman Leveling Guide.

Social Studies

Two Women Astronauts

by Marianne Lenihan

illustrated by Aleksey Ivanov

Genre	Comprehension Skill and Strategy
Fiction	• Sequence • Story Structure

Scott Foresman Reading Street 4.5.3

PEARSON
Scott Foresman

scottforesman.com

ISBN 0-328-13480-5
9 780328 134809
90000

Reader Response

1. Make two timelines. Show the sequence of events the author used to describe Sally Ride's and Mae Jemison's lives.

2. How are the two sections in Kim's report different?

3. Look back through the pages in this book to find a word that is unfamiliar to you. Then tell some things you could do to figure out the word's meaning.

4. Think about the two astronauts' lives. What do you think was the most difficult challenge each had to face?

Training Early at Space Camp

The two women astronauts you read about in this book had to wait until they were adults to begin training for a career in space flight. Today, however, children living in the United States can experience what space flight is like by attending Space Camp in Huntsville, Alabama.

The usual program for young people, ages nine to eleven, lasts for five days. Activities include flight and one-sixteenth gravity training simulators, IMAX® movies, rocket building, and simulated space shuttle missions. There are also programs for deaf and visually-impaired persons.

Named for our first woman astronaut, the Sally Ride Space Camp invites young girls and their mothers to experience the thrill of space exploration. Young girls who are interested in science and math can have a blast there!

Two Women Astronauts

by Marianne Lenihan
illustrated by Aleksey Ivanov

PEARSON
Scott Foresman

Editorial Offices: Glenview, Illinois • Parsippany, New Jersey • New York, New York
Sales Offices: Needham, Massachusetts • Duluth, Georgia • Glenview, Illinois
Coppell, Texas • Ontario, California • Mesa, Arizona

"Everyone thought my report was cool!" Kim told her parents. Kim's father smiled at her. "What's cool is how much you learned," he told her.

Kim nodded. "Now I really want to be an astronaut more than ever!" she told her parents. "These women did amazing things. I hope I get the chance to do great things too."

Kim's mother gave Kim a hug. "I wouldn't be surprised if one day a young girl writes a report about the story of your life!" she said.

"I hope so!" Kim said.

Finally, it was time for Mr. Burns to collect the students' reports. "Who wants to share a report with the class?" Mr. Burns asked. Kim's hand shot up. "I do! I do!" she said.

Kim took her report back from her teacher and stood in front of the class. She began, "Sally Ride and Mae Jemison are true heroes to me."

Kim took a deep breath when she had finished reading aloud her report. At first, her classmates and teacher were silent. Then they all started asking her questions.

"Class, your reports are due in two weeks. Remember, I want you to write about someone who has done something great! Any questions?" Mr. Burns looked expectantly at the class.

Kim stared at Mr. Burns. She didn't have a clue who she wanted to write about. Maybe when she got home, she could ask her dad. He always had good ideas.

Kim's father came home early from work that day. Kim told him about her writing assignment. "I don't know who to write about," she said. Kim was very worried.

Her father smiled. "Sure you do," he said. "What do you want to be when you grow up?"

Kim laughed. "An astronaut, of course! Why didn't I think of that?"

Kim got more and more excited. "Not only am I going to write about an astronaut," she said. "I'm going to write my report on two women astronauts!"

Kim got out her astronaut books and excitedly leafed through the pages. She knew just what she was looking for. There it was, pictures of Sally Ride and Mae Jemison, her two favorite astronauts in the whole world.

When Kim got to school the next day, she could hardly wait to tell Mr. Burns about her choices for the report. Kim explained to him that she had always had a real interest in space travel. "I want to go to Space Camp when I'm older," she said.

At lunch, Kim and her friends talked non-stop about their reports. "I think your idea is the coolest one of all," said Amy, one of Kim's friends. That made Kim more excited than ever.

Kim's report on Mae Jemison was now complete. She made a blue folder to hold both reports. She was proud of all her hard work. Kim felt a little sad too. "What's wrong?" asked Kim's mother.

"I learned so much about these astronauts and I wrote so much about them, that I almost feel like they are my friends," Kim said. "I miss them!"

Kim's mother smiled. "That shows what a great job you did!" she said.

The next morning, Kim brought her report to school. On the folder's cover she wrote the words "Two Women Heroes by Kim Yong."

Remember when I told you that I have never been a person who was interested in only one thing? I decided to write a book. The book would tell about some of my life and maybe convince both children and adults to explore new things and create their own incredible life story. My book's title is *Find Where the Wind Goes: Moments from My Life*.

Remember that it is never too early in life to dream big or help others.

Thanks for reading my story. Now it's time for you to write your own story. Oh, you don't need to write it with words. You can write it with the good choices you make and the awesome dreams you pursue. I just know that you will find where the wind goes—for you!

That evening, Kim searched the Internet for information. Next, Kim made an outline. Finally, Kim sat down at her computer and typed:

Sally Ride and Mae Jemison are true heroes to me. Sally Ride grew up in California, just like me. Sally and I also share the same interest in playing sports.

Unlike me, when Sally was young, she was not interested in the space program. She couldn't be interested because there wasn't any space program!

Of course, as Sally grew up, space exploration really took off. She was already very interested in science. Sally also enjoyed reading, and writing reports. William Shakespeare became Sally's favorite author. When it was time to begin college, Sally studied both science and Shakespeare.

Another exciting experiment I did in space was with South African frog eggs. Here on Earth, scientists know how long it takes frogs to develop from the egg stage into adult frogs. But no one knew if frog eggs would develop faster, slower, or at the same rate in outer space.

While on board for our eight-day space flight, we took notes on how long it would take the eggs to hatch. Can you guess what we discovered? The eggs hatched at the same rate in outer space as they did on Earth!

When I returned to Earth, I taught college classes. I am also the director of the Jemison Institute. Here, scientists and other experts from all over the world gather to work on scientific ideas that will help people in developing countries.

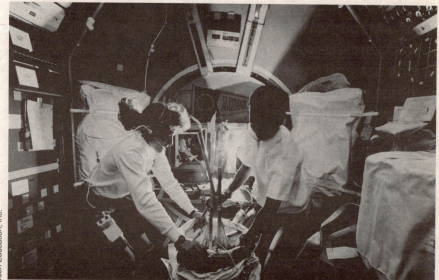

Mae Jemison and Jan Davis set up an experiment examining lower body negative pressure.

I even conducted an experiment on myself! I used something called biofeedback. Biofeedback is a way to train and calm your mind so it helps your body overcome pain or fear. I trained my mind to overcome space motion sickness.

What's motion sickness? You know that gravity is the force that keeps us on the Earth, right? Well, when astronauts first travel into space, their balance becomes all mixed up because there is not a lot of gravity in outer space. This makes most astronauts feel sick for the first few days. I wanted to try biofeedback as a way of helping myself and other astronauts resist motion sickness.

When we reached outer space, I began to experiment with biofeedback and it worked! Perhaps future astronauts will also try biofeedback.

Dr. Mae Jemison, September, 1992.

Sally began her college studies at Swarthmore College in Pennsylvania, and then attended Stanford University. Soon, Sally got more and more interested in space travel.

One day, Sally noticed an advertisement in the university's newspaper. The ad said that the National Aeronautics and Space Administration (NASA) was hiring astronauts for its new space shuttle program. NASA needed people who knew about astronomy and the other sciences. They were to be called mission specialists and run experiments while in space.

Up until that time, there were not any women astronauts, only men. If NASA was ready to hire scientists, maybe NASA was also ready to hire women. That meant Sally should apply!

I was accepted into the space training program in 1988. I was so excited!

For the next five years, I trained at NASA. I didn't get a lot of sleep because I was studying so hard. That didn't matter to me. All I could think about was going into space. I would also be the first African-American woman to become an astronaut. Can you imagine how proud I felt?

In 1992, I was assigned to fly on the space shuttle *Endeavour*. I would help to conduct over forty different experiments while in space.

When I was only sixteen years old, I entered Stanford University. I earned both a degree in chemical engineering and a degree in African-American studies. Then I became a doctor.

I wanted to help people in countries that needed better schools, hospitals, and more industry. So I joined the Peace Corps and was sent to Sierra Leone and Liberia.

I came back to the United States and opened my own doctor's office. I missed working in other scientific fields, so I applied to NASA as a mission specialist.

A thousand other women wanted to break into NASA's program, which at the time was only for men. Only thirty-five women would be chosen, and one of them was Sally! She had to take tests and be interviewed at the Johnson Space Center.

Soon, Sally made the team. It would be a year before Sally would be ready to take her first trip into outer space.

Sally's job was to study the part of the space craft called the remote manipulator system. This part of the shuttle is a giant jointed robot arm used to move cargo in the ship's payload bay. This arm also picks up or releases satellites.

Sally also had to stay in tip-top physical shape. To do this, she ran every day.

Even with all of Sally's training, she would not fly in the shuttle for a long while. Sally would help take pictures and supply wind and weather reports to the crew of the *Columbia*.

Sally was given a job at the Mission Control Center. She would be a *capcom*, which stands for "capsule communicator." Sally would be the only person allowed to speak to a spacecraft during a flight. She would share information from scientists and other experts.

Finally, Sally's big day arrived. She would be the first United States female astronaut!

Kim decided to write the second half of her assignment as if Mae Jemison were writing it. This is Kim's report.

Hello there! My name is Mae Jemison and I remember what it's like to be a fourth grader. When I was your age, I knew that someday I would be a scientist. Back then, there were only a few people of color working in the sciences. There were even fewer African-American women scientists. I was going to become a scientist whether the rest of the world liked it or not! I spent a lot of time at the public library in Chicago, Illinois, where I grew up, reading everything I could on the sciences.

Like you, I'm not only interested in science. I also love learning languages and can speak Russian, Japanese, and Swahili, which is an African language.

It was the summer of 1983, and all was cleared for a lift-off of the *Challenger*. Commander Bob Crippen led the way into the special room where the astronauts would dress in their space suits and prepare to board the space shuttle.

Many people had gathered to watch the launch. They held signs that read: "Ride, Sally Ride!"

The engines fired. The first United States woman astronaut was on her way!

Sally's first space trip lasted six days, two hours, and twenty-four minutes. Sally had the opportunity to do everything she had trained for, including operating the remote manipulator arm.

After her flight, Sally spoke to many groups about her experience in space.

Dr. Sally Ride speaks to the media on February 7, 2003, telling them about her Science Club festival for fifth to eighth grade girls.

Earth Science

Suggested levels for Guided Reading, DRA™, Lexile®, and Reading Recovery™ are provided in the Pearson Scott Foresman Leveling Guide.

Genre	Comprehension Skill and Strategy	Text Features
Nonfiction	• Main Idea and Supporting Details • Text Structure	• Chart • Diagrams • Graph • Time Line

Scott Foresman Reading Street 4.5.4

ISBN 0-328-13483-X

Danger:
The World Is Getting Hot!

by Johanna Biviano

Reader Response

1. Think about the book you just read. What are the main ideas of the book? Also give some supporting details from the book to expand on your answer.

2. Does the author present both sides of the issue? FInd places where the author mentions doubts about global warming.

3. Many of the words used in this book are made up of many parts, especially the scientific words. Some of these parts come from Greek or Latin words. Find words in the text that may have these Greek and Latin words in them:

   aer – air   *di* – two

   geo – earth   *inter* – between, over, past, or through

   How does the Latin or Greek root help you to understand the meanings of these words?

4. Many different types of scientists research the problem of global warming. Looking through the text, find information that may have come from:

   a. Meteorologists   **d.** Chemists

   b. Paleontologists   **e.** Geologists

   c. Zoologists

Glossary

anticipation *n.* the act of preparing for something before it happens

continent *n.* one of seven bodies of continuous land on the Earth's surface; Europe, Asia, Africa, North America, South America, Australia, and Antarctica

forbidding *adj.* uninviting or repellant

formidable *adj.* gives cause for fear, is difficult to overcome

hospitable *adj.* welcoming and homey

icebergs *n.* a detached piece of glacier floating at sea

salinity *n.* the quality of being saline, or having salt

Danger:
The World Is Getting Hot!

by Johanna Biviano

Editorial Offices: Glenview, Illinois • Parsippany, New Jersey • New York, New York
Sales Offices: Needham, Massachusetts • Duluth, Georgia • Glenview, Illinois
Coppell, Texas • Ontario, California • Mesa, Arizona

Here's How To Do It!

1. Make a list of things you normally do and want to change for the better. Write a list and label it "Old Way." Try to go through your day in your mind and list the things you do that use electricity or fuel power.
2. Make another column labeled "New Way" with ideas for the new way you want to do things. For example, you may have, "Mom drives me to school in the car," in your "Old Way" column. In the "New Way" column, you may write, "Take the bus instead." Make sure to leave room for a third column.
3. Place your list where you can see it often. Read it over, add new ideas to it, and try to keep your "New Way" ideas in your mind.
4. At the end of each day, keep a tally in the third column of how many times you actually did something from your "New Way" column. Each time you take the bus or walk instead of getting in the car, make a mark. By the end of a week, you will be able to show the changes you have made to help the environment.
5. Make sure you share your list with your friends and family. Inspire them to make changes too!

Now Try This

Trading Bad Habits for Good

In the battle against global warming, every person can help. You can help by watching how you use energy. The less energy you use, the less greenhouse gases are added to the atmosphere. You can start right away!

Old Way

New Way

What's the Weather Like Today?

What do you say when people ask you what the weather is like? If it's summertime, you might say, "It's hot." You might have snow where you are or heavy rain. The weather changes day to day, but most areas have pretty much the same kind of weather from season to season every year. That is called the climate.

Have you ever asked, "What is the climate like today?" You probably have not. The climate doesn't change from day to day.

Many scientists, however, ask, "What will the climate be like in five years? How about in 100 years?" They worry that the Earth's climate is changing, and that these may be harmful.

The Greenhouse Effect

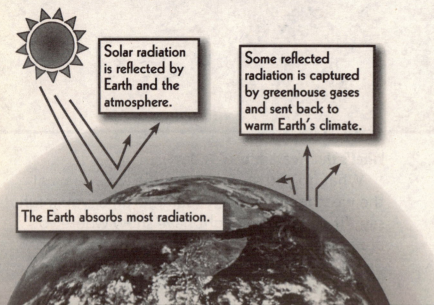

Because of greenhouse gases, more of the sun's warmth stays trapped on the Earth. This makes it hotter.

The Earth's Climate

Of all the planets in our solar system, Earth has the most **hospitable** climate for human life. Earth's climate has changed dramatically over time. These natural changes came gradually. Scientists worry today because the climate seems to have changed so quickly in the last 100 years.

The Environmental Protection Agency (EPA) reports that the Earth's overall temperature has risen one full degree Fahrenheit in the last 100 years. That may not seem like a lot, but it really is something to worry about.

How You Can Help

You can help by recycling. At home, you can start by watching how much electricity you use. Turn off the stereo, the television, and the computer when you are done using them.

You can also help by talking to your family and friends about conserving energy by carpooling, keeping cars tuned up and in good shape, and using buses and subways instead of driving.

The next time your family buys a light bulb, a toaster, a computer, or a car, do some research first! There are lots of energy-saving and low-emissions products on the market now.

Poorer Nations

The poorer nations of the world will have a hard time coping with global warming. Many of these nations depend on agriculture to survive. If storms or weather changes ruin their crops, many people would go hungry.

With fewer medical resources in developing nations, diseases could spread. Also, these nations are less likely to impose laws on their own industries to curb pollution. Why? Because they can't afford expensive new low-pollution factory equipment.

Recycling helps the environment.

The Temperature is Rising!

There is scientific evidence that humans are at least partly responsible for this.

The atmosphere is the air around the planet. Earth's atmosphere contains gases such as carbon dioxide, methane, nitrous oxide, water vapor, and ozone. These are called greenhouse gases because they act like the glass of a greenhouse. They trap the sun's rays in the atmosphere. If there were no greenhouse gases, the sun's heat would bounce back into space. The planet would be too cold for us!

Since the early 1800s, factories burning wood, coal and oil have poured pollutants into the air. The carbon dioxide in the air rose 30%.

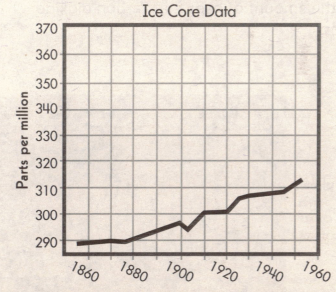

Since the 1800s, there is 30% more carbon dioxide in the air.

How We Add to the Greenhouse Effect

Cars, planes, and power plants all create greenhouse gases. In the last century, these gases have increased in the atmosphere at an alarming rate.

Whenever we burn wood, oil, gasoline, natural gas, or coal, we release carbon dioxide.

Methane is another greenhouse gas. Landfills are large sources of methane. Methane absorbs 20 times the amount of heat that carbon dioxide absorbs. Also, when we burn fossil fuels, nitrous oxide enters the air. Nitrous oxide absorbs 270 times the amount of heat that carbon dioxide absorbs.

Cars, planes, and power plants all create greenhouse gases.

Pollution from factories adds to global warming. Many factories have agreed to try to limit the amount they create.

New Laws for a Cleaner Environment

The government has passed special laws for industries. These laws limit the amount of greenhouse gas emissions. Factories and power plants must meet these guidelines.

Meanwhile, scientists and engineers keep trying out new ideas to protect the planet. In **anticipation** of low-emissions laws, car manufacturers have created low-emissions and fuel-efficient models. The government supports Energy Star products, from long-lasting light bulbs to more energy-efficient washing machines.

Recycling helps cut back on greenhouse gases. Americans can also help by keeping their cars tuned up, so they don't waste fuel. It helps to use public transportation and turn off lights when you leave a room.

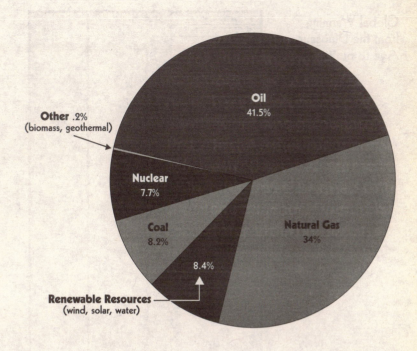

Non-Natural Gases

Carbon dioxide, methane and nitrous oxide all occur naturally. But because we have so much industry, we produce three more kinds of these dangerous gases. These gases are called hydrofluorocarbons (HFCs), perfluorocarbons (PFCs), and sulfur hexafluoride (SF6). These gases trap up to 11,000 times more heat than carbon dioxide!

There are also fluorocarbon gases that are used as propellants inside spray cans called aerosols. Many nations around the world have passed laws to make sure that we produce fewer aerosols.

Global Warming from the Dinosaur Age to our time.

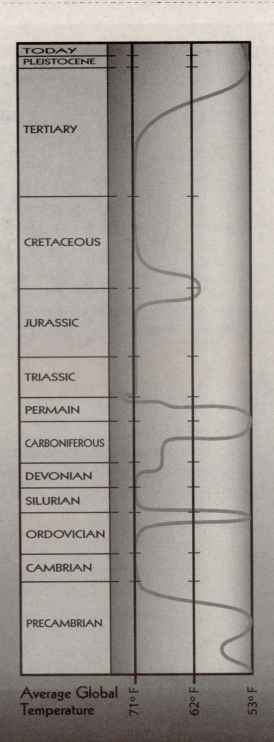

Emissions from industries and cars create smog—a smoky fog—over Los Angeles, California.

Is Help on the Way?

In the United States, the EPA helps collect information about global warming. It also tries to educate people about its effects.

Along with the IPCC, the EPA encourages industries to lower their emissions. It also wants industry to try to use technology, products, and practices that are better for the environment.

Industry is listening! In the United States, 29 states have made an Environmental Protection Plan.

How Will Global Warming Affect Our Health?

A warmer planet could be dangerous to the health of humans. Diseases spread by hot weather insects, such as mosquitoes, will become harder to control and spread to more areas.

People with asthma suffer from the heat. As we add greenhouse gases to the atmosphere, the lower atmosphere grows thicker and collects more pollutants.

Global warming is a global problem. Several nations created the IPCC, the Intergovernmental Panel on Climate Change, in 1988. This panel studies our global climate all over the world. In 1997, more than 160 countries signed an agreement called the Kyoto Protocol. These nations agreed to reduce their greenhouse gas emissions. The United States is not one of these nations.

Global warming could spread the diseases mosquitoes carry.

Is Global Warming a Fact?

Some scientists say that humans are not the primary cause of global warming. They believe that there may be other reasons why our planet has grown warmer.

They believe that what we call global warming is just a natural part of our planet's climate cycle. Since the beginning of life on Earth, the climate has changed from hot to cool and back again. At the coldest point in time, the Ice Age, much of the Northern Hemisphere was covered in glaciers. At the warmest times, there were no ice caps at the North or South Poles. Could we be headed toward another warm era in this pattern? It's hard to tell, as these patterns take hundreds of years to unfold.

If global warming continues, the Earth will get hotter and hotter.

Global warming may harm wildlife.

What Do We Know for Sure?

Global warming is a theory, not a fact. We can't be sure about its effects. But we can try to predict what is likely to happen. And from these predictions, we can take actions to help keep our Earth a safe place to live.

Scientists know for sure that we are producing many greenhouse gases. This makes it highly likely that humans are contributing to global warming. Some scientists predict that global warming will make Earth's weather wilder and more destructive in the future.

How Will Global Warming Affect the Environment?

As the planet warms, our environment will change. What might these changes be like?

The ice and snow at the North and South Poles could melt. This would raise sea levels all over the planet. Over the last century, the planet's sea level has risen 4-8 inches. This floods beaches and wetlands, and adds higher salinity to bays and rivers. Coasts become more vulnerable to storms.

When icebergs melt, they leave many animals homeless. The National Aeronautics and Space Administration (NASA) studied the ice cover in Greenland over a six year period. They noticed that Greenland's ice cover is thinning rapidly. Although it is harder to measure the change in a huge continent like Antarctica, the melting in Greenland is a bad sign.

Predictions About Our Weather

Although they cannot predict specifics, scientists have made some predictions for what will happen to our weather, if we continue to pump more greenhouse gases into the atmosphere.

Meteorologists are people who study climates. Along with other scientists, they worry about the harmful effects of global warming. Think about hurricanes, tornadoes, and other wild events. Think about the damage they cause.

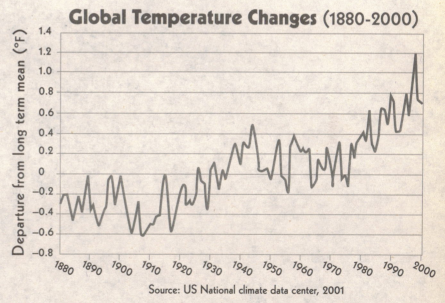

Source: US National climate data center, 2001

Temperatures have risen steadily over the 21st century.

How Will Global Warming Affect Our Weather?

Every year, hurricanes tear along the coast of the southern states and the Caribbean islands. They damage houses and harm people. These terrible storms occur in the tropics because they feed off warm air and water.

Global warming could produce terrible hurricanes.

Meteorologists fear that warmer global temperatures will allow storms to travel to places where they have never been before. They also fear that the storms could become even more **formidable** than any we have ever seen. These storms could reach cities in inland areas, which aren't equipped to deal with them.

Suggested levels for Guided Reading, DRA™, Lexile,® and Reading Recovery™ are provided in the Pearson Scott Foresman Leveling Guide.

LIFE ON MARS: THE REAL STORY

by Johanna Biviano
illustrated by Eric Reese

Genre	Comprehension Skill and Strategy
Fiction	• Draw Conclusions • Monitor and Fix Up

Scott Foresman Reading Street 4.5.5

PEARSON
Scott Foresman

ISBN 0-328-13486-4

Reader Response

1. What conclusion can you draw about how well Jim and Lisa know each other? Make a graphic organizer like the one below to show the clues that led you to conclusion.

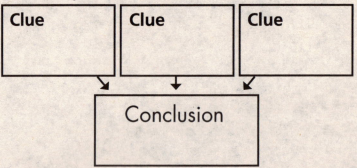

2. While you were reading, did you have any questions? What did you do to answer your questions?

3. On a separate sheet of paper, write down all of the words that were new to you as you read. If you think you can guess a word's meaning from the context, write down your guess. Look in the dictionary to see if your guess is correct. Make sure to write the correct meaning next to the word.

4. Lisa was afraid of Mars and Martians until she started learning about Mars. How are you able to get over your fears? Give an example of a fear you had and tell how you learned to deal with it.

Mars in Popular Culture

Everyone seems to love the idea of Martians! You can find them in books, movies, TV programs, and on the radio. In 1938, on Halloween night, Orson Wells broadcast a radio play, "The War of the Worlds," in which he pretended to broadcast a real Martian invasion. Thousands of people panicked, and fled for their lives!

In the 1960s, there was a TV comedy called "My Favorite Martian." This show was about a human-looking Martian who crashes his spaceship on Earth and befriends a man who hides him while he makes repairs on his ship. The Martian even had little antennae on his head!

Martians have attacked people in more than twenty films! These movies have thrilled audiences with special effects and frightening aliens, and some, like "Mars Attacks" and "Abbott and Costello Go to Mars," have made audiences laugh.

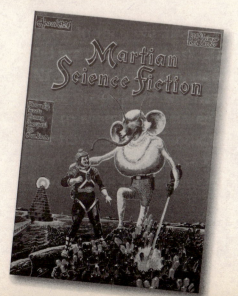

LIFE ON MARS: THE REAL STORY

by Johanna Biviano
illustrated by Eric Reese

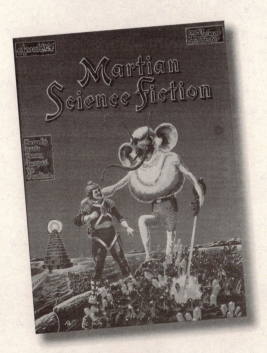

PEARSON
Scott Foresman

Editorial Offices: Glenview, Illinois • Parsippany, New Jersey • New York, New York
Sales Offices: Needham, Massachusetts • Duluth, Georgia • Glenview, Illinois
Coppell, Texas • Ontario, California • Mesa, Arizona

We looked through the telescope some more and then Dad and I went inside the house. Dad made hot chocolate. "You know what, Dad?" I said. "I'm not afraid of slimy green Martians anymore."

"That's good, Lisa!" Dad said. "Maybe someday you'll get to Mars for real."

"I hope so!" I said. "And you know what? I think that the next Martians anyone sees will probably be humans living and working on Mars! *We'll* be the Martians! And we're not slimy or green!"

23

I ran as fast as I could. I couldn't stop to catch my breath. My heart was pounding. There was a Martian running after me! The Martian was huge and green and slimy. It had six tentacles, three eyes, and a big blue mouth! Could I outrun it?

Then I felt it. Something wet wrapped itself around my ankle. I stumbled and fell. I couldn't move. But I could still scream.

"Don't eat me!" I shouted.

Then, to my horror, the Martian grabbed me by the shoulders with one of its big tentacles. I screamed again. "No! Leave me alone!"

To my surprise, it screamed back.

"Wake up, Lisa! Wake up, honey, it's just a dream! Open your eyes now," said Dad.

I rubbed my eyes. "I dreamed a Martian grabbed my ankle. It was going to eat me!"

Dad hugged me. Our dog, Hubert, leaped up on the bed and licked my face. "Lisa, you're watching too many scary movies," Dad said. "If there were huge scary Martians, we would know about them. And I know for a fact that there are no Martians in our house!"

"Okay, Dad," I said. "But can Hubert sleep on my bed tonight?"

Dad laughed. "Sure he can. Now get some sleep."

"The next morning at breakfast, my mom said, "Your father tells me you've been dreaming about Martians again."

"One Martian," I said. "He was invading Earth."

My mom smiled. "There's a better chance of us invading Mars. In fact, we already have."

"How did we do that?" I asked.

"Well, NASA, the government agency that runs our space program, has sent these robots called rovers to Mars. Rovers are small, wheeled vehicles that have cameras and can gather all sorts of information to send back to Earth."

"Did the rovers find Martians?" I asked.

That night, my dad took out our telescope and pointed it at the sky. "We can't see Mars, but it's up there," he told me.

I looked up at all the stars. I tried to imagine if there was life on any of them.

"You know, I read that there was a meteor from Mars that fell to Earth," Dad said. "It had tiny little organisms in it. They looked like bacteria. They were over a billion years old. They were also smaller than a human hair!"

"So that shows that life did exist on Mars once?" I asked. Dad nodded.

"We think it does," he told me. I was amazed.

"Do you think the Biosphere is proof that we can survive on a planet like Mars?" Mr. Teschi asked the class.

"I don't know," said Jim. "Mars has a lot of radiation in its soil. Could a Biosphere keep that out?"

"We don't know that, yet," Mr. Teschi said.

"And Biosphere 2 was on Earth," I said, "where all the plants grew in normal gravity. We don't know if a Biosphere would work on Mars. At least not yet."

Everyone in the class got a little quiet. I think we all wanted it to be possible to live and work on a place as cool as Mars.

Sunset on Mars

My mom gave me a hug. "They haven't found any life at all. At least not yet," she said.

I thought about Mars on my walk to school. My friend Jim caught up with me.

"Hey, Jim," I said, "did you know that we're exploring Mars?"

"Oh yeah? Well, what if the Martians don't want Mars to be explored?" Jim asked.

"Jim, there aren't any Martians," I said doubtfully.

"How do you know for sure? Maybe Martians are invisible," Jim said. "Let's ask our science teacher, Mr. Teschi. He knows everything."

That morning in science class, we asked Mr. Teschi about life on Mars.

"No one knows for sure," he said. "Why don't you two find out more about Mars for a science project?" That was something I was suddenly excited to do!

"Blast off to Mars!" Jim said.

Biosphere 2

At last, the day came for Jim and me to give our report. We told all the kids everything we knew about Mars. All the kids had questions. Finally, Mr. Teschi said, "You two have done an amazing job!"

Mr. Teschi told us that scientists were working hard to make it possible for humans to live on Mars. They were even trying to grow plants in space! Imagine trying to water a plant in zero gravity. The water would float around!

Then Mr. Teschi told us about Biosphere 2, a huge system of indoor environments sealed off from the outside world. Eight people had lived inside it for two years to learn how humans could survive without any help from the outside.

Mars, the red planet

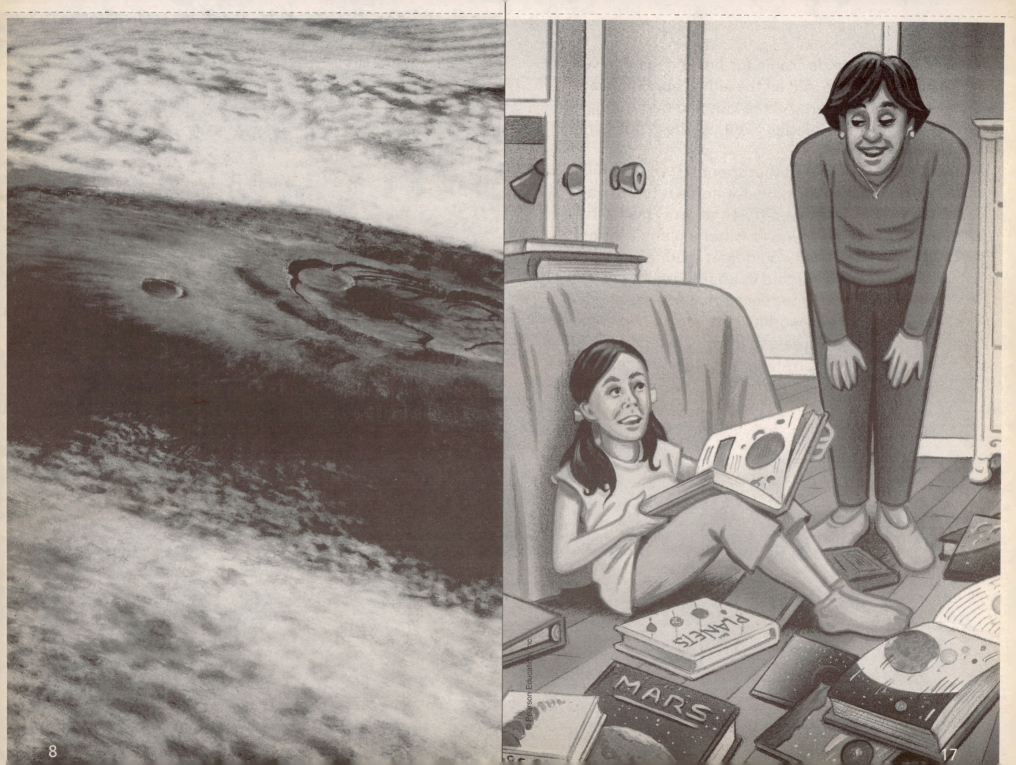

I couldn't wait to get to school. As soon as I saw Jim, I told him about my dream. I thought Jim might laugh at me, but instead he nodded. " Someday, maybe we will get to Mars," he told me. "I wish I had had that dream too!"

"Well, you were in it!" I told him.

All that week we worked on our report about Mars. We couldn't wait to give our talk in front of the whole science class! And a funny thing happened. The more I learned about Mars, the more my image of a slimy green Martian started to fade.

When I told my mom this, she smiled. "When you're afraid of something, sometimes the best thing to do is to learn all you can about it," she said. "I'm proud of you."

At the library, Jim and I got lots of books about Mars. We learned so many new things!

That night, when I fell asleep, I dreamed I was on Mars with Jim! I had read that humans couldn't breathe the thin air and that Mars was – 82°F, which was freezing. But in my dream, we were warm and breathing easily. We were riding a rover too! "I feel so light," I said. Jim told me that was because there was less gravity on Mars.

I know all sorts of impossible things can happen in a dream. And this was one dream from which I didn't want to wake up.

Olympus Mons is the highest peak on Mars.

Jim and I traveled across the dusty soil. Mars was so different from Earth! There weren't any oceans, trees, or plants. It looked like one big desert. Just then, we came to a huge series of canyons, rilles, and trenches.

"I read about this!" I said excitedly. "This is the Valles Marineres. And it's 2,500 miles long! That's as big as the United States!"

Just then, I heard a rumbling sound. "What was that?" I asked. I was a little scared. "Is it a—Martian?"

A Mars exploration rover

Suddenly, everything on Mars was getting hazy. "Lisa!" I heard, and the voice sounded familiar. I shut my eyes for a second. When I opened them again, I was in my bed on planet Earth! My parents were in my room.

"I dreamed I was on Mars!" I said. "And it was great!"

I was hungry, but nothing was growing on Mars, and there sure weren't any supermarkets. "Here," Jim said. He took a big chunk of chocolate out of his pocket and handed me half.

"Where did that come from?" I asked. Jim told me to remember that this was a dream. Anything could happen.

I looked at the sky. I was lonely for Earth. "How would we even know life if we found it?" I asked Jim. "What should we be looking for?"

"All life forms that we know of have carbon," Jim said. "Maybe we can find fossils. They would tell us if there was life here a long time ago." He looked down at Mars's surface. "I don't see any fossils, though, do you?" He was very disappointed, and so was I.

"If Mars doesn't have life, why do we care about it?" I asked.

Jim looked thoughtful. "Well, if Earth becomes too polluted, we might want to have the option of living on another planet."

"That's true," I said. "And if we could figure out how to live here, we could learn more about Mars firsthand. We wouldn't have to rely on a rover. We could learn about how life begins on a planet, and if there could be life on other planets."

Jim looked scared too. The sound grew louder. Suddenly, we saw what was making that noise. Two rovers were heading towards us. We could see their names printed along their sides: Spirit and Opportunity. Those were the same two rovers that had landed on Mars on January 4, 2003. They were collecting soil samples and taking pictures.

"Let's go this way," Jim said. "I see something over there."

We came to an area that looked like a dried stream. "There are supposed to be big sheets of ice underneath the surface of Mars," Jim said. "Do you think there could be something living in the ice? Like Martians?"

"Wait," I said. "Back on Earth, scientists have found microscopic organisms that don't need the sun's energy to survive. They can be as deep as 3,300 feet below the surface, hibernating inside layers of frozen ice and soil. If they're thawed, these organisms come back to life! Could Mars have this kind of life?"

"It could if Mars had water!" Jim said excitedly.

Both of us stared at the dried stream bed. Living things had been found in freezing temperatures on Earth. Maybe they would also be found here! I wasn't thinking about slimy Martians anymore. I was thinking of tiny life forms. And this time, I wished I could see them!

Scientists believe that if there is life on Mars, it will be in the water under the surface.

Suggested levels for Guided Reading, DRA™, Lexile,® and Reading Recovery™ are provided in the Pearson Scott Foresman Leveling Guide.

Social Studies

The Women's Movement

Genre	Comprehension Skill and Strategy	Text Features
Nonfiction	• Cause and Effect • Answer Questions	• Captions • Diagram • Map • Glossary

Scott Foresman Reading Street 4.6.1

PEARSON
Scott Foresman

scottforesman.com

ISBN 0-328-13489-9

9 780328 134892

by Lara Bove

Reader Response

1. Using a chart similar to the one below, show what caused suffragists to be jailed. What were some effects of suffragists being jailed?

Cause	Effect

2. What were bloomers? How can you find out more about bloomers?

3. Look through the book and find examples of verbs ending in –ing. Pick two sentences with –ing endings and try to rewrite them without using –ing.

4. Use the map on pages 12 and 13 to find out which states allowed women to vote between 1890 and 1900.

Glossary

abolitionists *n.* people who actively tried to end slavery.

attire *n.* clothing; what a person wears.

cumbersome *adj.* difficult to deal with.

rivals *n.* people who want and try to get the same thing as another or do better than another; competitor.

spectators *n.* people who are watching an event.

suffrage *n.* the right to vote.

suffragists *n.* people who actively tried to get women the right to vote.

The Women's Movement

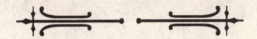

by Lara Bove

Editorial Offices: Glenview, Illinois • Parsippany, New Jersey • New York, New York
Sales Offices: Needham, Massachusetts • Duluth, Georgia • Glenview, Illinois
Coppell, Texas • Ontario, California • Mesa, Arizona

Here's How to Do It!

1. Think of an issue that is important to you. You might want to improve education for the poor. You might want to help care for homeless people. Or you may have another entirely different idea.
2. Look back at the three activist steps on page 22. Then think about and write down your answers to these questions.
- Who are you trying to make aware of the issue? How will you make them aware?
- Why is change needed? How can you help people see this?
- What leaders need to be convinced? How will you do this?
3. How will things be better if your changes are made? Write a paragraph describing how the world will be better.
4. Make a plan of action. Outline the steps you will take to change your classroom or world. Then put your plan into action!

Now Try This

Be an Activist

An activist is someone who tries to change society or government. Because many people do not like change, activists are not always popular. Activists, however, can be recognized for their courage.

An activist does three things:
1. Makes people aware of an issue.
2. Helps people see that change is needed.
3. Convinces the leadership to make the change.

Women's Suffrage

Voting rights among men and women have not always been equal. While many white men have always had the right to vote, women's voting rights have been restricted in terms of where they could vote and in which elections. In 1869 women could vote in Wyoming. At that time Wyoming was only a territory. It became a state in 1890 and gave women full voting rights, including voting for President of the United States. Soon other western states such as Colorado, Idaho, and Utah gave women the right to vote too.

In other states women could vote in some local elections. In 1920 the Nineteenth Amendment, or improvement, to the U.S. Constitution became law. That gave women the right to vote in all elections.

Women and some men worked hard to make voting rights equal for everyone. Their work is known as the women's **suffrage** movement. Suffrage is the right to vote.

Women vote in Wyoming Territory.

Seneca Falls

The women's suffrage movement began in Seneca Falls, New York. The year was 1848, and Elizabeth Cady Stanton and Lucretia Mott, two leaders in women's rights, organized a meeting. They put a notice in the newspaper to let people know about the meeting. They called it a women's rights convention.

The Women's Rights Convention took place over two days, and three hundred people attended. Many women who came brought their husbands with them. A few women **suffragists** read speeches. Frederick Douglass, an enslaved man who had escaped to freedom, also spoke. A well-known speaker, he was a powerful man in the fight to end slavery. Douglass spoke strongly in support of women's rights.

The newspapers covered the convention, but the stories were not favorable. In general, Americans at that time did not think women should be voting, and this included most women. Many American women saw their role as being mothers and wives. They did not think that they needed to vote.

Elizabeth Cady Stanton

The suffragists did not give up. They held more protests in August 1918. The police arrested them, and the newspapers showed pictures of the prisoners. The women began wearing black armbands. They were saying that justice was dead.

The amendment finally passed in both the House and the Senate in June 1919. The women still had a lot of work to do. They needed thirty-six states to ratify, or approve, the amendment.

The first three states passed the amendment in June 1919. Those states were Wisconsin, Illinois, and Michigan. The last state to pass the amendment was Tennessee, on August 18, 1920. Women had finally won the right to vote. It was a long struggle—only one woman who had attended the Seneca Falls convention was still alive. She was the only one to live to see the dream become reality.

Prisoners Gain Public Support

The women continued to picket, and things got much worse. The police continued to arrest them, and the judges gave harsher sentences. By the fall some women were sent to jail for sixty days.

The conditions in jail were horrific. The women were treated roughly, even abused, and their food was rotten and sometimes had worms inside.

This did not seem to change the attitude of politicians, since people who picketed for this cause were still being arrested. Suffragists worked hard to let the public know how badly they were being treated, and people became more and more sympathetic to the cause.

At the end of November 1917, the prisoners were all released, but the suffragists still had not completed their task.

In January 1918 the House passed the Susan B. Anthony Amendment, but it did not pass in the Senate. Another year would go by before that would happen.

Women celebrate their right to vote.

At the end of the two days, the convention passed many resolutions, or goals, that the women wanted to achieve. One goal was that women should have the right to vote. Since laws affected women and men alike, women wanted to take part in electing the people who passed the laws. They would have to work hard to make this possible.

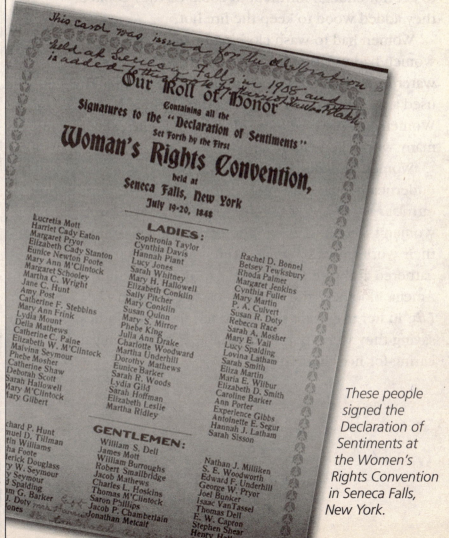

These people signed the Declaration of Sentiments at the Women's Rights Convention in Seneca Falls, New York.

Clothing

In the 1800s fashion was strict. The clothes women wore made it difficult for them to do their work, and they worked hard. Women cooked on wood and coal stoves. They collected wood, put it in the stove, and made a fire. They waited for the fire to get hot enough for them to cook. As they cooked, they added wood to keep the fire hot.

Women had to wash clothing by hand. Some women had water pumps, but others had to carry water from a well or stream to do their washing. They used a washboard and scrubbed the clothing by hand. Women also sewed clothing for their families, and many worked on family farms.

Women wore long, heavy dresses with petticoats underneath. Because women's fashion was so **cumbersome** and got in the way of their work, some women thought wearing bloomers would make their work easier. Bloomers were long, baggy pants gathered at the ankle. Bloomers were named after Amelia Bloomer, who edited a magazine called *The Lily*. In her magazine she described the new clothes, saying they were more comfortable for gardening and caring for her children.

Because the women could not be charged with picketing, which was a legal activity, they were charged with obstructing traffic. The women were found guilty and were fined twenty-five dollars each. They chose to serve three days in jail rather than pay the fine.

Less than a week later, the pickets began again. The women were again arrested. In the end these women also spent three days in jail.

Picketing at the White House

Soon women began picketing in front of the White House. Their first picket was on January 10, 1917, and after that they came almost every Monday through Saturday. The women picketed in all kinds of weather. In the beginning, President Wilson treated them quite well. He smiled as he drove by them and offered them coffee on cold days.

In April 1917 the United States officially declared war on Germany, and once again, people asked the suffragists to wait for the war to end. They would not wait. They continued their daily pickets at the White House.

By June of 1917 the President was not as friendly with the picketers. When he had Russian diplomats visiting, the marchers carried a banner that embarrassed him. It said that the United States was not a democracy. After all, women couldn't vote.

Wilson said that the women had to stop picketing, and if they did not they would be arrested. Alice Paul consulted with lawyers, who said the women had a legal right to picket. The women continued to picket, and they were arrested. In fact, more than twenty women were arrested in one week.

Women picket for their rights in front of the White House.

Elizabeth Cady Stanton loved bloomers. She said that women needed more freedom with their attire. Bloomers gave women more freedom to move about.

Today it seems silly that people would have been upset by women wearing bloomers, but they were. In fact the activists gave up wearing bloomers by 1854 because they did not want people to focus on what they were wearing. They wanted people to listen to what they were saying. Since they were asking for the right to vote, women knew they needed voting men to give them that right.

This woman is wearing bloomers.

Slavery And The Women's Movement

Even in the 1800s there were more serious problems than the clothing women wore. Slavery was still legal in half the country.

Many of the women's rights activists were also **abolitionists.** This means they believed slavery should be abolished, or stopped. A woman named Sojourner Truth had been an enslaved person. She had escaped to New York and become a leader in the fight to end slavery. Though she could not read or write, she was a powerful speaker.

In 1851 Sojourner Truth spoke at a women's rights convention in Ohio. No one wrote down her words while she spoke. Later someone wrote it down from memory. In her speech titled "Ain't I a Woman?" she said that if a man says women should be helped into carriages, lifted over ditches, and given the best of everything, why hasn't she been helped. "Ain't I a woman?" she asked.

Sojourner Truth continued to support women's rights. In 1853 she spoke in New York City. This time many **rivals** came. They sat in the meeting, making a lot of noise so no one could hear the speakers. Sojourner Truth put them in their place. She spoke to them, telling them they could not stop the women's movement, and she promised that women would get their rights.

The suffragists held parades in New York City and Washington, D.C. Thousands of people marched in one parade in New York City. Sadly, some of the **spectators** caused some trouble for the people marching in the parade. A crowd of people in the middle of the street would not let the marchers pass. The crowd yelled and spit at the marchers, and they even tripped and shoved them. One hundred marchers ended up in the hospital, but the police did not do anything. All of this was printed in the newspapers.

In 1914 World War I began. The suffragists did not want to see the war stop their movement. They had waited during the Civil War, and when that war ended, they got nothing. So this time they persevered. President Woodrow Wilson ran for a second term in 1916. He made campaign promises to keep the United States out of the war.

Wilson also promised Carrie Chapman Catt that he would support women's suffrage, but it was not his priority. Nevertheless, he gained women's support. Wilson apparently did fairly well with female voters in the dozen or so states that allowed women to vote in 1916.

Signs of Success

As you know, in Wyoming, women could vote beginning in 1869, when Wyoming was a territory. When Wyoming became a state in 1890, it was the first state with women's suffrage. Three years later, Colorado gave women voting rights. Carrie Chapman Catt, an active suffragist, worked to get women's suffrage in the West, and she succeeded in Utah and Idaho.

Though it took a few years, several other western states gave women voting rights as well. Women got voting rights in Washington State in 1910. The next year women in California got the vote. Oregon, Arizona, and Kansas passed women's suffrage in 1912.

Women's suffrage parade, New York City, 1912

Sojourner Truth

People Who Made It Happen

Susan B. Anthony

In 1872 Susan B. Anthony voted illegally. Three weeks later, on Thanksgiving Day, a federal marshal came to her home and arrested her. She was released after her lawyer posted bail, but her trial was rigged and she was found guilty. She was fined one hundred dollars. Anthony refused to pay the fine, and the government never tried to collect it.

Lucy Stone

Lucy Stone married Henry Blackwell in 1855. She did not take his last name, which was rarely done in the 1850s. In fact she could not sign legal documents as Lucy Stone. Stone was ahead of her time in other ways. She said she would not pay taxes on her home since she couldn't vote. She said it was taxation without representation. The state took some of her furniture as payment for the taxes.

Lucy Stone

How an Amendment To The Constitution Is Ratified

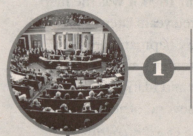

1 An amendment goes to the House of Representatives. Two-thirds of the representatives must pass it. If they do not, it stops there.

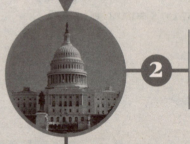

2 If it passes in the House, it goes to the U.S. Senate. Two-thirds of the senators must pass it. If they do not, it stops there.

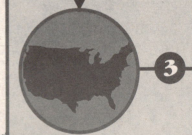

3 If it passes in the Senate, it goes to the state legislatures. Three-fourths of the legislatures must pass it. If they do not, it is rejected.

There were only forty-eight states in 1920. Today there are fifty states. So today it takes thirty-eight states to ratify, or approve, an amendment.

The NWSA

The NWSA held its first meeting in 1869. In Washington, D.C., Susan B. Anthony asked Congress to pass a sixteenth amendment to the Constitution which would give women the right to vote. Soon it was being called the Susan B. Anthony Amendment.

Congress considered the amendment in 1878, nine years after Anthony first asked for it. When Senator Sargent, from California, introduced the amendment, it did not pass.

The women, however, did not give up. They traveled all across the country making speeches, leading marches, and circulating petitions. Because there were no radios or televisions in the late 1800s, people could not hear or see the speakers unless they went in person. Without planes, cars, or sometimes even paved roads, the suffragists traveled by horse-drawn carriages and on trains. They did not let the difficulty of travel stop them because they believed so strongly in their cause.

The women's movement merged into one group in 1890, and this time the group was called the National American Woman Suffrage Association (NAWSA). Elizabeth Cady Stanton was its first president.

Alice Paul

Alice Paul grew up in a Quaker home. She went to college and then graduate school. That level of education was unusual for women at the time. In 1906 Paul went to England where she joined the women's suffrage movement and was jailed three times for her beliefs. In 1909 she came back to the United States, became a suffragist leader, and led marches and other protests. She went to jail three more times and even staged a hunger strike in jail.

Lucretia Mott

Lucretia Mott grew up in Boston, Massachusetts, and became a teacher. Her interest in the women's rights movement first began when she learned that she would be paid half the salary that a male teacher would be paid. Mott also worked to end slavery. She and her husband helped many runaway slaves along the Underground Railroad, a network of safe places for enslaved people to stay as they escaped north to freedom.

Alice Paul   *Lucretia Mott*

A Movement Tested And Divided

In the 1850s Americans were afraid a war would break out. They did not want to think about women's rights. They were thinking about slavery and war.

The Civil War began in 1861, when Abraham Lincoln was President. President Lincoln made a deal with the suffragists, promising to support them after the war. The war ended in 1865, and a few days later, President Lincoln was killed. Andrew Johnson became president, but he did not support women's rights.

The suffragists lost hope in the federal government. Things got even worse when the leaders of the women's rights movement ended up forming two different groups. Lucy Stone started the American Woman Suffrage Association (AWSA). Elizabeth Cady Stanton and Susan B. Anthony started the National Woman Suffrage Association (NWSA).

The AWSA had both women and men as members. They worked at the state level, trying to get each state to grant suffrage to women. The NWSA was thought of as a more extreme organization than the AWSA. It allowed only women as members, and it sought to change federal laws. The NWSA felt it was more effective to focus on passing federal laws, rather than trying to change laws in each state.

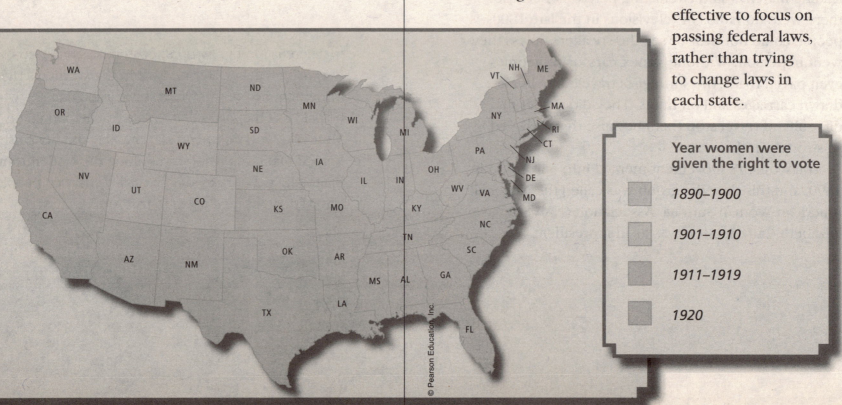

Year women were given the right to vote

- 1890–1900
- 1901–1910
- 1911–1919
- 1920

Biography

JIM THORPE
The Greatest Athlete in the World

by Eric Oatman

Genre	Comprehension Skill and Strategy	Text Features
Nonfiction	• Fact and Opinion • Text Structure	• Map • Captions • Heads • Glossary

Scott Foresman Reading Street 4.6.2

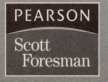

ISBN 0-328-13492-9

scottforesman.com

Reader Response

1. King Gustav V told Jim that he was the greatest athlete in the world. Was the King giving his opinion or stating a fact? Find at least two other facts and two other opinions in the book. Write your findings in a chart similar to the one below. You may include the statement given above.

Fact	Opinion

2. Most authors of biographies write them in time order—chronologically. List the important events in Jim Thorpe's life in that order.

3. What are the different meanings of the words *land* and *reservation*?

4. What information did you learn from one of this book's captions that is not in the main text?

Glossary

amateurs *n.* athletes who play without being paid.

boarding schools *n.* schools with buildings where students live during the school term.

decathlon *n.* a ten-event track and field contest.

manual *adj.* done with the hands.

pentathlon *n.* a five-event track and field contest.

semiprofessional *adj.* getting paid to play a sport part-time.

reservation *n.* land set aside by the government for a special purpose.

society *n.* the people of any particular time or place.

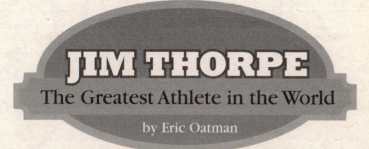

JIM THORPE
The Greatest Athlete in the World

by Eric Oatman

PEARSON
Scott Foresman

Editorial Offices: Glenview, Illinois • Parsippany, New Jersey • New York, New York
Sales Offices: Needham, Massachusetts • Duluth, Georgia • Glenview, Illinois
Coppell, Texas • Ontario, California • Mesa, Arizona

Now Try This

Sports World

Jim Thorpe was a top performer in just about every sport he tried. As you know he was a track and field star. He was also excellent at baseball, basketball, ice hockey, and tennis. He made golfing and figure skating look easy.

How much do you know about these sports and others? Here's your chance to find out!

Research the history of a sport you want to learn about. Jot down your answers to as many of these questions as you can:

- Who invented the sport?
- What equipment is needed to play it?
- Is the sport played in other countries? Where is it played? Do Americans play the sport? If so, when did they begin playing it, and where?
- Why do people like to play the sport or watch it?
- What fun facts might call people's attention to the sport?

Turn what you learn into an advertisement. Make a poster to persuade people to play or watch your sport. Attach a picture of someone playing it. Cut it out from a magazine, download it, or draw one. Use the poster on the next page as a model. After you have finished, display your poster so your classmates can learn about the sport and what makes it fun!

~ Jim Thorpe ~

One day, in 1907, in Carlisle, Pennsylvania, a young man walked past several high jumpers and their coach. The jumpers were having trouble getting over the bar.

The young man asked the coach if he could try. The coach was surprised that he wanted to try in work clothes—overalls and heavy work boots—but the coach said he could. He warned the young man that the bar was almost six feet off the ground. The young man stepped back, ran at the bar, and cleared it easily.

The coach, a man named Pop Warner, could not believe it! He immediately wanted the young man on his track team.

The young man's name was Jim Thorpe. Soon he was wearing the uniform of the Carlisle Indian Industrial School, and winning almost every event he entered.

Jim Thorpe loved to compete.

~ Chasing Horses ~

Jim was born on May 28, 1887, near Prague, Oklahoma. At the time, Oklahoma wasn't a state, but was called Indian Territory. The Thorpes, who were Native Americans, lived there on land reserved for members of their nation, the Sauk and Fox.

Jim's ancestors were not all Native Americans. His father was part Irish, and his mother was part French. Jim's mother and father were brought up as Native Americans, and so were Jim and his ten brothers and sisters. No one could have been more proud of his Native American roots than Jim.

In work that involved the whole family, Jim's father trained and sold horses. When a horse broke away, Jim would chase and catch it. Those long sprints helped make him stronger and build stamina, the ability to keep going when everyone else is too tired.

He was always willing to take on a physical challenge. He would race his twin brother Charlie from tree to tree, or he would dare his friends to try to throw a stone or hit a baseball farther than he could. When he hunted and fished, he wanted to be the one to bring home the biggest deer and the largest fish. Sometimes he ran the twenty miles from his home to the school and back again at the end of the day.

Jim hurls a heavy metal ball in the shot put event at the 1912 Olympic Games in Stockholm, Sweden.

In 1950 nearly four hundred sportswriters and broadcasters named Jim the most outstanding athlete of the first half of the twentieth century. A movie about his life, *Jim Thorpe All American,* was released in 1951.

Jim died on March 28, 1953, in California. In 1954 two Pennsylvania towns agreed to merge and call the new town Jim Thorpe. Jim is buried there, in the only town in the United States believed to have been named after an athlete.

After his death, recognition of Jim's greatness kept coming. In 1963 he was elected to the National Football League Hall of Fame. In 1982 the IOC realized that it had broken its own rules in taking Jim's medals away and gave copies of them to his family in 1983. Today the college football award for the Best Defensive Back is named after Jim Thorpe.

Honors such as these make it clear that the man who stunned Pop Warner in 1907 with his high jumping skill was one of a kind. He was the greatest athlete that America has ever produced.

Jim led Carlisle's football team to victory after victory, making him the nation's most famous football player.

~ The Sauk and Fox Nation ~

Jim Thorpe's roots were in the Sauk and Fox Nation. Until the early 1700s, the Sauk and the Fox were neighbors in the forests of northern Michigan. Driven west by other Native American nations and white settlers, they moved to separate villages on the Illinois side of the Mississippi River. During the early 1800s, they were forced west into Iowa and then into Kansas. They joined as the Sauk and Fox Nation after 1869, when they were moved to Indian Territory which is now Oklahoma. Today fewer than four thousand Sauk and Fox live on or near reservations in Iowa, Kansas, Missouri, and Oklahoma.

In 1880 sixty different nations lived in the Indian Territory. By law, only Native Americans could live there, but during the 1870s and 1880s, white settlers came. At first, U.S. soldiers drove them away, but then the U.S. government changed its mind and let settlers claim western parts of the territory.

Soon after Jim was born, the government divided the land reserved for Native Americans. It gave a 160-acre lot to each family and sold any leftover land. The goal was to turn all Native Americans into farmers. This was because, at the time, most Americans were farmers, and the government wanted Native Americans to adopt the ways of American **society.**

Jim Thorpe is ready to tackle.

In 1932 U.S. Vice-President Charles Curtis invited Jim to watch the opening ceremonies of that year's summer Olympics in Los Angeles. Like Jim, Curtis was part Native American.

~ Football and Farewell ~

Jim liked football better than baseball. He played for professional football's best team, the Canton (Ohio) Bulldogs, where Jim then stayed as a player and coach until 1920.

He played football for eight more years. He wore the uniforms of the New York Giants, the Chicago Cardinals, and the Cleveland Tigers. When he retired, he was forty-one years old.

Life after football was difficult for Jim. For someone who had known only sports, it wasn't easy to find work. The Great Depression also made it hard because during this time, many people could not find jobs.

In 1932, the Depression's worst year, U.S. Vice-President Charles Curtis invited Jim to attend the Olympics in Los Angeles. When he arrived, the 105,000 people in the stadium rose to applaud him.

Jim moved many times during the 1930s and 1940s. He worked as an actor in California and on the recreation staff of the Chicago Park District. He helped write a book on the history of the Olympics, became active in the affairs of the Sauk and Fox Nation, and lectured on Native Americans and sports.

But most Native Americans didn't want to be "Americanized." They preferred to live on reservations, where land belonged to the entire nation. They wanted to maintain their own customs, languages, and beliefs, but, unfortunately, they had little choice. By chopping up the land into lots, the U.S. government did away with some of the Native American customs.

In 1889 the states of Texas, Kansas, Missouri, and Arkansas outlined Indian Territory. At this time the Sauk and Fox Nation owned 750,000 acres of land. Today the Sauk and Fox have only eight hundred acres left. Indian Territory became part of the state of Oklahoma in 1907.

~Indian Territory in 1889~

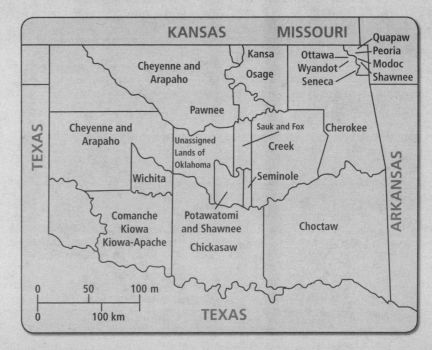

As part of the plan to bring Native Americans into the mainstream of American life, the government set up **boarding schools.** Their goal was to teach Native American children to speak English, learn a trade, practice farming, and leave their nation's ways behind them. Jim was only six years old when he was sent to live at a boarding school on the Sauk and Fox **reservation.** When he was nine, his twin brother, Charlie, died of pneumonia.

Before and after: Like many Carlisle students, Thomas Torlino, of the Diné, arrived at the school in Native American dress. The attempt to "Americanize" him began with a change of clothing and a new haircut.

Jim sent his medals and cup to IOC headquarters in Switzerland, where they gathered dust. The public didn't seem to care. They loved Jim and wanted to see him play. Pro teams fought to hire him. He played major league baseball for six years. He played in the outfield for the New York Giants, the Cincinnati Reds, and the Boston Braves.

~ Homecoming ~

Returning to the United States, Jim found even more fame. About fifteen thousand people had turned out in Carlisle, Pennsylvania, to welcome him home. A week later, he was honored at a parade in New York City and then another parade in Philadelphia. Jim had left the United States as the most famous football player in the nation, and had returned as its most famous all-around athlete.

That fall Jim was once more the power behind Carlisle's victories on the football field. His team played the U.S. Military Academy (Army) on Thanksgiving Day. In one play, he ran the length of the field—one hundred yards—to score a touchdown. Referees called the play back because a Carlisle player had made an illegal move. On the very next play, Jim ran ninety-seven yards for a touchdown, and this time it counted. The final score was Carlisle 27, Army 6. Jim had scored 22 of those points. Once again, Jim was named to the nation's All-American team.

Sadly, Jim's world came crashing down around him in January 1913. A newspaper reported that he had been paid to play semi professional baseball in 1909 and 1910. Olympic rules banned professional athletes from competing against **amateurs.** Jim had known nothing about these rules, but the International Olympic Committee (IOC) demanded that he had to return his gold medals.

Jim never got over his brother's death and ran away from the school many times. When he was twelve, to keep him in school, his parents sent him to another boarding school farther from home. His mother died while he was there, and he ran away again to work on a horse ranch for a few years.

In 1904, when Jim was seventeen, his father persuaded him to finish his education at the Carlisle Indian Industrial School in Pennsylvania, the nation's oldest boarding school for Native Americans. It educated about one thousand children who came from more than seventy Native American nations, from grade school through high school.

At school students were not allowed to speak their native languages. They were taught academic subjects in the morning, and in the afternoons, the boys were taught industrial arts—carpentry, blacksmithing, and the types of **manual** labor used in farming. Girls learned domestic arts, such as sewing and baking.

Shortly after Jim entered Carlisle, his father died. Jim returned to Indian Territory and found work on a farm, but Carlisle lured him back in 1907, when he was twenty years old. That was the year that Pop Warner—and Jim—learned that the young man from Oklahoma had a special gift for sports.

~ The Man Who Invented Modern Football ~

Jim Thorpe's first coach was Glenn "Pop" Warner. Warner coached for many years at many colleges. His teams won three times more games than the number they lost.

Warner was twenty-two years old before he played his first game of football. His teammates at Cornell University called him "Pop" because he was older than any of them. After graduating in 1894, Warner became a coach and worked to improve the sport of football. He taught kickers how to make the ball spiral and sail through the air. He had his players line up with one hand on the ground instead of two. He created shoulder pads and thigh pads to protect the players, and had numbers sewn onto their jerseys. These things had never been done by anyone before.

Jim wanted to play football, even though he seemed to be best at track and field events. He ran, jumped hurdles, high jumped, long jumped, and threw the discus, shot put, and javelin. Pop Warner, however, didn't think that Jim, at 144 pounds, was heavy enough to play college football. Although Carlisle wasn't a college, many of its athletes, like Jim, were old enough to be in college, so most of the school's opponents were college teams. In 1908, Warner finally gave in, and Jim played as a substitute on the football team.

Modern-day pentathlete

The pentathlon that Jim Thorpe ran was unlike the modern version. The modern pentathlon tests competitors' skills in horseback riding, pistol shooting, fencing, swimming, and cross-country running.

A month after the Lafayette track and field meet, Jim sailed to Europe to compete in the 1912 Olympic Games being held in Stockholm, Sweden. Although legend has it that Jim didn't train while on the ship, he ran laps and exercised each day with the rest of the U.S. team.

Once he got to Stockholm, Jim was almost a one-man track team. He competed in two track competitions, the **pentathlon,** which had five events, and the **decathlon,** which had ten events.

The pentathlon required him to compete in the long jump, the javelin throw, the 200-meter dash, the discus throw, and the 1,500-meter run. In the decathlon, Jim faced the long jump, discus, and javelin events again. The seven other events included in this competition were the shot put, the high jump, and the pole vault; the 100-meter, 400-meter, and 1,500-meter foot races; and the 110-meter hurdles.

Jim swept both contests. He earned 8,412 points out of a possible top score of ten thousand in the decathlon, making this performance a record that would not be broken for fifteen years.

After Jim won the decathlon, Sweden's King Gustav V, in praising Jim as the greatest athlete in the world, gave him a drinking cup lined with gold and jewels in the shape of a Viking ship.

Jim left Carlisle in 1909 to play two seasons of **semiprofessional** baseball in North Carolina. That was not usual for college players; the money was good, and like today, college athletes weren't allowed to play for money.

In 1911 Pop Warner called Jim back to Carlisle. Jim had put on forty pounds of muscle— just what he needed, Pop felt, to excel at football.

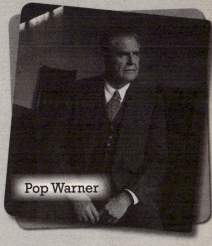
Pop Warner

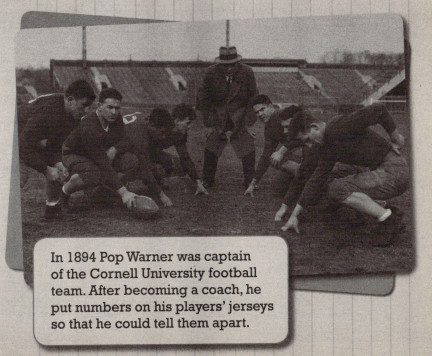
In 1894 Pop Warner was captain of the Cornell University football team. After becoming a coach, he put numbers on his players' jerseys so that he could tell them apart.

Jim excelled at football, indeed. As a halfback, he carried the ball from touchdown to touchdown. No one was better at punting or kicking the ball over a goalpost. On defense, he was one of the team's top tacklers.

In front of a crowd of thirty thousand people at Harvard College, Jim won fame as a football player. That afternoon Jim made a six-point touchdown and four three-point field goals. When the game was over, Harvard had put fifteen points on the scoreboard, and Jim had scored all of Carlisle's eighteen points to win the game. After the season's end, he was named an All-American, one of the best players in the entire country.

Jim also continued to excel at track and field events. Harold Bruce was the track coach at Lafayette College in Easton, Pennsylvania. His team was one of the best in the country. In May 1912, he invited the Carlisle track team to compete at a meet in Easton. The day of the meet, Bruce and forty members of his track team went to the train station to welcome the Carlisle team, and there they saw Warner get off the train with five young men.

When Bruce asked where Warner's athletes were, Warner said they were standing right next to him.

Bruce could not believe what he was hearing. This was an important day at Lafayette, and the school's graduates were visiting from all over the country. His team had expected a hard-fought meet, but Warner's team of five didn't seem like much of a challenge.

Bruce told Warner that he had forty-six men on his team and that there were eleven events. He said that Warner's five team members would not stand a chance. Not only that, he said the spectators would be bored silly!

Warner had confidence—Bruce's comments did not scare him.

Jim won five events that day and came in third in one other. Two of his teammates finished first and second in three races, and another teammate won the high hurdles. The final score: Carlisle 71, Lafayette 41.

Jim competes in the track and field broad jump event.

Suggested levels for Guided Reading, DRA,™ Lexile,® and Reading Recovery™ are provided in the Pearson Scott Foresman Leveling Guide.

Genre	Comprehension Skill and Strategy
Fiction	• Literary Elements: Theme • Summarize

Scott Foresman Reading Street 4.6.3

ISBN 0-328-13495-3

9 780328 134953

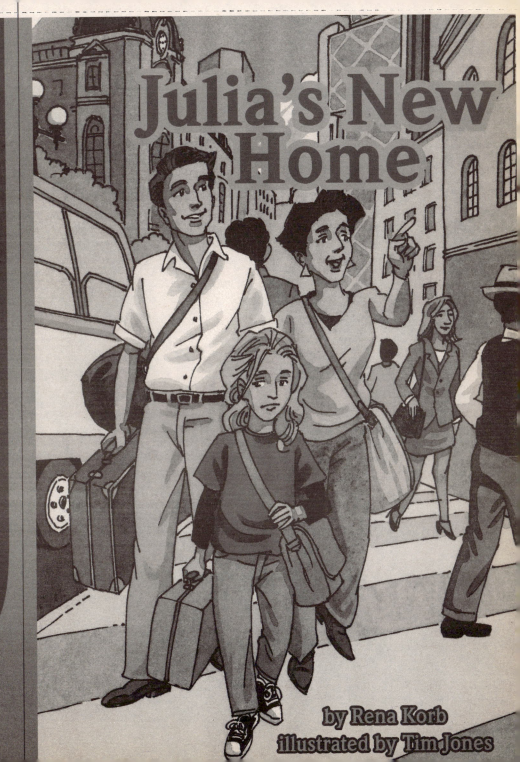

Julia's New Home

by Rena Korb
illustrated by Tim Jones

Reader Response

1. On page 19, Julia realizes that she has figured out the secret to living in Santiago? What is the secret?

2. Summarize the adventures that Julia and her mother have in Santiago.

3. Read the first page of the book. What is a high-rise apartment? How can you tell?

4. Give one example of a way that Julia finds life the same in Chile as it is back home in Boston. Give one example of a way that she finds life different.

The City of Santiago

In 1541 a Spanish explorer named Pedro de Valdivia built a new city along the Mapocho River. He named the settlement Santiago. The surrounding land was called Chile. For close to 300 years, the land was ruled by Spanish governors.

By the early 1800s, the people of Chile wanted to be free from Spain. Between 1810 and 1818, Chileans fought the War of Independence. After the victory, Santiago became the new capital of the country of Chile.

Today, Santiago is a modern, exciting city with a population of more than five million. Santiago has a subway system, several airports, many banks and businesses, and a stock exchange.

The city also is rich in culture. Chileans and tourists alike enjoy visiting the city's museums, sightseeing among the old Spanish buildings, or simply relaxing in the beautiful parks.

Julia's New Home

by Rena Korb
illustrated by Tim Jones

Editorial Offices: Glenview, Illinois • Parsippany, New Jersey • New York, New York
Sales Offices: Needham, Massachusetts • Duluth, Georgia • Glenview, Illinois
Coppell, Texas • Ontario, California • Mesa, Arizona

"*Me gusta tu camisa,*" Isabel said.

Julia looked down at her brand-new bright red shirt. "*Muchas gracias,*" she answered. Only then did she realize that something amazing had just happened. She had understood Spanish!

Julia and Isabel spent the rest of the afternoon together. Julia could not understand everything Isabel said, but the girls also used gestures.

At the end of the day, Julia was sad to leave. That's when Mrs. Miller told her the news. "You girls are going to the same school." Then she translated so Isabel could understand.

"Cool!" the new friends exclaimed at exactly the same time.

Later that day, they went for a walk. Outside Señora Rojas's house stood Doña Eva, and a girl who looked just about Julia's age. *"Buenos días!"* Senora Rojas said. She greeted Julia's mother by kissing her on both cheeks and smiled warmly at Julia.

Then she introduced the girl *"Ésta es mi sobrina. Se llama Isabel."*

"She's Doña Eva's niece," her mother explained to Julia.

"Buenos días, Isabel," Julia said. *"Me llamo Julia."* That was another sentence she had learned. It means, "Hello Isabel. My name is Julia."

Julia Miller stood on the balcony of her high-rise apartment and stared gloomily at the street below. Other people might find the scene pretty, but not Julia. She had already looked at the white tips of the Andes Mountains and counted the palm trees lining the streets.

Julia had lived in Santiago, Chile, for just a week, and she did not like it one bit. She missed Boston, where she used to live.

She remembered that terrible day when she found out they were moving! As soon as Julia came home from school, she knew something was wrong. Her father was never home that early and her mother had looked serious. Then they told her the news. They were moving to Santiago, Chile!

Julia's father had been offered a wonderful new job. "What about your job?" Julia asked her mother.

"I can write books anywhere," said her mother. Her mother wrote books for children. "I can't imagine anything more exciting than living in another country!"

Her father noticed Julia's trembling lips. He put his arm around her. "We would never make this move if we didn't think you'd love Chile," he told her.

So far, Julia didn't love Chile at all! They had arrived in January. In Chile, the school year ran from March to December. That meant she wouldn't even have the chance to make friends for months!

At home it would be winter and she could ski and ice skate. Here, it was very hot.

It was finally time! School would start in two more weeks! Julia was excited and nervous.

She looked at the school supplies she and her mother had bought. There were shiny new pens and smooth notebooks. "I hope these are good choices," Julia said. "I want to look like everyone else."

"You will look like everyone else," her mom said. "Remember that school uniform!"

Julia groaned aloud. At her school, everyone had to wear a uniform. Her uniform was a boring gray skirt, white blouse and red necktie.

The rodeo was so thrilling. Julia watched with excitement as teams of riders chased a bull around the ring. They used their horses to nudge the bull to a stop along the railing. If they hit that spot, they'd get more points.

After the teams competed, the judges awarded trophies. The huasos took turns dancing with the queen of the rodeo.

"That was fun," Julia mumbled sleepily on the ride home.

Even her name had changed. In Spanish, there was no "J" sound. Instead, it was pronounced like an H. Now everyone called her "Hulia."

One night, Julia's dad announced he wanted to take his girls out to dinner. "Yum!" Julia said, jumping up and ready to go. She hadn't had a good hamburger since they arrived in Chile.

"Better go change," said Julia's mother. "People don't wear shorts and t-shirts out to dinner, here."

"They don't?" asked Julia. She changed into a dress, but she felt grumpy about it.

One weekend, Julia's dad came with them to the rodeo. It was called *la fiesta huaso*. "You two are having so much fun exploring, I want to explore, too!" he said.

Julia loved the exciting rodeo. She thought that huasos looked a little bit like American cowboys. Instead of big tan cowboy hats, the huasos wore flat-brimmed black hats made of felt. Instead of a cowboy shirt, they wore colorful *mantas*, which were like ponchos, only shorter.

"I think there's a secret to living here," Julia told her parents. "Santiago is like Boston. But different!" Her parents laughed.

Julia loved walking around the city. She always saw something new. There were the video arcades called flippers. She loved the post office that was in an old palace.

Another day, when they were walking, they recognized Señor Ruiz's wife, Señora Rojas!

"Son los Millers!" Señora Rojas called out with a wave. Julia's mother stopped, and the two women talked for a few minutes in Spanish. To Julia's surprise, she realized she could make out a word here and there.

It was so hot outside. Julia noticed that no one, not even the smallest kids, were wearing shorts.

"Boy, if I have to wear long pants or dresses every time we leave the house, this is going to be a long summer!" she said.

They took an elevator to the top floor of a tall building. As soon as they got out, a hostess greeted them in Spanish, *"Buenas noches."* Julia did not speak Spanish but her parents did.

"She said 'good evening,'" Julia's mother told her.

Julia picked up the menu. "Big mistake," she thought. "I don't understand it!" she said.

Julia's parents helped her. There were so many new foods. *Humitas* were corn kernels mixed with onions and spices and then wrapped and baked in corn husks. "I bet you'd love *pastel de papas*. It's just like shepherd's pie," said Julia's father.

Julia's parents sampled several traditional Chilean treats. *"Es rico!"* Julia's mom exclaimed, biting into an *empanada*. "That means it's delicious. It's just ground meat, olives, and some spices. It's like a hamburger wrapped in dough."

The next day Julia's mom took her on a walk. The people walking by spoke a constant stream of Spanish. Julia had no idea what they were saying.

Julia tried to explain to her mother how she felt. "It looks sort of like Boston," she said. "There are cars and stores, but nothing is quite the same. I haven't seen a single hamburger place yet."

The dinner table was covered with traditional Chilean treats. There was a salad of chopped onions and tomatoes, a meat casserole called *pastel de choclo,* and a special pumpkin stew. Julia recognized a plate piled high with empanadas.

Remembering how her mother had enjoyed them at the restaurant, Julia took a small bite. Her mother was right! They were delicious. She wrinkled her forehead, trying to think what her mother had said. *"Es rico!"* she told the table.

Over the next month, Julia and her mother continued to explore the city. One day they found a crafts fair. Women dressed in colorful costumes sold silver jewelry. There were traditional crafts made by the Mapuche Indians. After looking carefully, they chose a silver headband for Julia.

Other days they took the subway to the center of Santiago to visit the city's many museums. Julia particularly liked the history museum.

"Why don't we get a snack?" her mom said. They stopped at a café. Julia's mom got a drink and Julia picked out a cookie. "You want to pay?" Julia's mom said, handing her a bill.

Julia stared at the money in her hand. Along the bottom she read "*Cinco mil pesos*" and in the corner it said 5,000. She was holding 5,000 pesos. "So much money!" she exclaimed.

"Not really," Julia's mother laughed. "Five thousand pesos is only a bit more than eight dollars." Julia's mother sighed. "There is one thing I don't like about Chile. They often don't have coffee."

Julia realized that, like herself, her mom missed some things about life back home. Knowing that, made her feel a little less alone.

Julia's mother was right! Julia met her hostess, Señora Rojas, and the Señora's mother, Doña Eva. She also met an uncle, a married son and his wife, and three teenage children.

Then she met her father's boss. "I am Señor Ruiz," he said.

"But I thought your last name was Ruiz García!" she exclaimed. "What happened to the rest of your last name?"

Everyone in the room laughed. For a moment, Julia felt embarrassed. "Most people in Chile have two last names," he said. "One from their mother and one from their father. People usually use only their father's name in day-to-day life."

One day, Julia and her family were invited to dinner at the house of her father's boss. His name was Eduardo Ruiz García.

Julia's mother laid out a skirt for her. "I hate wearing a skirt," Julia muttered, but she put it on without a fight. She even made sure her fingernails were clean without being told.

After a short drive, the Millers pulled up in front of a quaint, old home. Julia followed her parents to the door, holding a box of candy to give to their hosts. Julia's mother murmured, "Don't be surprised if Daddy's boss has a big family. Many generations in Chile often live under the same roof."

After their snack, they stopped to watch some kids playing soccer. One boy was playing by himself. He kicked the ball and bounced it off his knee. Then he bounced it off his head! "He's really a great player," Julia said.

The boy saw her watching. *"¿Le gusta el fútbol?"* he asked with a smile. When Julia did not answer, the boy repeated his question. This time Julia made out the word football. However, all she could say was *"No hablo español,"* which meant "I don't speak Spanish." How could she make friends if she couldn't speak the language?

Julia's mother worked the next day. Julia turned on the television to fill up the silent apartment. She immediately saw one of her favorite television programs. But the actors and actresses spoke in Spanish!

Julia turned to a show she remembered seeing and found she could figure out some of the words. To her surprise, she even understood a bit of what they were saying.

All that afternoon, Julia watched Spanish shows. She especially loved variety shows. She wrote down Spanish words. Imagine! Learning Spanish by watching TV!

Suggested levels for Guided Reading, DRA,™
Lexile,® and Reading Recovery™ are provided
in the Pearson Scott Foresman Leveling Guide.

Science

Science

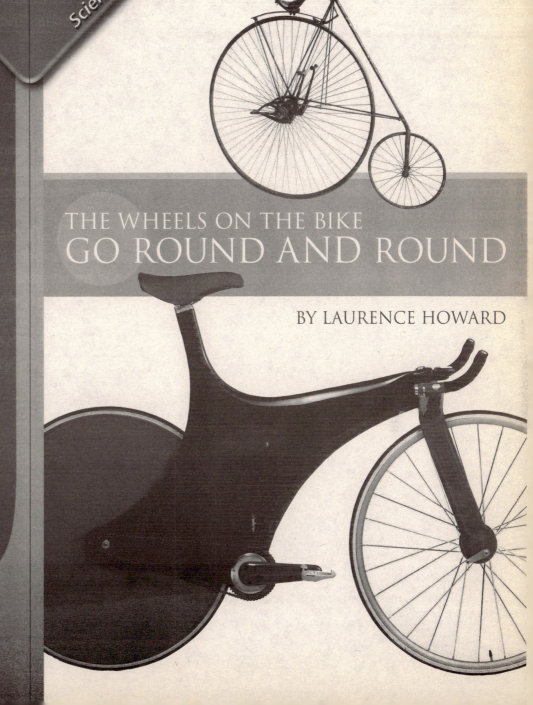

THE WHEELS ON THE BIKE
GO ROUND AND ROUND

BY LAURENCE HOWARD

Genre	Comprehension Skill and Strategy	Text Features
Nonfiction	• Generalize • Ask Questions	• Table of Contents • Captions • Labels • Glossary

Scott Foresman Reading Street 4.6.4

PEARSON
Scott Foresman

scottforesman.com

ISBN 0-328-13498-8

9 780328 134984

90000

Reader Response

1. Make a general statement describing what bicycles were like in the 1800s.

2. What questions do you have about the forces of motion that act on a bike? Where can you find the answers to your questions? Write your questions and answers in a chart similar to the one below.

Questions	Answers

3. One of the vocabulary words is *pneumatic*. What other word starts with *pneum-*? Why do you think that other word starts with the same letters?

4. Look at the different bicycles on pages 11 through 13. How are they the same? How are they different?

Glossary

acceleration *n.* the act of speeding up.

amateur *adj.* not done for money or as a profession.

deceleration *n.* the act of slowing down.

drag *n.* the force acting on an object in motion, in a direction opposite to the object's motion.

force *n.* energy or power that may cause, change, or stop the motion of an object.

friction *n.* resistance to motion of two moving objects or surfaces that touch, or the act of rubbing one thing against another.

motion *n.* movement.

pneumatic *adj.* filled with air.

traction *n.* ability to push against a surface without slipping.

THE WHEELS ON THE BIKE
GO ROUND AND ROUND

—— BY LAURENCE HOWARD ——

PEARSON
Scott Foresman

Editorial Offices: Glenview, Illinois • Parsippany, New Jersey • New York, New York
Sales Offices: Needham, Massachusetts • Duluth, Georgia • Glenview, Illinois
Coppell, Texas • Ontario, California • Mesa, Arizona

Here's How to Do It!

1. Gather together materials to make a poster. What colors and materials will you use to grab people's attention?
2. Using the information you have found, make a poster advertisement that would be useful to bicycle lovers who have just moved to your city or town. Organize the poster's information clearly and in a way that is easy for people to read and understand.
3. Your advertisement will show newcomers and other cyclists what is available to them. Perhaps you could get permission to hang your poster at your school, or somewhere in your community, for people to see and use.

Now Try This

Spread the News About Biking

Using the Internet, the library, and any other sources you can think of, do a careful exploration of cycling organizations and activities that exist in your area. Include stores or catalogs that sell anything having to do with cycling.

Don't forget to find out what arrangements your local government has made to meet the needs and protect the safety of cyclists. There may be special bike trails or paths that have been set aside for cyclists.

Often, there are biking laws and other rules about where people may cycle, how cyclists must behave, what they must wear while they are cycling, and how automobile drivers must act around cyclists.

The Internet is a treasure trove of information about bicycles.

CONTENTS

CHAPTER 1
Early Bicycle History   4

CHAPTER 2
Modern Bicycles   8

CHAPTER 3
Bicycle Science and Superstars   14

Now Try This   22

Glossary   24

Chapter 1 *Early Bicycle History*

The wheel was invented more than five thousand years ago, when people realized they could move heavy objects by rolling them over something round. Later on, people discovered they could move themselves on wheels too. Before the invention of what we know today as the bicycle, people created many different versions of self-moving vehicles.

Velocipede

Many people thought Armstrong's illness would leave him too weak to win races, but he did not let that slow him down, and he did not give up. Despite having to endure months of painful medical treatments, Armstrong came back to win race after race, including the Tour de France, the most important race in cycling.

As you have learned, the bicycle has come a long way since the creation of running machines, which didn't even have pedals, and high wheelers, which were highly dangerous. Comfort, safety, and science have played important roles in the development of self-moving vehicles. As interest in bicycles grew, inventors built many different kinds of them to suit a range of interests, abilities, and terrains. Cyclists can take to the roads, the race tracks, the mountains, and more with the specialized bikes of today.

What kind of bike have you used before? What kind of bike do you own, or what kind of bike would you like to have? Did you learn about new varieties of bicycles that might be of interest to you, now that you have read this book? As you can see, the bicycle is a great invention to use for traveling, for sport, and for fun.

A hobbyhorse from the 1800s (top)
and modern BMX racing (bottom)

In 1817, a German nobleman named Baron Karl von Drais created the *draisienne*. Von Drais' invention had two wheels, and the front wheel could be turned left or right. The draisienne, or *hobbyhorse,* was made of wood and could only move when the rider walked or ran. It was also known as the running machine.

In the 1860s, when pedals were attached to the front wheel of a hobbyhorse, the *velocipede* was born. Can you see why the word *velocipede* means "fast foot"?

Because it provided a very bumpy, bouncy ride, the velocipede was also called the "boneshaker." At the time, streets were made of cobblestones, and the hobbyhorse had wood and iron wheels. Ouch! Back when this great-grandfather of the bicycle was popular, indoor tracks were created so people could ride without serious injury.

In the early 1870s, after people had become tired of the boneshaker, English cycle makers introduced a bicycle with steel rims, solid rubber tires, and a front wheel that was much larger than the back one. Why? Making one turn of the pedals equaled one circle of the front wheel. The larger the front wheel, the farther you could travel on one turn of the pedals.

One problem with these high-wheeled bicycles, or *high wheelers*, was the danger of falling off. They were built to be fast, not safe. The rider sat high off the ground on a seat over the large front wheel, and some front wheels were over five feet tall. Just getting on and off was a real challenge, and to be safe, they needed a very smooth road. Even a pebble or small pothole might cause the rider to lose control and fall head over heels. High wheelers also had spokes, which gave support to lighter types of wheels, making them as strong as heavier wheels.

The next advance in the development of bicycles was the introduction of **pneumatic** tires—rubber tires filled with air under pressure. These tires provided bicyclists a much smoother, more comfortable ride than just hard wood or metal.

This unusual high wheeler had a large rear wheel.

Spoke

Lance Armstrong in the 1996 Olympics (left) and the 2004 Tour de France (below)

Three years later, medical tests showed that Armstrong had cancer. He required two operations, and doctors only gave him a 50 percent chance of getting well. Fortunately, medical treatment helped Armstrong beat his illness. Only five months after Armstrong was told he had cancer, he was back training on his bicycle!

As of 2004, Lance Armstrong had won six Tour de France bicycle races in a row. The Tour de France is a three-week bicycle race, with a course that passes through several European countries and covers two thousand to twenty-five hundred miles.

Armstrong was born September 18, 1971, and he grew up in Plano, Texas. Encouraged by his mother to get involved in sports, Armstrong became a professional triathlete when he was just sixteen. In a triathlon, athletes compete in a contest of swimming, bicycling, and running. When Armstrong finished high school, he decided to concentrate only on cycling. His practice rides were so long that when he finished, his mother had to come with her car to pick him up.

The first summer after Armstrong finished high school, he qualified for the 1989 junior world championship cycling race held in Moscow, Russia. In 1991, he won the United States **amateur** cycling championship, and he participated in the 1992 Olympics.

Through hard training, Armstrong has become one of the world's best cyclists. In 1993 he won ten championships, and also began to share his success with others by starting a junior racing program for kids.

Finally, in 1885, science and inventive creativity produced the *safety bicycle*. This new invention had two same-sized wheels that reduced the chance of falling off, and also had pedals that were connected to the rear wheel by means of gears and a chain. This was different from earlier bikes, which had their pedals connected directly to the front wheel. On the high wheeler, the size of the wheel controlled the speed of the bicycle, but on a safety bicycle, the speed was controlled by the difference in size between the two gears.

The safety bicycle's two equal-sized wheels made it easier and safer to ride than the high wheeler.

Chapter 2 *Modern Bicycles*

By 1900, an important invention had been created, called the *derailleur*. This device allowed the rider to choose different combinations of front and rear gears. Different combinations of gear sizes allowed the rider to travel at any speed while pedaling at a comfortable rate. A large front gear combined with a small rear gear would make the bike go fast, and a small front gear combined with a large rear gear would make the bike go slowly. Modern racing bicycles and mountain bicycles often have twenty or more speeds.

Two of the greatest bicycle racers of all time are Marshall "Major" Taylor and Lance Armstrong. Both had to overcome severe difficulties in their efforts to be champions.

Born in 1878 in Indiana, Marshall Taylor was African American, at a time when African Americans were not given the same opportunities as white people. Luckily, Marshall received a bicycle from a friend, and before long, cycling was his favorite activity. By watching experts, he taught himself bike tricks and quickly became an expert at bike tricks himself.

Soon, Marshall started entering bicycle races, and a bike shop in his town paid for some of his equipment and expenses. Marshall liked to wear an army uniform with lots of military decorations on it, and that is why people started to call him "Major."

Marshall Taylor won national sprint races in 1899 and 1900. A sprint is a short, fast race. By 1901, everyone thought of him as the world champion bicycle sprint racer, and fans from many countries admired Major Taylor. His champion performances and the records he set made it easier for other African Americans to become professional athletes in America.

Marshall "Major" Taylor

At the beginning of the twentieth century, the safety bicycle became popular throughout the United States and around the world. Factories produced bikes in huge quantities, which made it possible to sell them for a price the average worker could afford. People joined biking clubs, and bike races became popular.

The bicycle craze slowed down with the rise in popularity of the streetcar and other mass transit systems, and for many years following the 1910s, bicycles were thought of as children's playthings. Over the next few decades, major improvements in bicycles consisted of making them lighter and stronger, and providing better ways to switch gears.

Worries about air pollution, physical fitness, and the cost of gasoline gave bicycles a new popularity with adults in the 1960s, '70s, and '80s. In 1984, seventy-six million bicycles were sold in the United States, an amount more than double the thirty-one million automobiles sold that year. Bikes have become so popular that a whole world of activities has developed around them. There are many bicycling clubs in the world, and there are many kinds of bicycles.

In the late 1900s, bicycles grew in popularity.

Interest in bikes encouraged inventors to create many new types of bicycles, and mountain bikes were created in the 1970s. They are made with fat tires, which rarely go flat and help the bike move faster on dirt trails. Treads, or deep groves in the tires, help the bicycle grip the terrain. Mountain bikes also have strong, heavy frames to match the rough mountain environment on which they are made to travel. They usually have comfortable seats and twenty-seven speeds.

Track-racing bikes have a very light frame, and their tires are made to grip the track. They have no brakes, light wheels that only move when the pedals are moved, and handlebars that are set low to reduce the **force** of air. When the rider sits low to the handle bars, it reduces **drag**—which is caused by air pushing against a surface area—the smaller the area, the less drag. Drag slows down a bike's movement.

A bicycle called a BMX (Bicycle Motocross) is made to race on dirt roads and to do tricks and stunts. BMX bikes are lightweight and have few parts, their wheels are tiny to keep their weight low, and BMX bike frames are designed to survive falls and crashes. For safety, BMX bikes usually have more than one kind of brake, for slowing down quickly and preventing accidents.

Newton's first law of motion says that an object stays at rest until a force acts on it. Once a force acts on it and it starts moving, it keeps moving in the same direction until another force acts against it.

Many forces contribute to and oppose a bicycle's motion. As you know, the force that gets a bicycle accelerating, or moving, is pedaling, and the force that safely slows down and stops a bike is the friction caused by braking. Using hand brakes on a bicycle pushes a rubber pad up against the side of the tire, and this friction makes the bike come to a stop.

Also, the tire's ability to push against the ground without slipping is called **traction**. Traction is the sticking friction of an object on a surface on which it is moving. The tire grips the road so the bicycle can move forward, but if the road is too rough it can create too much friction, which can slow down or stop a bicycle.

Drag, as you read earlier, is a force that slows down motion, and drag is caused by air pushing against you and the bicycle as you move. If you were biking up a hill with the wind in your face, for example, drag would slow you down, and another force that would slow you down would be gravity. When biking down the hill, however, the pull of gravity would help you speed up.

© Pearson Education, Inc.

Gravity and pedaling would cause *acceleration* downhill. Drag from the air and friction from the wheel brake would cause *deceleration*.

Chapter 3 *Bicycle Science and Superstars*

If you want to understand what makes a bicycle work, you need to know about **motion** and force. Motion is another name for movement, and force is something that causes an object to be pushed or pulled. Speeding motion up is called **acceleration**. This happens when you pedal faster and faster on your bike. Slowing down motion is called **deceleration**—this can happen when you stop pedaling, or when you apply the brakes.

Isaac Newton, a mathematician and physicist, figured out how motion works, and he broke it down into three rules called the laws of motion. The one we will concentrate on is Newton's first law.

Wheel brake

Track-racing bike

BMX bike

Road bikes

Road bikes are designed for speed, and they are faster than any other bicycle. Because of their speed, professional bike racers use road bikes, but they are also fine for just riding around the neighborhood. They have very light frames, a thin seat, ten or more speeds, and extremely thin, but incredibly strong, tires that rarely slip or slide, even in the rain.

Recumbent bike

Tandem bike

Hybrid bikes combine some of the features of mountain bikes and road bikes. For example, they have the comfortable seats of mountain bikes and the narrow tires of road bikes. Their frames are stronger than those of road bikes, but they are not as heavy as the ones used for mountain bikes. Hybrid bikes are used on streets and solid trails, and most hybrids have twenty-one or more possible speeds.

Recumbent bicycles let the rider sit in a position that is half way between sitting and lying down. They have comfortable, stuffed seats, and the pedals are placed forward, toward the front wheel rather than under the rider.

Two-wheelers that are made especially for children normally have one speed and coaster brakes. Coaster brakes work by firmly pedaling backward, which creates **friction** on the rear wheel. Friction is when two surfaces rub together. A braking device inside the wheel hub, or the center of the wheel, creates drag on the wheel, causing the bike to stop.

There are also bicycles built for two riders called tandem bikes. They have two seats, two sets of handlebars, and two sets of pedals; and they are available in the styles of mountain, hybrid, road, and recumbent bikes.

Earth Science

EXPLORING THE MYSTERIES OF SPACE

by Gini Douglass

Genre	Comprehension Skill and Strategy	Text Features
Nonfiction	• Graphic Sources • Monitor and Fix Up	• Captions • Labels • Glossary

Scott Foresman Reading Street 4.6.5

ISBN 0-328-13501-1

Reader Response

1. Look at the pictures and reread the captions in this book. How do the captions and pictures help you understand space exploration?

2. Do you have any questions about a particular subject that you have just read about? What are some strategies you could use to find out more information about this subject?

3. Homonyms are words that are spelled the same but have different meanings. Use the word *hatch* as a verb in a sentence. Name another homonym and give its definitions.

4. Reread page 5. Using a chart similar to the one below, write astronomers' names on the left and their view of the universe on the right.

Astronomer	View

Glossary

astronomers *n.* experts in the science that deals with the Sun, Moon, planets, stars, etc.

data *n.* facts from which conclusions can be drawn; things known or admitted; information.

debris *n.* scattered fragments; ruins; rubbish.

galaxy *n.* a group of billions of stars forming one system.

geocentric *adj.* viewed or measured from Earth's center.

heliocentric *adj.* with the Sun at the center.

satellite *n.* an astronomical object that revolves around a planet; a moon.

24

EXPLORING THE MYSTERIES OF SPACE

by Gini Douglass

PEARSON
Scott Foresman

Editorial Offices: Glenview, Illinois • Parsippany, New Jersey • New York, New York
Sales Offices: Needham, Massachusetts • Duluth, Georgia • Glenview, Illinois
Coppell, Texas • Ontario, California • Mesa, Arizona

Here's How to Do It!

1. First, before you sit down to write your letter of welcome, you may want to take some time to brainstorm. What are the most important points you want to make?

2. You may want to mention some important moments in the history of space exploration in order to inspire your crew. Think about some of the exciting discoveries and missions that have taken place in the past. What do you think was the most inspiring moment in space exploration history?

3. You may want to thank your crew for joining you on this mission, and congratulate them on their success as astronauts. Be sure to tell them how much you will appreciate their hard work.

4. As you may know, space missions always have powerful and memorable names. Some of the earlier space missions have had names such as Mercury, Apollo, and Endeavor. If you could choose an inspiring name for your mission, what would it be? How will this name reflect the goals of your mission to work at the International Space Station?

Now Try This

Lead a Mission to the International Space Station

Now it's your turn to go on a mission into space—a mission of the imagination. At this very moment on the International Space Station, a crew of astronauts is hard at work conducting experiments and helping with its construction. By the time construction on the Space Station is completed, it will have taken forty-five missions to get the job done.

Several crews on many different missions have already traveled to the International Space Station to contribute their skills toward its completion. Teamwork has been the key to making these missions possible. If you could be the commander of the next mission to the International Space Station, what would you like to say to your crew? Why not start by writing a letter of welcome!

Have you ever gazed up at the night sky and wondered about the mysteries of the universe? For instance, do you ever wonder how big the universe is or what it might be like to travel through space and see far off stars and galaxies up close? Have you ever wanted to know exactly how long it would take to travel to another planet in our solar system? What are you seeing when you spot a shooting star? If you have ever found yourself asking such questions, you will be happy to know that you are not alone. Human beings have been gazing up at the sky and wondering about the mysteries of space since the dawn of time.

Over the past few thousand years, humans have been driven by a need to understand and explain the universe, and this desire to understand the mysteries of the universe is something that comes naturally to us all. You may remember being a small child and asking questions about the way the world works. Perhaps you saw a bird fly by, and you wondered how that was possible. Or, perhaps you wondered why the Moon appeared to be round and full on some days, and shaped like a banana on others. We humans are born with a deep sense of curiosity about the world around us, and it is our curiosity that inspires us to learn about the world in which we live.

Just as we are curious about what lies beyond our solar system and our **galaxy,** the Milky Way, early **astronomers** had a strong desire to understand what they were seeing in the sky. Long before technology was available to assist them, early astronomers were able to make accurate guesses about the planets and stars. For example, by observing the positions of the Sun and Moon in the sky, early astronomers were able to create calendars that were very similar to the calendars we use today, and early astronomers even took the time to map the position of every visible star in the night sky.

Copernicus (top) believed in a heliocentric universe. His diagram shows the Sun as the center of the solar system (bottom).

Human space exploration is still a relatively new enterprise, but it is amazing to consider the progress we have made. We must pay tribute to the many brave astronauts who have risked their own safety so that humankind could benefit from their brilliant work in space. Today, human space exploration has become a truly international effort, and people from many different countries have contributed their ideas and knowledge to the cause of space exploration.

Russia and the United States, along with fourteen other countries, are working together to complete the International Space Station (ISS). The International Space Station is large enough for astronauts to live and work inside it. The first piece of the station was launched in November of 1998, and since then many sections have been added to it—it is currently the length of three school buses. By the time it is completed, it will be about the length of a football field. Scientists hope that their work at the ISS will bring us closer to our goal of visiting and living on a planet such as Mars.

Human beings have never stopped striving to learn more and more about our place in the universe. The more we learn, the more we realize how much is still unknown to us. People once believed that the planet Earth was the center of the universe, but we now understand that it is a tiny part of a vast universe yet to be explored.

Americans witnessed one of the most important moments in human history. Armstrong, commander of the Apollo 11 mission, became the first man to walk on the Moon. His words upon setting foot on the lunar surface were, "That's one small step for man, one giant leap for mankind." Today, Armstrong's words remain as unforgettable as the triumphant success of the Apollo 11 mission.

Armstrong and Aldrin's visit to the Moon lasted a little longer than two hours, but the effect of their visit on the imagination of the American people and the world would last much longer. Following the success of the Apollo 11 mission, we continued to strive to reach new heights in space.

American and Russian astronauts (left) train for life aboard the ISS (right).

As early as 280 B.C., a Greek man named Aristarchus suggested that we live in a **heliocentric** universe, with Earth revolving around the Sun. Scientists did not accept his views. If Earth was moving, why couldn't they feel it? They believed that the universe was Earth-centered, or **geocentric.**

Over time ideas about space changed. As a result of the work of astronomers such as Nicolaus Copernicus (1473–1543) from Poland, we came back to the sun-centered view of the solar system. When we understood that Earth was not the center of everything, we saw that the universe was much more vast and unknown than we had previously imagined.

As a new view of the universe continued to take shape, another revolutionary event occurred. In 1608 a man from the Netherlands named Hans Lippershey invented the first telescope-like instrument called a looker. Astronomy would never be the same again, and humanity was on its way to exploring the far distances of space through a telescopic lens. The first person to use a telescope to study space was the Italian astronomer Galileo Galilei. Galileo lived from 1564 to 1642, and he made several important discoveries during his lifetime. Galileo was the first to observe dark spots on the sun called sunspots, and he observed the craters and peaks that exist on the surface of the Moon. By using a telescope, Galileo was also able to prove Copernicus's claim that the planets in our solar system revolved around the Sun.

As time went on, astronomers used telescopes to observe space. Astronomers learned more and more about the planets in our solar system, and our idea of space began to take on more and more detail. In 1705 Edmond Halley claimed that comets were in orbit around the Sun, and that one in particular would pass by Earth every seventy-six years. It is now called Halley's Comet.

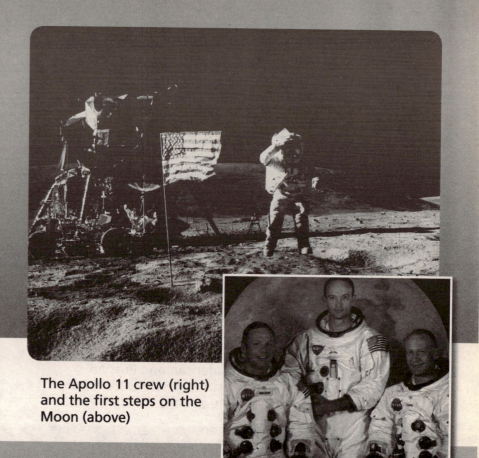

The Apollo 11 crew (right) and the first steps on the Moon (above)

In 1967 NASA began a series of missions into space called the Apollo missions. In 1969, after learning as much as possible about how to travel safely on the Moon, NASA launched the Apollo 11 mission. On July 20, astronauts Neil A. Armstrong and Edwin E. Aldrin, Jr., landed safely on the Moon's surface in a lunar module designed to carry them to their destination. Millions of people back on Earth watched the incredible events unfold on TV.

Many people have volunteered to take the giant leap into outer space. It all began in 1961, four years after the Soviet launch of Sputnik 1. The first person to travel to outer space was a Russian man named Yuri Gagarin. Gagarin orbited Earth once in a spacecraft called the Vostok 1, and his flight lasted one hour and twenty-nine minutes. Today, astronauts are able to stay in space for much longer, but back in 1961, Gagarin's mission was nothing short of miraculous.

After Yuri Gagarin's trip, an American astronaut named Alan B. Shepard, Jr., became the second human being, and the first American, to orbit Earth. Following these two moments in space history, the race between the Soviet Union and the United States intensified. While the Soviet Union seemed to be more interested in doing scientific research in space, the United States was determined to send the first human being to the Moon. This became the main focus of our space program, and a matter of national interest.

In 1961 President John F. Kennedy challenged the American people to put a man on the Moon by the end of the decade. Kennedy inspired the nation, especially the many dedicated people at NASA who worked, through trial and error, to make this dream a reality.

Halley's Comet (above) and Edmond Halley (far right)

It turns out that Halley's Comet does exist, and its orbit has been witnessed by many people throughout history. Today we know that comets are actually made up of lumps of ice and dust that travel from the outer areas of the solar system toward its center, the Sun. When comets get closer to the Sun, the heat turns the ice into steam, and the jets of gas they emit form long tails that can be seen from Earth. Halley's Comet made its most recent appearance in 1986, and a number of countries sent out spacecraft to snap some photos of the famous comet. The next chance we will have to see Halley's Comet will be in the year 2062!

When you see a streak of light in the night sky it may appear as if a star is falling toward Earth. What you are actually seeing is a bit of space **debris** called a meteoroid. It is believed that meteoroids are formed when asteroids collide in space. Asteroids are made of rock or metal, and they orbit the Sun in a region between Mars and Jupiter called the Asteroid Belt. Italian astronomer Giuseppe Piazzi discovered the first minor planet, or asteroid, called Ceres, in 1801. It was estimated to be 930 km (578 miles) in diameter, which is about the same size as Texas!

The 1800s was an exciting time in the history of astronomy. At this time, astronomers were learning more about the planets and their orbits, or revolutions around the Sun, and beginning to understand more about the universe in the process. For example, in 1846, the eighth planet from the Sun, Neptune, was discovered.

Scientists figured out that according to Newton's laws of motion, there was something not quite right about the orbit of Uranus, the seventh planet from the Sun. Scientists predicted that another planet, now called Neptune, might exist beyond Uranus, which would explain the disturbance of Uranus's orbit. They were right.

The mathematician and physicist Isaac Newton (top) described how and why objects move in his three rules known as Newton's laws of motion. His work helped scientists discover the planet Neptune (bottom).

The satellite Galileo, which was launched into space in 1989 by the space shuttle Atlantis, provided us with more evidence that our solar system is a mysterious and enchanting place. Galileo's mission was to travel to the planet Jupiter. Once it arrived, after traveling more than six years, the satellite collected **data** about Jupiter and some of its moons. It was hoped that Galileo's mission would last for about two years, but the hardworking satellite ended up sticking around for eight! As a result of Galileo's mission, we were able to learn more information than ever before about Jupiter's atmosphere and about some of Jupiter's moons.

Unmanned missions into space continue to be an essential aspect of our space program, and scientists are currently hard at work designing new spacecraft and planning new missions that will stretch the boundaries of our imaginations even further. What these unmanned missions have taught us is that we are but a small piece of the puzzle that is the universe.

Nevertheless, what we lack in size, we make up for in spirit. The information we have learned about our universe at each step of our space program has motivated us to continue our exploration, and human space travel has been, perhaps, the most dramatic and inspiring form of space exploration to date.

Over the past four decades, other important unmanned space missions have brought back astonishing pictures of the distant places in our solar system and beyond. The Hubble Space Telescope, named after the astronomer Edwin Hubble, was launched into space in 1990. NASA and the European Space Agency (ESA) created and designed the Hubble together. The Hubble Telescope is actually a floating observatory, orbiting Earth at the rate of five miles per second. It takes the Hubble telescope only ninety-six minutes to make one complete orbit of Earth.

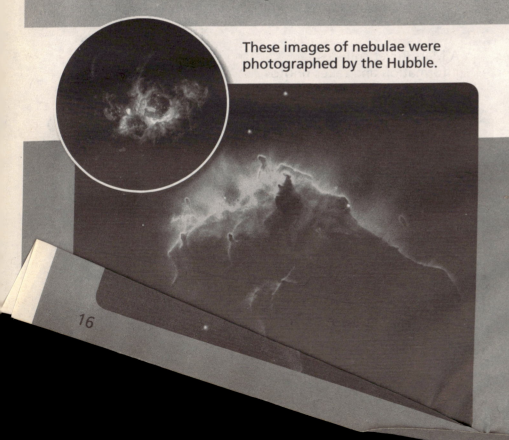

These images of nebulae were photographed by the Hubble.

Neptune was actually observed in 1612 by Galileo. Galileo observed Neptune, but he concluded that the enormous blue object was a star rather than a planet. During the few days that Galileo had the opportunity to observe Neptune, he noticed that its position seemed to change slightly. Ordinarily, this might have suggested to him that what he observed was something other than a star, but unfortunately, Neptune slipped out of his view before he could determine that it was indeed a planet and not a star. Of course, we now know that there is only one star in our solar system: the Sun.

The case of Galileo's near discovery of a new planet shows how much our understanding of the solar system and outer space has changed in only a few centuries. In fact, astronomers at the beginning of the 1900s were not aware that any galaxies beyond our own galaxy, the Milky Way galaxy, existed.

This is the W. M. Keck Observatory in Hawaii (left) and an interior view of its telescope (below).

Unmanned aircraft and satellites were very important to both space programs at the time, and they continue to be essential to space programs today. For instance, even though the technology we have created has allowed us to travel to the Moon and other regions of space, we are still unable to travel to the surface of the planet Mars. For human beings, the trip still would be too risky. Our technology has not caught up with our dream to visit another planet in person, which is why robotic missions have been so important.

A Mars Rover collects information and takes photos of the red planet's surface.

Although relations were not very good, the competition between the Soviet Union and the United States inspired each country to make great progress in space exploration. Achieving human space travel became a priority for both nations, and NASA's goal was to make human space travel a reality. Just twelve years after the launch of Sputnik 1, the United States sent astronauts to the Moon.

The United States and Soviet Union continued to launch more satellites and robotic aircraft into space, and the dream of sending a human being into space would soon become a reality. Before this could be accomplished, however, it was important that unmanned missions collect as much information as possible about the conditions humans would face during space travel.

Unmanned missions into space have brought back crucial information that allowed us to prepare for human space flight. Sending an unmanned aircraft or satellite into space has many benefits. Unmanned (or robotic) spacecraft and satellites can go farther into space and can remain in space for longer periods than spacecraft carrying humans. Also, since there is no need to worry about supporting and protecting human life, the level of risk is much lower.

Astronomers began to notice what looked like cloudy patches of distant stars, and they concluded that these patches were part of the Milky Way galaxy. In the 1920s a man named Edwin Hubble studied these same patches of stars, and he realized that he was, in fact, observing other galaxies!

Astronomers and scientists in the 1900s continued to observe and study the mysteries of space. These scientists used powerful telescopes to search for far-off planets and stars, and they also began to understand that new forms of space exploration were possible. Soon, they began to develop the technology that would make space exploration a reality.

The technological advances of the 1900s brought about a new effort to explore deep into space, and modern space exploration took on a whole new dimension. Up until that time period, our exploration of space was limited to what we could observe from Earth. Though we learned a great deal about space from what we observed through powerful modern telescopes, scientists and astronomers knew that we could learn even more by traveling through space itself. If we could find a way to get beyond Earth's atmosphere, then we could gain a whole new perspective of our solar system and outer space.

It soon became evident that rockets were the secret to making space exploration possible. As early as A.D. 1045, the Chinese had used rockets for military purposes. A Russian scientist named Konstantin Tsiolkovsky, who lived in the mid-1800s to early 1900s, had made important discoveries regarding rocket science and space flight. Tsiolkovsky's discoveries were essential to our understanding of how rockets could be used to launch space ships.

In 1919 an American scientist named Robert Goddard began to experiment with rockets. Goddard was the first to suggest that a rocket could one day reach the Moon. Many people made fun of Goddard and his ideas, but history would soon prove that his ideas were not so crazy after all.

Goddard worked with the U.S. government during World War II, using the rocket technology he developed to aid in the war effort. At the same time, scientists in other countries worked to develop their own programs in rocket science. In 1957 the Soviet Union (now called Russia) launched the world's first man-made **satellite,** Sputnik 1, into orbit around Earth. A few months later, the United States launched its own satellite, Explorer 1, into space.

NASA was created partly in response to the successful launch of Sputnik 1 (above) and the Russian space program.

In 1958 a very important, government-sponsored organization called the National Aeronautics and Space Administration (NASA) came into being. NASA became the center of technological and scientific research for the American space program and remains its headquarters today. NASA was established, in part, in response to the successful launch of the satellite Sputnik 1 by the Soviet Union. In the years following World War II, the governments of the United States and the Soviet Union did not have a good relationship, and the two countries each lived in fear that the other would move ahead in the race to explore space.